The publishers wish to thank the following artists for contributing to this book:

Bob Bampton: p.6 (bottom left); Owain Bell: pp.47 (top right), 57 (top right), 69 (top left), 87 (top right), 91 (top right), 132 (center right), 181 (top left); Peter Bull: pp.26 (top left, center right), 51 (center left), 61 (top right), 73 (top left, center right and bottom right), 77, 79, 119, 138 (bottom left), 174; Tony Chance of Garden Studio: p.123; Kuo Kang Chen: pp.40/41, 108/109; Peter Dennis of Linda Rogers Associates: pp.35, 86, 128, 138; David Eddington of Maggie Mundy Illustrators' Agency: p.8 (bottom right), 68 (top right), 134 (center right), 137 (top right), 178 (center right); Eugene Fleury: pp.8/9, 24/25, 27, 54/55, 74/75, 135, 167; Chris Forsey: cover, pp.10, 64/65, 66 (top and center left), 120/121, 164/165; Jeremy Gowar: pp.168/169; Peter Kestevan of Garden Studio: pp.80, 171; Bernard Long of Temple Rogers Artists Agents: pp.18/19, 82/83, 148/149; Kevin Maddison: pp.35 (bottom left), 38 (top right), 58 (top right), 78 (center right), 114 (top right), 132 (top left), 142 (top right), 183 (top right); Josephine Martin of Garden Studio: pp.16 (top right and bottom left), 32/33, 106/107; Eva Melhuish of Garden Studio: pp.59 (bottom right), 88, 144/145; Michael Roffe: pp.160/161; John Scorey: pp.6 (bottom right); 66 (bottom right), 87 (left), 130/131; Swanston Graphics: p.52 (top right).

First American edition, 1992

Copyright © 1991 by Grisewood & Dempsey Limited. All rights reserved under International and Pan-American Copyright Conventions. Published in the United States by Random House, Inc., New York. The Random House Library of Knowledge is a trademark of Random House, Inc. Originally published in Great Britain by Kingfisher Books, a Grisewood & Dempsey company, in 1991.

LIBRARY OF CONGRESS CATALOGING-IN-PUBLICATION DATA
The Random House library of knowledge : first encyclopedia / by Brian and Brenda Williams. — 1st American ed.
p. cm.
Originally published in Great Britain by Kingfisher Books in 1991.
Includes index.
Summary: A first encyclopedia containing over 500 brief entries, illustrations, and maps.
ISBN 0-679-83059-6
1. Children's encyclopedias and dictionaries. [1. Encyclopedias and dictionaries.] I. Williams, Brian. II. Williams, Brenda. III. Random House (Firm) IV. Title: Library of knowledge.
AG5.R26 1992
031—dc20 91-32817

Manufactured in Spain 10 9 8 7 6 5 4 3 2 1

Abbreviations

Some words are abbreviated, or shortened, in the encyclopedia. The table below explains what the abbreviations stand for.

Measurements and Abbreviations

in	inch
ft	foot
yd	yard
mi	mile
sq mi	square mile
mph	miles per hour
oz	ounce
lb	pound
qt	quart
gal	gallon
°F	degrees Fahrenheit
mm	millimeter
cm	centimeter
m	meter
km	kilometer
km/h	km per hour
g	gram
kg	kilogram
°C	degrees Celsius
c. (before a date)	circa (about)
B.C.	before Christ
A.D.	*anno Domini* (refers to any time after the birth of Christ)

The Random House Library of Knowledge™

First Encyclopedia

By Brian and Brenda Williams

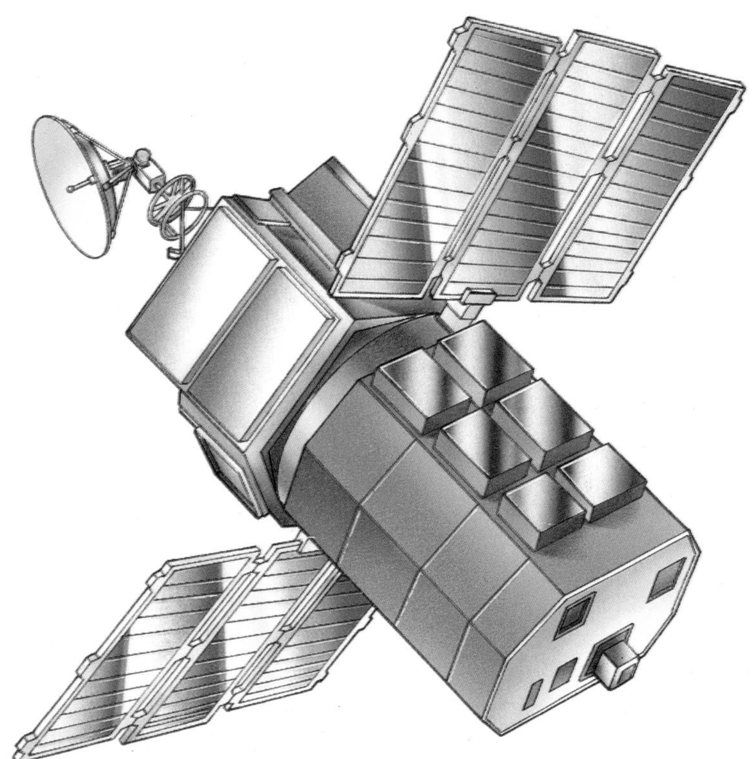

Random House New York

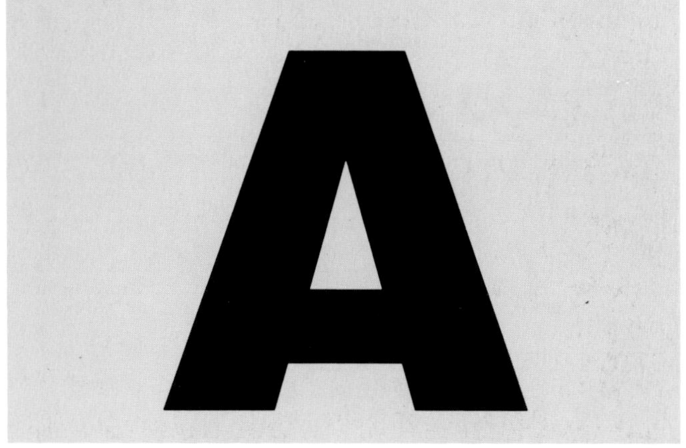

aardvark

The aardvark is a mammal that lives in southern Africa. Its name means "earth-pig." It uses its strong claws to dig and to rip open termites' nests. The aardvark laps up the insects with its sticky tongue. See **mammals**.

▼ The aardvark has a long snout and donkeylike ears. It can dig at an amazing speed.

abbey see **church**

Aborigine

The Aborigines were the first Australians. Thousands of years ago they came to Australia from Asia. They were skilled hunters and could find food and water even in the desert. One of their weapons was the boomerang. Today about 100,000 Aborigines live in Australia.

acid

Acids are chemical substances. Some acids are poisonous. They burn our skin and turn metals into liquid. But acids also have many uses. Stomach acids digest food. The sour taste of a lemon is caused by citric acid in the juice.

▼ Some substances change color when put into an acid. Litmus, a dye, turns red in acid. It turns blue in a base or alkali, such as baking soda dissolved in water.

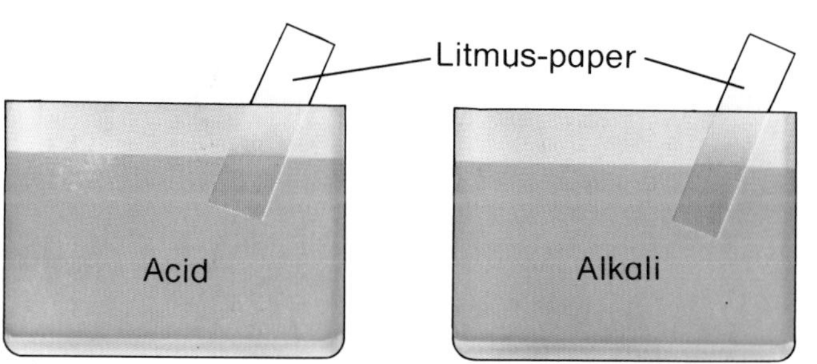

FIND OUT FOR YOURSELF

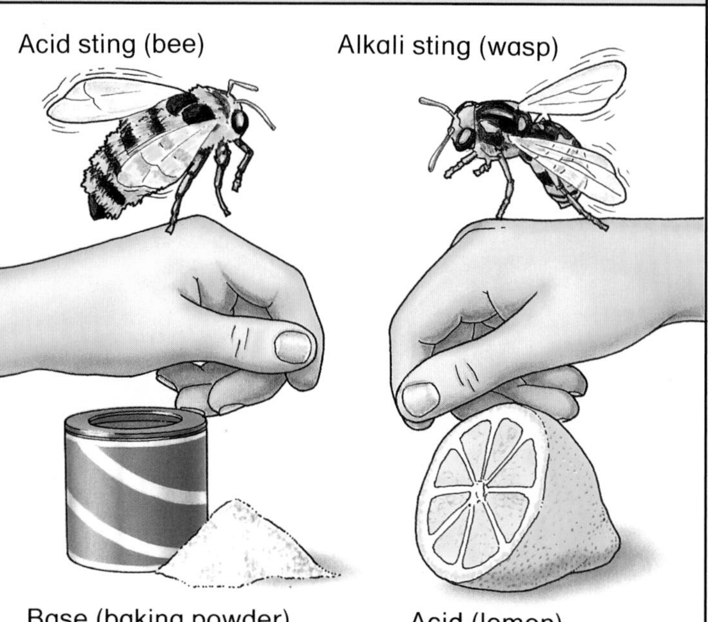

Bases are chemicals that "neutralize," or act against acids. A bee sting contains acid. Baking powder (an alkali) takes away the pain. A wasp sting contains an alkali. Putting lemon juice (an acid) on a wasp sting neutralizes the alkali and eases the pain.

actor see **drama**

advertising

The first advertisements were shop signs, such as a boot outside a shoemaker's shop. Today many businesses advertise to tell people about their goods or services. Some advertisements appear as words and pictures in print. Others are performed by actors on radio and television. People who make up advertisements think up catchy slogans and songs to help people remember each advertisement.

▲ Advertisements must catch the eye, so that people see and remember them. Advertisers use different ways to display their messages.

LIFE STORY

Aesop

According to legend, Aesop was a Greek slave who made up stories called fables. Though his fables have animal characters, they also show how people behave. Aesop may not have been a real person. Some people believe he lived on the Greek island of Samos about 2,500 years ago.

Aesop may have been freed from slavery because of his wonderful stories. A fable is a story with a moral, or hidden meaning. One of Aesop's fables is about a race between Tortoise and Hare. Hare raced far ahead and, sure of winning, stopped for a nap. Slow but steady Tortoise kept going and plodded past the sleeping Hare to win the race.

Africa

Africa is the second biggest continent. In the north is the hot, dry Sahara Desert. Central Africa is hot and wet, and there are thick rain forests. There are wide grassy plains called savannas in eastern Africa. Africa has mighty rivers, including the Nile, Zaire (Congo), Niger, and Zambezi. It also has very large lakes, such as Lake Victoria. The highest mountain in Africa is Kilimanjaro.

The first people appeared in Africa over four million years ago. Today there are many different ethnic groups in Africa with different customs and languages. Many African countries were once European colonies.

agriculture see **farming**

AFRICA

Africa is a continent of contrasts. It has mountains, deserts, forests, grasslands, and great cities. It has many wild animals; some are becoming rare. Africa is home to many groups of people, with different languages and ways of life. Many Africans live in small villages, although industry and cities are growing rapidly.

▲ Africa has a very long coastline and many of its people live in small villages beside the sea. They catch fish from sailing boats.

▲ Mt. Kilimanjaro is Africa's highest mountain. An extinct volcano, it rises to 19,340 ft (5,895 m).

▼ Cairo, the capital of Egypt, is Africa's biggest city. It stands on the banks of the Nile, the greatest of Africa's rivers.

FACTS AND RECORDS

Area: 11,706,165 sq mi (30,319,000 sq km)
Number of countries: 52
Population: 648,000,000
Largest country: Sudan (967,494 sq mi [2,505,813 sq km])
Largest city: Cairo (Egypt) 9,851,000
Longest rivers: Nile, Zaïre, Niger
Biggest lake: Lake Victoria
Largest deserts: Sahara, Kalahari, Namib
Biggest island: Madagascar
Greatest waterfall: Victoria Falls (5,580 ft [1,701 m] across)

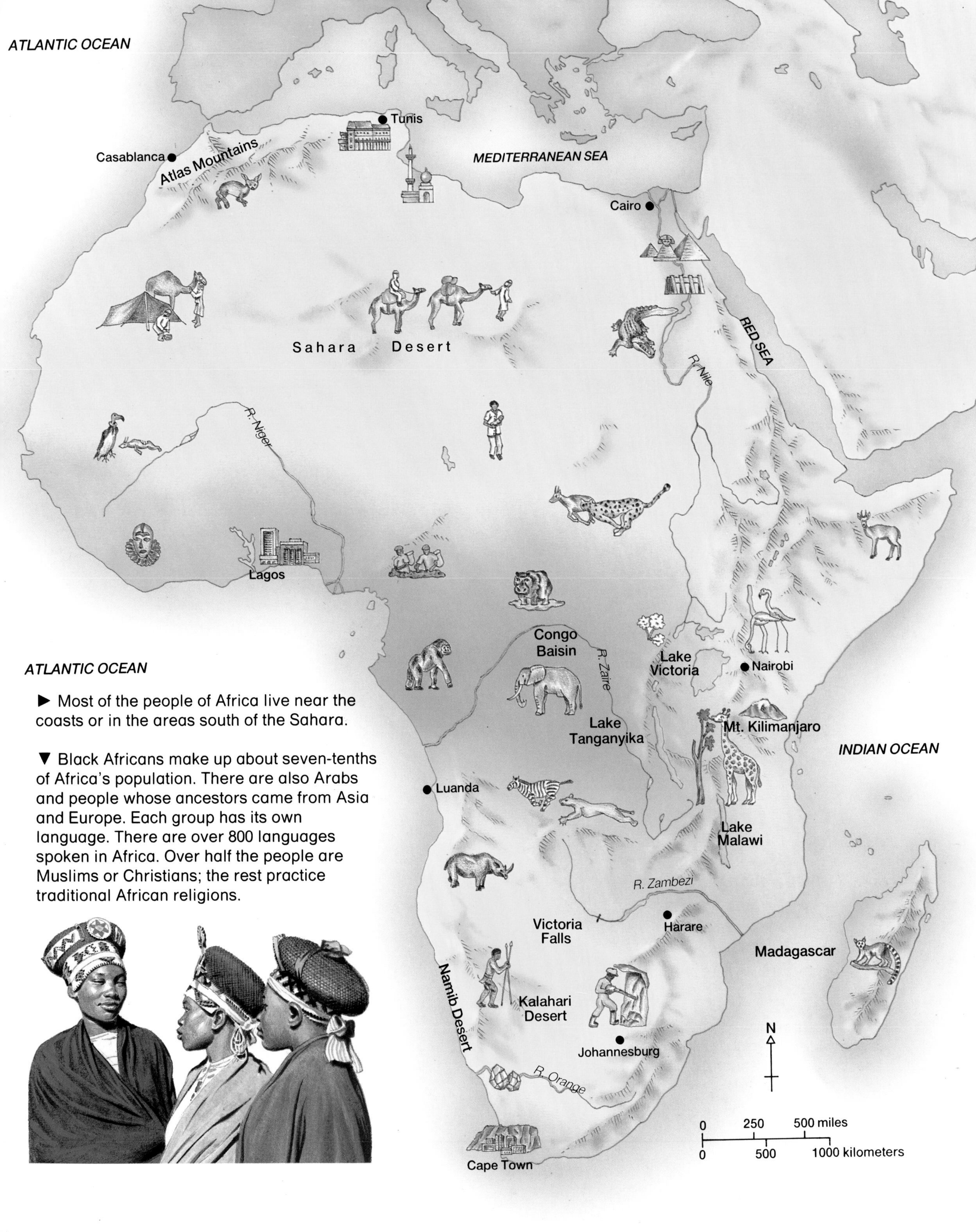

► Most of the people of Africa live near the coasts or in the areas south of the Sahara.

▼ Black Africans make up about seven-tenths of Africa's population. There are also Arabs and people whose ancestors came from Asia and Europe. Each group has its own language. There are over 800 languages spoken in Africa. Over half the people are Muslims or Christians; the rest practice traditional African religions.

AIR

Air is all around us. The earth is wrapped in a "skin" of air, the atmosphere. The different layers of the atmosphere are shown in the picture. The higher you go, the thinner the air becomes. There is no air at all in space. Without air, there would be no life on earth. Animals breathe air, and plants use air to help feed themselves.

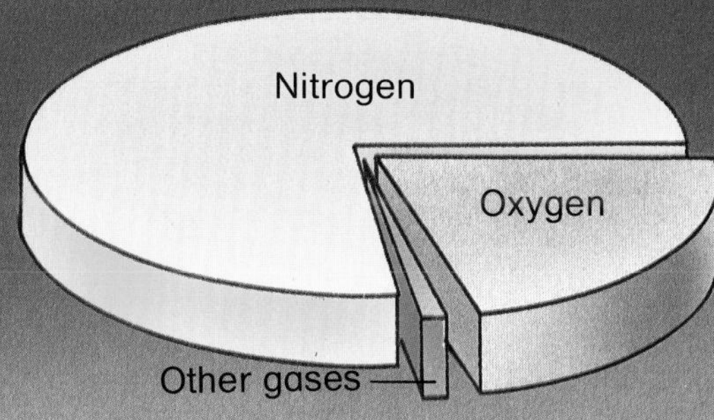

▲ Air is a mixture of gases. The pie chart above shows you that the main gases in the air are nitrogen and oxygen. There are small amounts of other gases.

▲ Gases from cars and factories cause air pollution. They form an extra layer in the atmosphere, so less of the earth's heat can escape into space. This "greenhouse effect" may make the earth warmer.

FIND OUT FOR YOURSELF

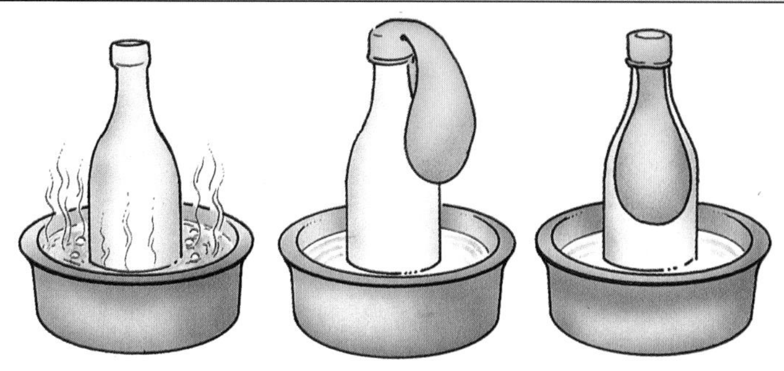

Stand a bottle in warm water. The heat makes the air inside expand (take up more space). The pressure of air inside the bottle increases. Fit a balloon over the neck of the bottle and stand the bottle in cold water. As the air in the bottle cools, the pressure drops. Because the pressure of the air outside the bottle is greater, it pushes the balloon into the bottle and inflates it.

Air can push up as well as down. A skydiver falls quickly until the parachute opens to meet the upward push of the air. In an aneroid barometer, below, rising air pressure will push in the sides of a thin metal box, moving a pointer on a scale.

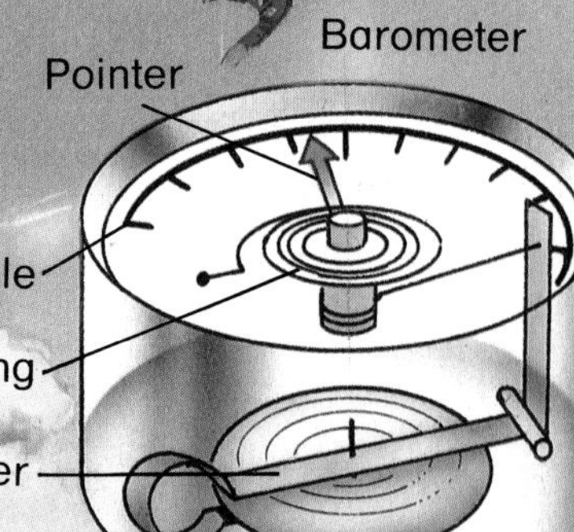

A

aircraft

Airplanes, airships, and balloons are aircraft. Airplanes, or "planes," have curved wings. As the plane's engines push it through the air, air flows around the wing. Because of the wing's shape, the air pushes up underneath it. This "lift" keeps the plane flying.

▼ A modern airliner can fly at 375 mph (600 kph) high above the clouds and can carry as many as 400 passengers. It can fly nonstop across oceans and continents. Some airliners have two jet engines, others have four. On most jets, the engines are under the wings.

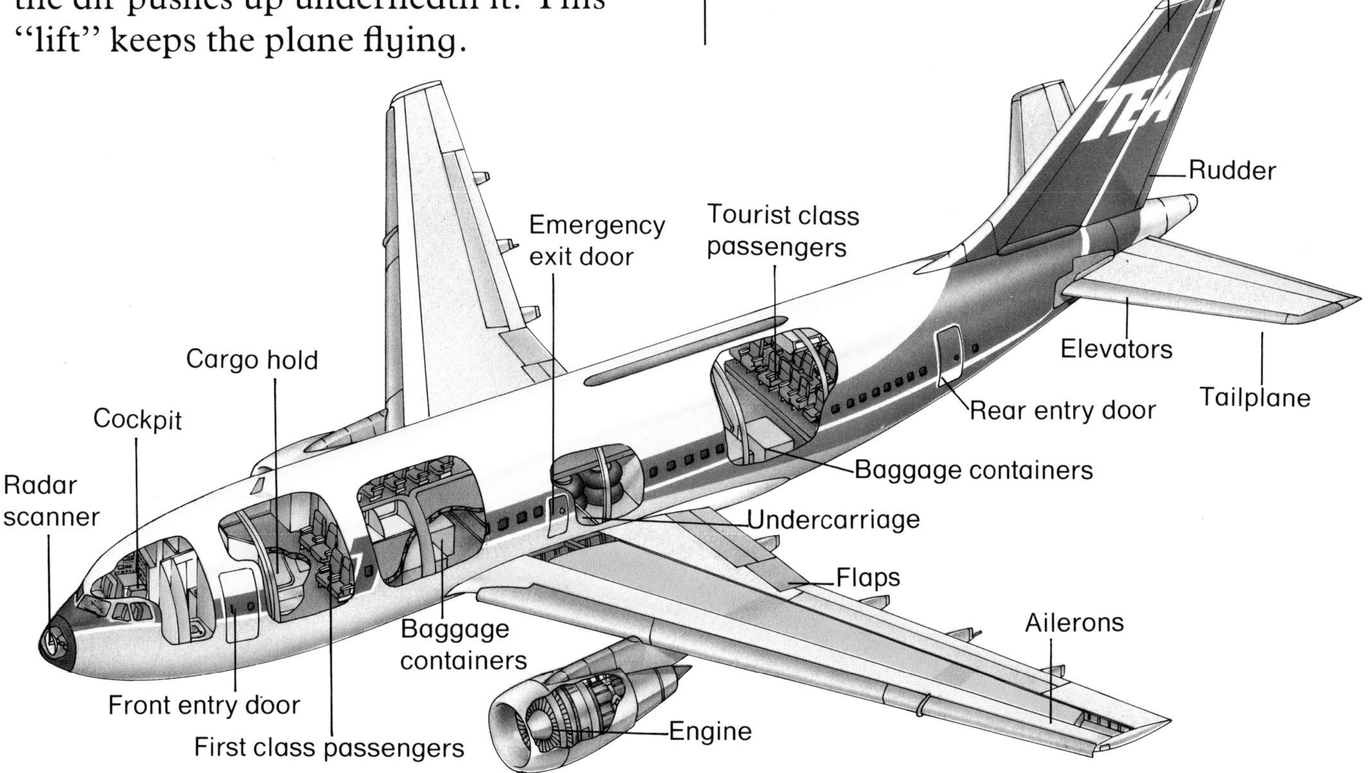

Airships and balloons have no engines. They are filled with gas or hot air. Gliders do not need engines, either. They can soar on rising currents of warm air. Most modern airplanes have jet engines, which shoot out jets of hot gases to push the plane along. Some planes have propellers that spin in the air and "screw" the plane forward. All early airplanes had propellers. Helicopters have rotors, which are thin wings that spin like upward-pointing propellers.

See **balloons and airships**, **engines**, **helicopter**, **Wright brothers**.

airport

An airport is a place where airplanes take off and land. At a big, busy airport planes arrive and leave every few minutes. Airports have long strips of concrete, called runways, on which planes take off and land. People called air traffic controllers use radio and radar to track aircraft flying near each airport. The controllers tell pilots when it is safe to take off and land. Airports are very busy places. Airport workers load cargo, check and clean planes, and look after the passengers. A big airport is like a small town, with parking lots, hotels, stores, banks, restaurants, and offices.

AIRCRAFT

A balloon looks very different from a helicopter. A Concorde can fly much faster than a glider. Yet all are aircraft. For thousands of years people dreamed of flying like the birds. Not until this century did the dream come true. Today, aircraft carry passengers across oceans and continents in a few hours.

▶ The Montgolfier brothers built this hot-air balloon in 1783. Two men, Jean Pilâtre de Rozier and the Marquis d'Arlandes, flew in it. No one had ever flown safely before.

Montgolfier balloon

▼ The German airship *Hindenburg* was three times longer than the biggest modern airliner, the 747 jumbo jet.

Boeing 747 airliner

Zeppelin

▲ In this little plane, *The Spirit of St. Louis*, Charles Lindbergh flew alone across the Atlantic in 1927. It took him 33.5 hours.

Spirit of St. Louis

▼ Orville and Wilbur Wright built their *Flyer* and taught themselves how to fly.

Wright brothers' *Flyer*

FACTS AND RECORDS

In 1903 Orville Wright flew an airplane for just 12 seconds — the beginning of the age of flight.

The first nonstop flight across the Atlantic was in 1919, by the British fliers Alcock and Brown.

The world's fastest aircraft was the rocket-engined X-15, which reached a speed of 4,534 mph (7,297 km/h) in 1967.

In 1989 a Boeing 747 airliner flew nonstop from England to Australia in 20 hours, 9 minutes.

Stealth bomber

▲ The American Stealth bomber has an unusual "flying wing" shape. In flight, it is almost "invisible" to radar beams that spot ordinary aircraft.

Concorde

▲ Concorde first carried passengers in 1976. It is the world's only supersonic airliner. It flies at over 1,300 mph (2,090 km/h).

▼ Some very fast jets have "swing wings." The wings are held straight for slow flight and fold back when the plane is flying fast.

▼ The Bell XS-1 was the first plane to fly faster than sound (670 mph [1,078 km/h]), in 1947.

Bell XS-1

Swing-wing jet

Helicopter

Glider

▲ A glider has no engine. It uses rising air currents, called thermals, to soar as high as 46,000 ft (14,000 m).

▲ The helicopter was developed in the late 1930s. Its rotor blades act as wings and propellers. The helicopter can fly upward and downward. It can also hover.

Harrier

◀ The Harrier jump-jet can take off and land vertically, like a helicopter, by swiveling its engine nozzles.

A

LIFE STORY

Alexander the Great

Alexander the Great was born in 356 B.C. His father, Philip, was king of Macedonia, a kingdom in what is now Greece. Aristotle, a famous Greek philosopher, was Alexander's teacher.

After Philip was murdered, Alexander became king. He swiftly conquered the other Greek kingdoms. Then he dared to attack the mighty Persian empire. At a town called Gordium was a massive knotted rope. People believed that whoever could untie the knot would rule the world. Alexander boldly cut the knot with his sword.

Alexander won battle after battle. He defeated the Persian king Darius. He conquered Egypt and founded a city called Alexandria. He wanted to conquer India, but his soldiers persuaded him to turn back.

Alexander was only 33 when he died in 323 B.C. Without him to lead his vast empire, it soon broke up.

alphabet

We use alphabets to write the words that make up languages. An alphabet is a group of letters, or signs. Each one stands for a sound.

The first writing was picture writing. Eventually the pictures became simple picture signs, then letters. Most European alphabets come from the Roman alphabet. Chinese, Greek, and Russian have different alphabets.

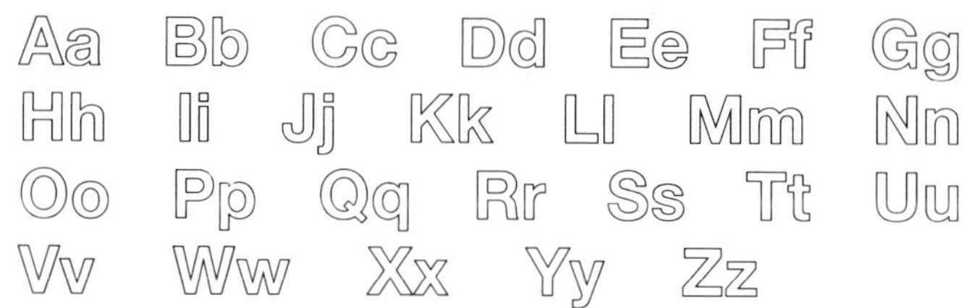

▲ The English alphabet has 26 letters. They are written as capitals (uppercase) or small (lowercase).

Amazon

The Amazon River in South America is 4,000 mi (6,437 km) long. Because so many smaller rivers feed into it, the Amazon pours more water into the ocean than any other river.

Amazon birds

DID YOU KNOW?

The Amazon rain forest is amazingly rich in plant life. A patch of jungle about one square mile (two and a half square km) may have 3,000 different kinds of plants. Forest trees reach up 200 ft (60 m) toward the sunlight. Only a little sunlight reaches the ground.

The Amazon begins its journey in the Andes Mountains. It flows east, through thick rain forest, the largest tropical forest on earth. The Amazon flows into the Atlantic Ocean. See **South America**.

America see **Canada, North America, South America, United States of America**

American Indians

When Europeans sailed to America in the 1400s, they called the people they met "Indians." The Europeans did not know about America. They thought they had sailed to the Indies, islands in Asia. The Indians had lived in America for thousands of years. Some were farmers, others hunted and fished. Some Indians lived in the forests, others on the plains. Indians also settled in the jungles of Central and South America.

▲ These Indians live high in the Andes Mountains in South America. They travel to town to sell their crops.

The Maya, Aztec, and Inca Indians built great civilizations. The Indian way of life changed forever when Europeans arrived. See **Incas and Aztecs**.

DID YOU KNOW?

There were no horses in America when the first Europeans arrived. Wild horses had died out. Horses were brought from Europe in the 1600s. Plains Indians such as the Sioux and the Cheyenne became expert horse riders.

amphibians

Amphibians are cold-blooded animals. Like reptiles and birds, amphibians lay eggs. Amphibians spend part of their life on dry land, and part in water. They can breathe air and move around on land. But nearly all amphibians must return to water to lay their eggs.

The first prehistoric animals to move from water to land were the first amphibians. Present-day amphibians include toads, frogs, newts, salamanders, and caecilians. See **prehistoric animals**.

AMPHIBIANS

Amphibians are animals such as frogs and salamanders. They spend part of their lives in water and part on land. All amphibians lay their eggs in water — in rivers, ponds, or on a drop of water trapped in a leaf. The eggs hatch into swimming tadpoles, which soon grow legs and can crawl onto dry land. Amphibians eat insects and other small creatures.

THE GIANT SALAMANDER

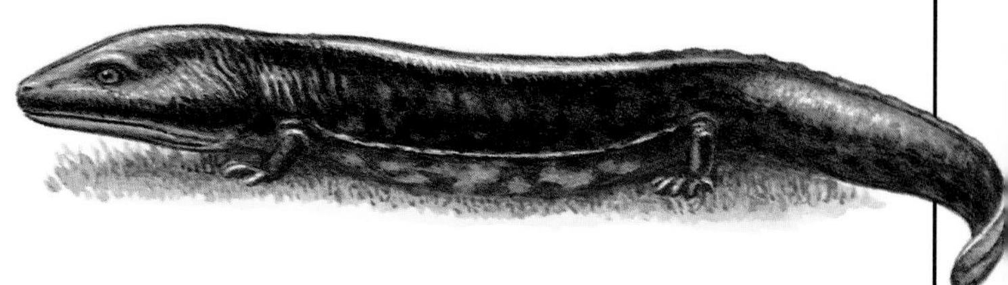

Most amphibians are small animals. The biggest amphibian in the world is the Chinese giant salamander. One of these huge amphibians measured 6 ft (1.8 m) from nose to tail (as tall as a grown man) and weighed 143 lb (65 kg).

▲ Tree frogs are good climbers. Many frogs "sing" by puffing out their throats with air.

▲ Newts can breathe through their skin.

▲ The midwife toad carries its eggs on its back until the tadpoles hatch.

◀ The Mexican axolotl is a tadpole that never grows up. It has gills, but never develops lungs.

LIFE CYCLE OF A FROG

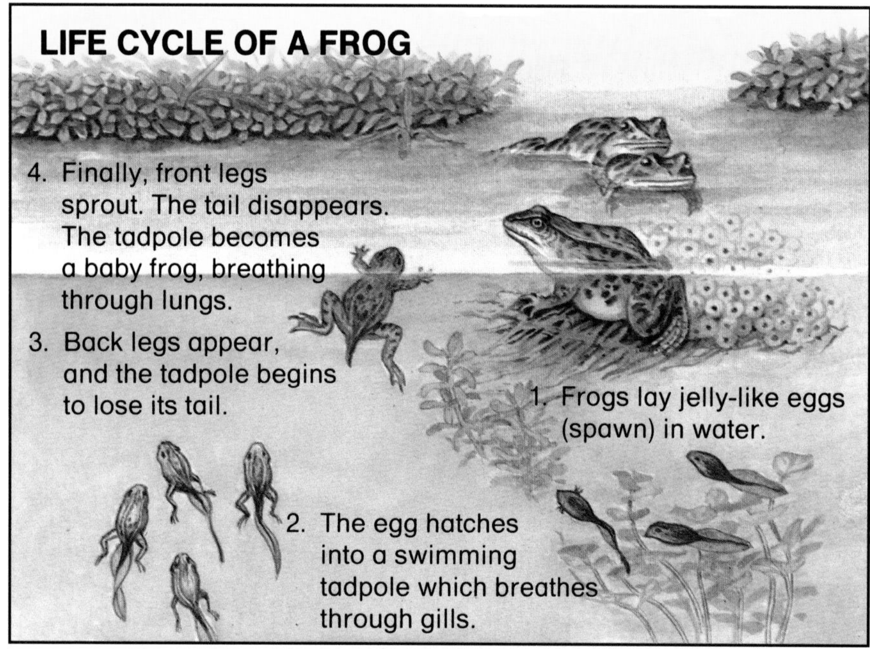

WHY BRIGHT COLORS?

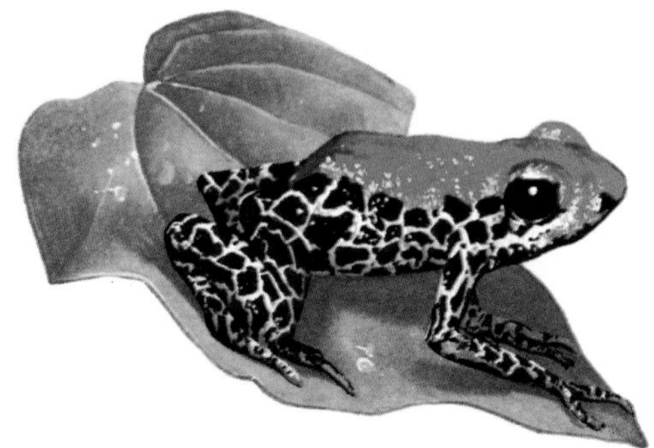

Most frogs are the color of leaves or mud. This helps them to hide from enemies, such as snakes. But some frogs have a deadly poison in their skin. poisonous frogs are brightly colored. The colors warn other animals to keep away.

Andes Mountains

The Andes Mountains run the length of South America. The highest peak is Aconcagua, which is 22,835 ft (6,960 m) high. Lake Titicaca is the highest large lake in the world. See **South America**.

Anglo-Saxons

The Anglo-Saxon people came to England from Germany about 1,500 years ago. They set up kingdoms, the most important of which was Wessex. Many English words are Anglo-Saxon.

▲ Archeologists found this Anglo-Saxon helmet in a tomb at Sutton Hoo, England.
► Alfred the Great (849–899) ruled the Saxon kingdom of Wessex and fought against Danish invaders.

▼ The Anglo-Saxons lived in villages. Their houses were made of wood, thatch, and mud. Nobles lived in great halls. The villagers lived by farming.

animals

It is usually easy to tell the difference between a plant and an animal. Most animals can move by themselves. Most plants cannot. Plants make their own food. Animals cannot; they eat plants or other animals. Animals have brains and nervous systems. Plants do not, but a few plants behave like animals, and a few tiny animals behave like plants.

Animals can be divided into two groups. Animals with backbones are called vertebrates. Animals without backbones are called invertebrates. The main animal families are listed below.

Animals range in size from tiny blobs of floating jelly to enormous whales. They have developed over millions of years. Some have changed as the earth has changed, but others have died out. See **prehistoric animals**.

ANIMAL CLASSIFICATION

Vertebrates (animals with backbones)
Fishes: More than 30,000 species, or kinds
Amphibians: About 4,000 species
Reptiles: More than 6,500 species
Birds: About 8,800 species
Mammals: More than 4,000 species

Invertebrates (animals without backbones)
Insects: More than 1 million species
Crustaceans (crabs, lobsters): 25,000 species
Mollusks (snails, slugs, octopuses): 128,000 species
Plus: Many thousands of spiders, starfish, worms, corals, jellyfish, sponges, and others.

ANIMALS

Animals live in every part of the earth, in the water, in the air, and on land. The area where an animal lives is called its habitat. Here are some important habitats. Herds of grass-eating animals live on the plains. Forest animals live among the trees. Desert animals can live with little water. Polar animals have thick fur to keep warm.

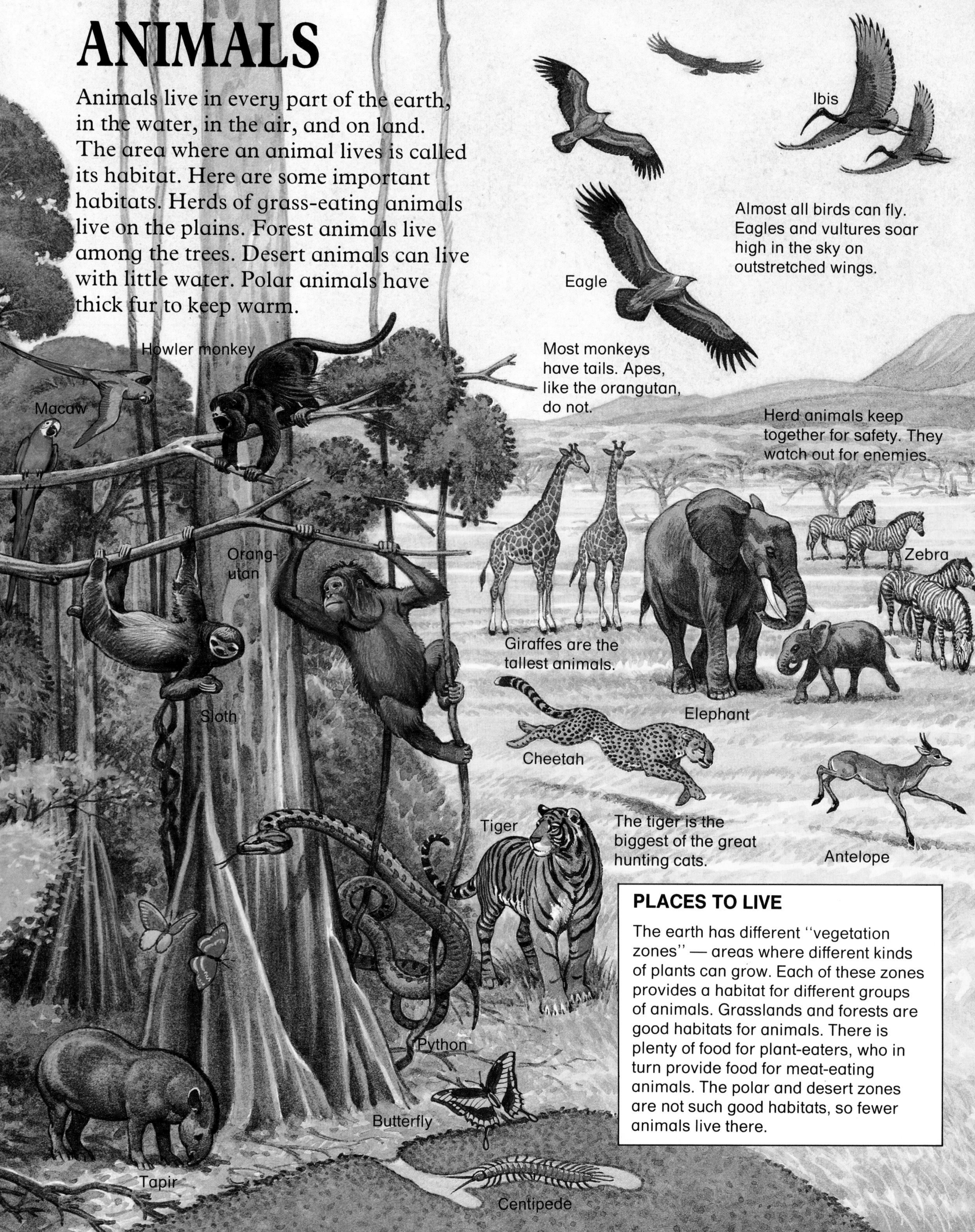

PLACES TO LIVE

The earth has different "vegetation zones" — areas where different kinds of plants can grow. Each of these zones provides a habitat for different groups of animals. Grasslands and forests are good habitats for animals. There is plenty of food for plant-eaters, who in turn provide food for meat-eating animals. The polar and desert zones are not such good habitats, so fewer animals live there.

◀ Many different kinds of animals and birds live in a woodland habitat.

▲ Tiny living things called plankton drift in the seas. They are eaten by other animals, including the giant blue whale.

The octopus is a mollusk.

Fish have no lungs. They use gills to breathe in water.

Polar bears have thick fur and seals have layers of fat to help keep out the cold.

A

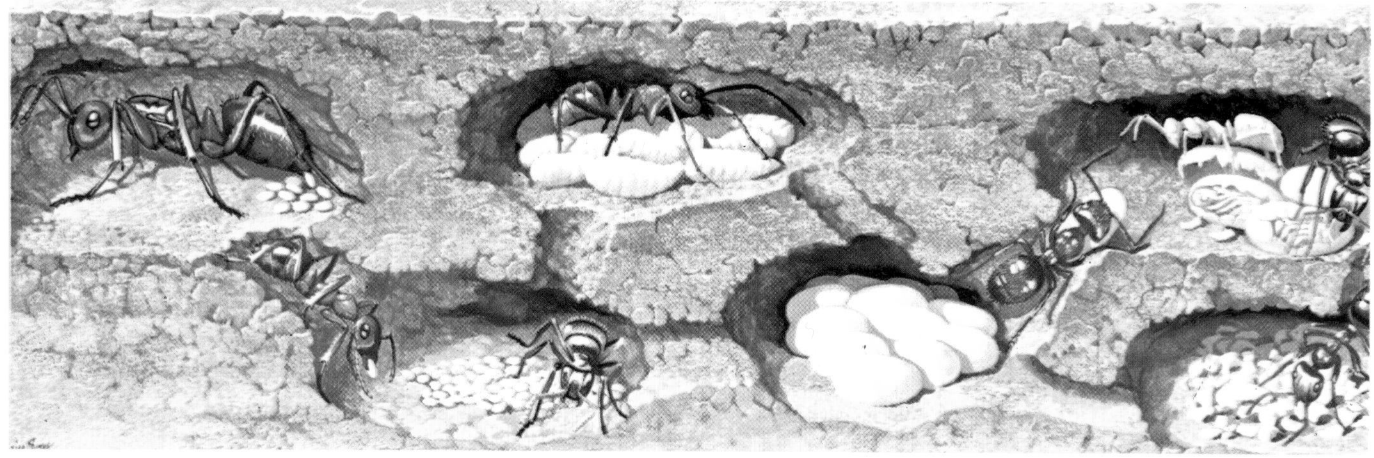

▲ Inside an ants' nest, the queen (1) lays eggs. Workers care for the eggs (2) as they grow and turn into larvae (3) and cocoons (4). New workers emerge (5). Waste material is stored in a garbage chamber (6).

ant

Ants live in groups called colonies. One colony may contain as many as a million ants. Ants are found all over the world. They build nests on or under the ground, or in trees. Each colony has a queen. After she mates with a winged male, the queen spends her entire life laying eggs. Worker ants look after the eggs and collect food for the colony; soldier ants guard the nest. A colony of army ants will eat any animal that cannot escape. See **insects**.

Antarctic see **Arctic and Antarctic**

antelope

Antelopes are plant-eating mammals. Like cows, they chew the cud. This means that they grab mouthfuls of grass, swallow it, and chew it properly later. Antelopes live in groups called herds. They are always watchful for enemies. Some herds of antelope live on the grassy plains of Africa. Other antelopes live in small groups in forests. Male antelopes use their horns to fight during the breeding season. The biggest antelope is the eland. The smallest is the dik-dik, which is the size of a rabbit.

apes

Apes are the mammals most like humans. Unlike monkeys, apes do not have tails. They can stand upright, but usually move around on all fours, especially in trees. The biggest ape is the gorilla. Gorillas and chimpanzees live in the forests of Africa. The gibbon and orangutan live in Southeast Asia.

▼ These apes live in Asia. The gibbon is acrobatic. The orangutan moves more slowly.

Apes live in small groups. They eat mostly fruit, leaves, and roots, but chimpanzees will eat monkeys and other animals. Apes are intelligent. They can learn to use simple tools, and tame chimpanzees have learned some words in human language. See **mammals**.

archeology

Archeologists uncover the past. They find and study ruined buildings, buried treasure, even old pots. Often they excavate, or dig out, their finds. They may find a grave under farmland, a Roman temple beneath a new office building, or a sunken ship on the seabed. Even a tiny piece of broken pottery can tell an archeologist what life was like hundreds or even thousands of years ago.

archery

An archer shoots an arrow from a bow. Longbows and crossbows were favorite weapons before guns were invented. Today archery is a sport.

architecture

Architecture is the art and science of designing buildings. An architect draws detailed plans for the builders to follow.

Some of the greatest architecture of the past was made by the ancient Egyptians, Greeks, Romans, Arabs, Indians, and Chinese. In Central and South America, the Aztecs and Incas made impressive buildings. In the 1500s, European architects copied the simple but graceful Greek and Roman classical style. Later architects preferred more decoration. Modern architects plan airports, factories, schools, office buildings, shops, houses, and sometimes whole towns. Architecture should be pleasing to look at, as well as comfortable and safe for people to live and work in. See **buildings**.

▼ Architecture has produced different styles of buildings for different purposes over the centuries.

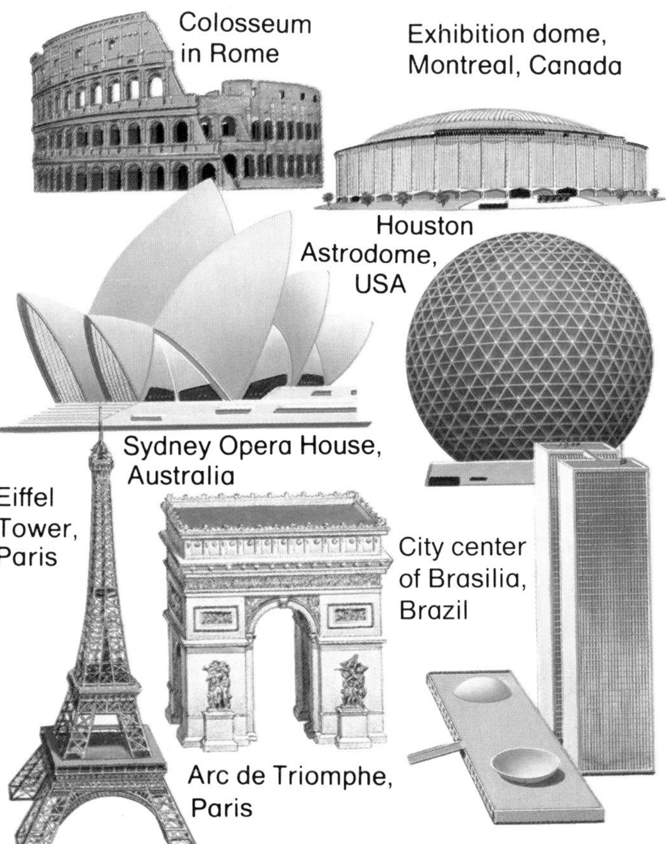

▲ The Arctic and Antarctic are covered with snow and ice. Winters are long and cold, and summers short. The picture shows three Arctic animals.

Arctic and Antarctic

The earth's coldest places are close to the North Pole, in the Arctic, and the South Pole, in the Antarctic. These are the polar regions. The Arctic is mostly frozen sea, surrounded by land. The Antarctic is an ice-covered land continent, surrounded by cold sea. In places the ice is thousands of yards thick. It is so cold that very few plants can grow, and there are few land animals. But the seas are rich in fish, which are eaten by penguins, seals, and whales. The Arctic is home to Eskimos and some other hunting peoples, but only scientists live in the Antarctic.

Aristotle

Aristotle was a Greek scientist and philosopher (a person interested in why life is as it is). He lived more than 2,000 years ago. Aristotle was taught by another philosopher, Plato. Their ideas still interest people today. See **Greece**.

armadillo

The armadillo lives in North and South America. Its body is protected by bony armor. When frightened, an armadillo rolls into a ball, so no enemy can hurt it. Armadillos eat insects and roots, using their strong claws for tearing and digging.

▲ The armadillo is a timid animal. It can run fast to escape an enemy and can dig burrows with its powerful claws.

armor

In ancient battles, soldiers fought at close range with swords, spears, clubs, and bows and arrows. For protection, they wore armor. Roman soldiers wore leather and metal armor. In the Middle Ages, knights wore coats of chain mail,

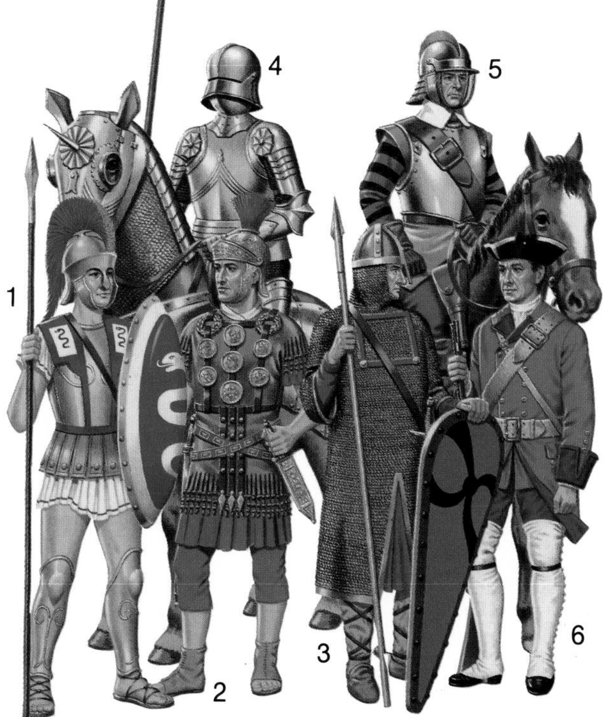

▲ Armor through the ages: (1) Greek (2) Roman (3) Norman (4) Medieval knight (5) Roundhead of the 1600s (6) By the 1700s, soldiers no longer wore body armor.

made from iron rings looped together. Later, they wore heavy suits of steel-plate armor. By the 1700s guns had made armor out of date.

art

Through art, people express how they see and feel about the world. An artist's work can delight, shock, or puzzle us. The arts include painting, sculpture, literature, music, dance, theater, and architecture. The first artists were Stone Age cave painters. Art is fun to do for yourself. Everyone can enjoy great art through museums, theater, television, art galleries, books, and records.

◀ This huge statue of the prophet Moses was made in the early 1500s by the Italian artist Michelangelo. He was one of the greatest artists of the period known as the Renaissance, or rebirth of learning, in Europe in the early 1500s. Michelangelo was helped in his work by assistants.

DID YOU KNOW?

The famous cave paintings at Lascaux, France, are about 20,000 years old. They are pictures of the animals prehistoric people hunted.

The impressionists were a group of French artists of the 1800s. At first, some people made fun of their paintings, but today impressionist paintings are worth enormous sums of money.

Asia

Asia is the largest continent. It stretches from Turkey in the west to the Pacific Ocean in the east. About a third of the earth's land is in Asia.

More than three in every five of the earth's people live in Asia. They are a mixture of races and religions. The two largest Asian countries are China and India. Each has more people than any other country. Most of the U.S.S.R. is in Asia. Japan is the leading industrial country in Asia. The Middle East, especially Saudi Arabia, is rich in oil.

Asia has many kinds of land and climate. There are tropical forests and jungles. There are hot, dry deserts and cold tundra plains. There are wide steppes, or grasslands. Asia has the world's greatest mountain range, the Himalayas, and some very long rivers.

Asia has a long, rich history. Great civilizations rose and fell there. Five great religions – Buddhism, Christianity, Hinduism, Islam, and Judaism – began in Asia. See **religion**.

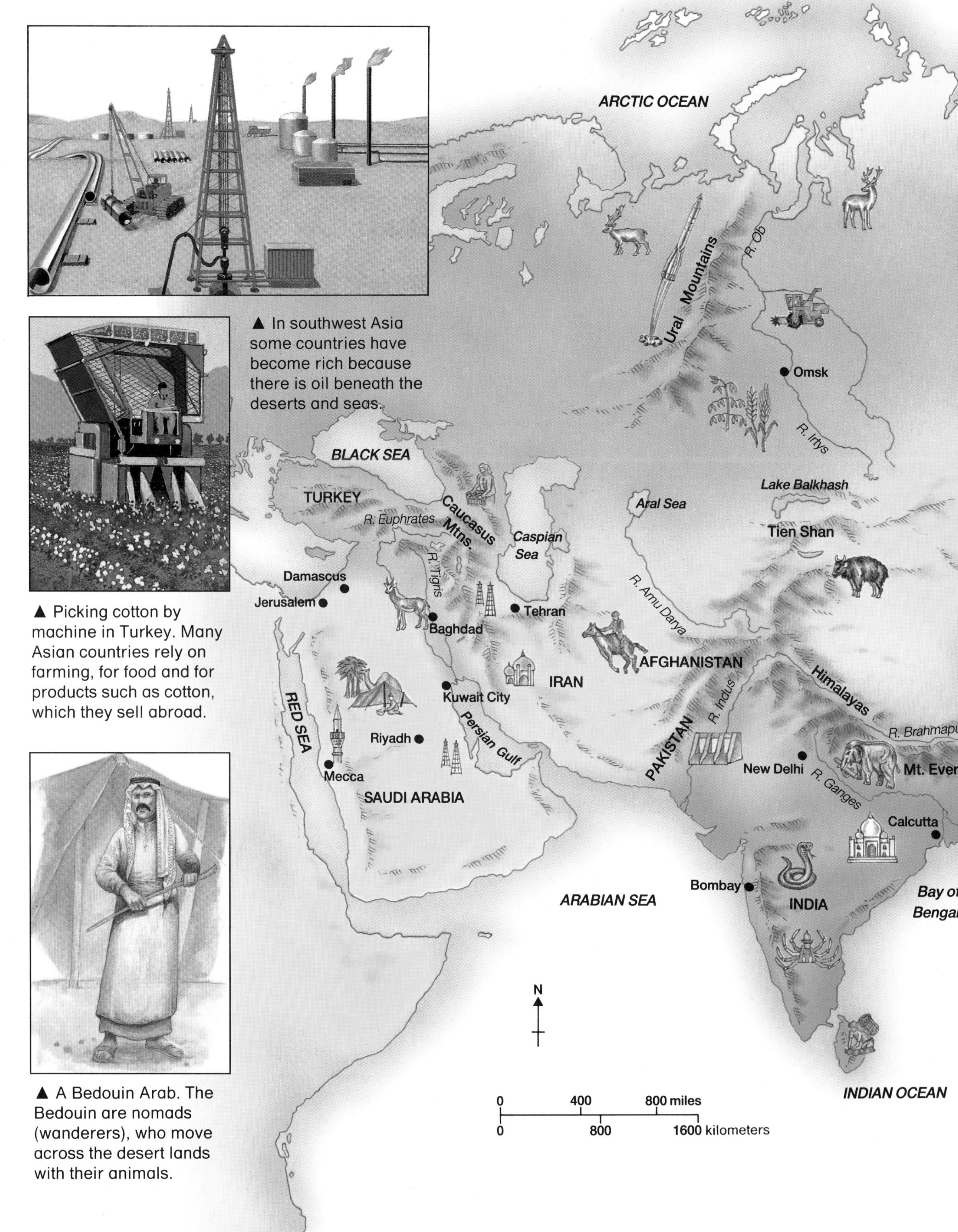

▲ In southwest Asia some countries have become rich because there is oil beneath the deserts and seas.

▲ Picking cotton by machine in Turkey. Many Asian countries rely on farming, for food and for products such as cotton, which they sell abroad.

▲ A Bedouin Arab. The Bedouin are nomads (wanderers), who move across the desert lands with their animals.

ASIA

Asia is the biggest continent. It stretches from the Arctic in the north to the equator in the south. It covers nearly a third of the earth's land surface. Asia has many different types of land and climate. In central Asia are the world's highest mountains, the Himalaya. Many people live in the warm, wet monsoon lands of south Asia.

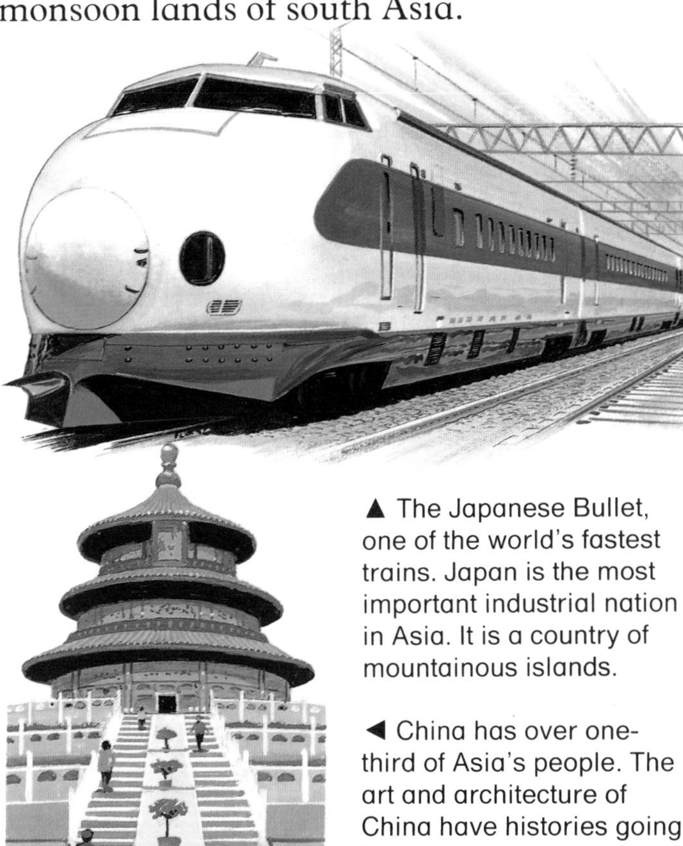

▲ The Japanese Bullet, one of the world's fastest trains. Japan is the most important industrial nation in Asia. It is a country of mountainous islands.

◀ China has over one-third of Asia's people. The art and architecture of China have histories going back thousands of years.

FACTS AND RECORDS

Area: 17,139,000 sq mi (44,390,000 sq km). This includes 75 percent of the U.S.S.R. and 97 percent of Turkey.
Number of countries: 39
Population: 3,108,000,000, excluding U.S.S.R.
Largest country (excluding U.S.S.R.): China (3,705,369 sq mi [9,596,916 sq km])
Country with most people: China (1,160,017,000)
Largest city: Tokyo-Yokohama (Japan) 26,952,000
Highest mountain: Mt. Everest
Longest river: Chang Jiang (Yangtze)
Largest lakes: Caspian Sea, Aral Sea, Lake Baikal

A

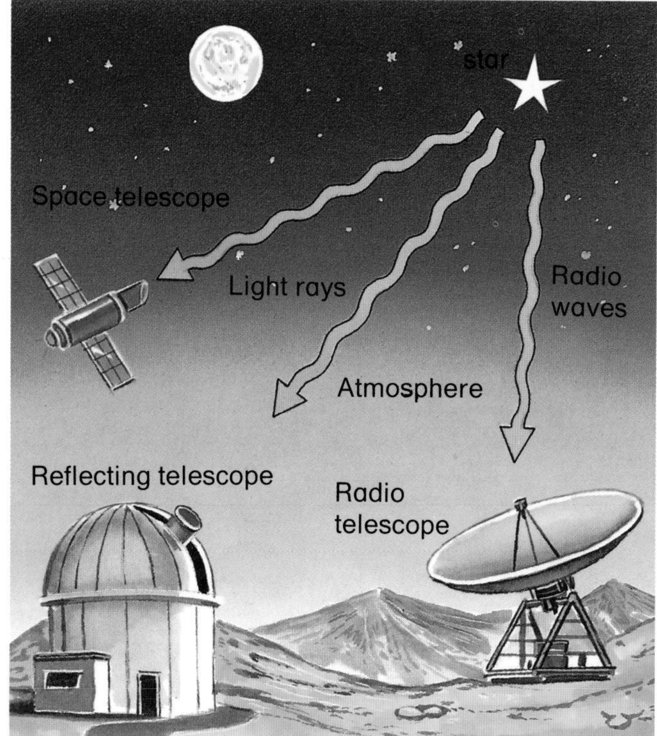

▲ Astronomers use radio telescopes to study radio waves from stars. A space telescope, above the earth's atmosphere, sees stars more clearly than one that is placed on the ground.

astronomy

Astronomy is the study of the stars. Ancient astronomers thought, wrongly, that the stars affected people's lives. They drew maps of the stars, and they noticed that some stars moved. These wandering stars were planets. Today astronomers use telescopes on the ground and in space. They can detect stars so far away that light from them takes hundreds of years to reach earth. See **moon**, **solar system**, **star**, **universe**.

Atlantic Ocean

This is the earth's second-largest ocean, after the Pacific. It separates Europe and Africa from America. The North Atlantic Current is a warm current of water that flows across the Atlantic.

atom

Everything in the universe is made of atoms. An atom is very tiny. It is the smallest unit of a chemical element (such as iron) that behaves like that element. One atom measures about .04 millionth of an inch across. Under the most powerful microscope, it looks like a fuzzy white dot. Atoms can be divided into even smaller units. The center of an atom is the nucleus. It is made of protons and neutrons. Spinning around the nucleus are electrons. Each element has its own arrangement of protons, neutrons, and electrons in its atoms. See **nuclear energy**.

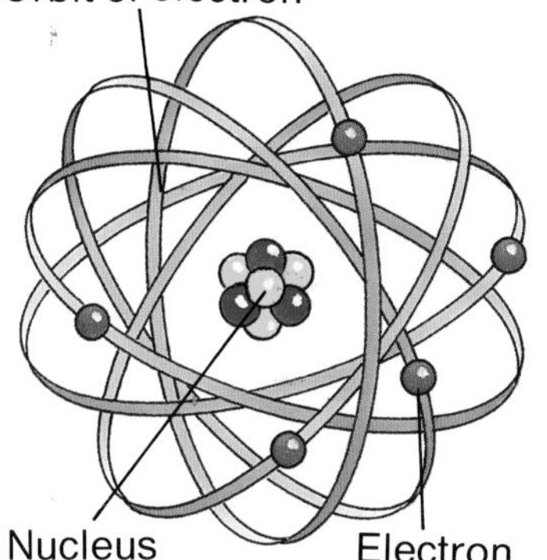

◀ Inside the atom. The center of the atom is the nucleus, made up of protons and neutrons. Around the nucleus are electrons. Every element is made of atoms. Each element's atoms are arranged differently.

Australia and Australasia

Australia is the smallest continent. Neighboring island countries, including New Zealand, Papua New Guinea, the Philippines, and islands in the Pacific, are sometimes described as being in Australasia, or Oceania.

Australia and its neighbors were first settled by Asian and Pacific people thousands of years ago. Aborigines lived in Australia. Maoris settled in New Zealand. Dutch sailors from Europe explored Australia in the 1600s. From the 1700s, Britain ruled Australia and New Zealand. Most of the countries of the region are now independent.

AUSTRALASIA

Australasia includes Australia and its Pacific Ocean island neighbors, including New Zealand. Some of the people settled there thousands of years ago. Others came from Europe and Asia in recent times. Natural wonders include the Great Barrier Reef, the world's longest coral reef.

FACTS AND RECORDS

Area (land): 3,273,259 sq mi (8,477,749 sq km)
Number of countries: 11
Population: 24,015,500
Largest country: Australia (2,966,183 sq mi [7,682,422 sq km])
Smallest country: Nauru (8 sq mi [21 sq km]), about 8,000 people
Largest city: Sydney, Australia (3,623,600)
Highest mountain: Mt. Wilhelm (Papua New Guinea)
Longest river: Darling (Australia)

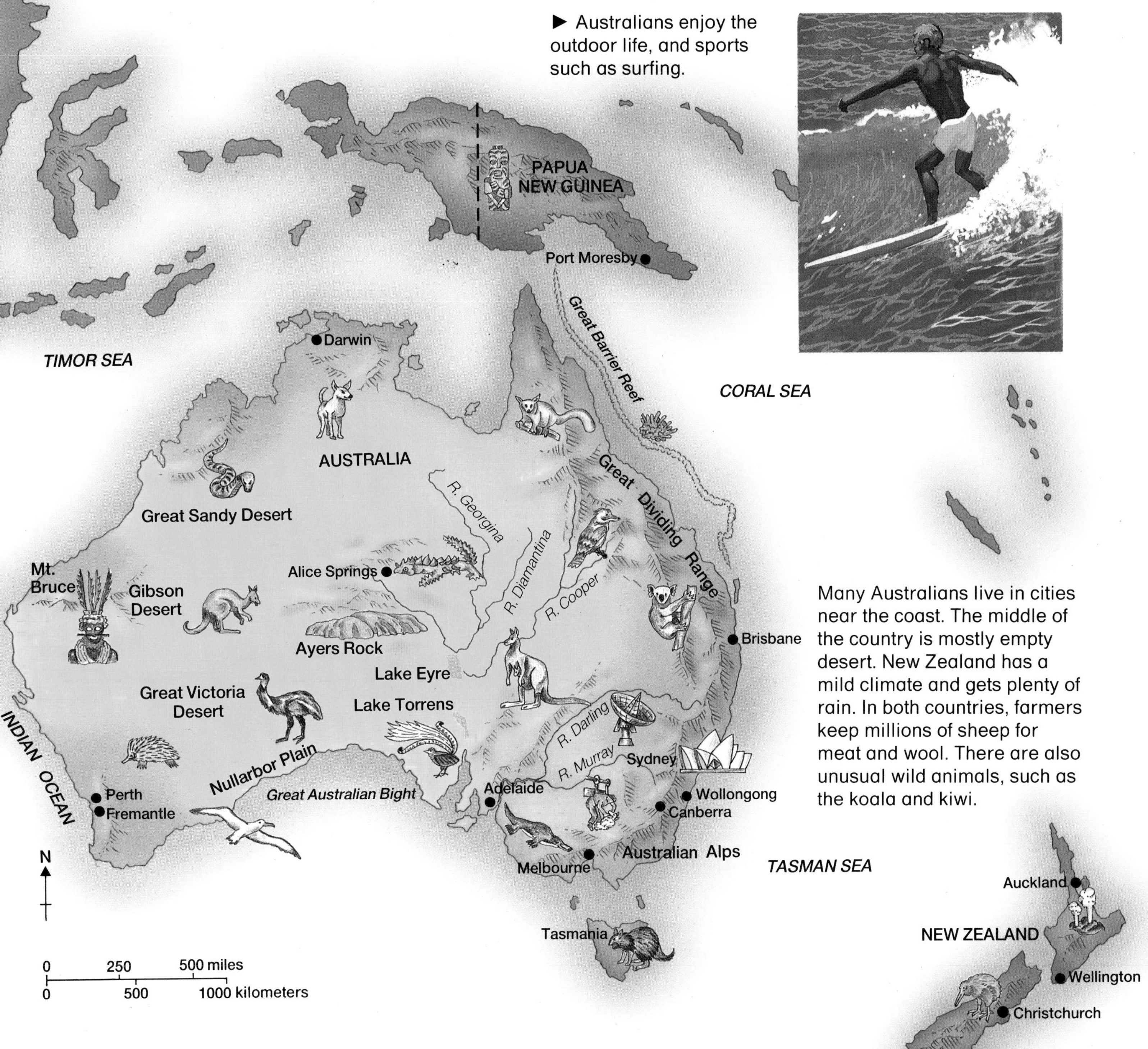

► Australians enjoy the outdoor life, and sports such as surfing.

Many Australians live in cities near the coast. The middle of the country is mostly empty desert. New Zealand has a mild climate and gets plenty of rain. In both countries, farmers keep millions of sheep for meat and wool. There are also unusual wild animals, such as the koala and kiwi.

B

Bach
The Bach family of Germany produced many excellent musicians. Johann Sebastian Bach (1685–1750) was one of the world's greatest composers. He was also a brilliant organist. Bach wrote hundreds of pieces of music, many of them for choirs and for use in church.

▼ Bach was one of the great composers. Here he is shown playing the organ, with a group of musicians.

bacteria
Bacteria are tiny living things, so small you can see them only through a powerful microscope. They are found in soil, water, and air. Bacteria make food go bad, and some cause diseases. But many are also useful to us.

badger
Badgers are relatives of weasels. The European badger has a black and white striped head, thick gray fur, and short legs. Badgers live in burrows called sets. They come out after dark to find food.

ballet
Ballet is dance performed on the stage to music. It began in the 1600s in France and Italy. In the early 1900s the Russian Ballet became world-famous. Ballet dancers train hard to learn set positions and movements. See **dance**.

balloons and airships
A large balloon can be a flying machine. In 1783, two men "flew" in a basket attached to a hot-air balloon. Today, people fly in balloons for fun.

An airship is a sausage-shaped balloon with engines and propellers. Airships were invented in the 1850s.

► In 1783, two Frenchmen, Jean Pilâtre de Rozier and the marquis d'Arlandes, made the first flight in a hot-air balloon. The balloon was made by the Montgolfier brothers.

DID YOU KNOW?

The German airship *Hindenburg* was 804 ft (245 m) long. It was destroyed by fire in 1937. This disaster ended transatlantic airship flights.

B

bamboo

Bamboo grows so tall that it looks like a tree, but it is really a giant grass. Bamboo grows best in hot countries. The hollow stems are used to make houses, baskets, boats, and water pipes.

▲ Bamboo has many uses. It can make houses, household items such as drinking mugs and baskets, and even birdcages.

bank

Banks protect people's money and pay them interest on their savings. Savings and loan associations lend money to people who need a loan — for example, to pay for a new house or new machines in a factory. There are also international banks that lend money to businesses all around the world.

barometer see **air**

bat

Bats are the only mammals able to fly. A bat has wings of skin stretched between its long bony fingers. Bats fly at night, using echo signals to avoid objects in their way. See **mammals**.

battery

The electricity from a battery is made by chemicals inside it. Dry batteries are used in flashlights and radios. Some can be recharged again and again. A car has a wet battery, containing weak acid. See **electricity**.

battles see **wars**

bear

Bears are powerful mammals, with furry coats and sharp claws. The biggest are the Kodiak bears of Alaska. Almost as big are the brown grizzly bear and the white polar bear.

▼ Female bears give birth to their babies, or cubs, in winter. In spring, the mother begins to teach her cubs how to look after themselves.

B

beaver
Beavers are rodents that live in forests, beside streams. They swim well, using their webbed feet and oarlike tails. They eat bark, shoots, and roots. American beavers are nature's dam builders. First they cut tree branches, using their sharp front teeth. They build a dam across a stream using branches, mud, and stones. Water blocked by the dam makes a pond. In the pond, the beavers build a snug dome-shaped den.

bee
Bees are busy insects. They fly to and from flowers, collecting nectar and pollen for food. Without the bees' visits, many flowers could not make seeds. Some kinds of bees live alone, in burrows. Others live in large colonies. They build a nest called a hive. In each hive there is one queen, some males, or drones, and many worker bees. The workers care for the eggs laid by the queen, and rear the young. They collect nectar to make honey. They build wax cells inside the hive, some for the young bees and some in which to store honey. Honeybees collect pollen in baskets on their back legs. People keep bees to collect the honey. See **insects**.

◀ Many six-sided cells make up the honeybees' comb, where they store the honey.

LIFE STORY

Beethoven
Many people admire the music written by Ludwig van Beethoven. It can be sad and delicate, or stirring and full of energy. Beethoven wrote nine symphonies for the orchestra, as well as other pieces for singers, piano, and small groups of stringed instruments. He also wrote an opera and religious music.

Beethoven was born in 1770, in Bonn, Germany. He could play the harpsichord, violin, and organ by the time he was 10. In 1787 the composer Mozart heard him play, and he said that Beethoven would be a great musician. Beethoven became a famous pianist as well as a great composer. Later he grew unhappy and quarrelsome, because he was going deaf. This was a terrible hardship. Beethoven never heard some of his greatest music played. He composed it in his head, unable to hear either the orchestra or the applause of the audience. He died in 1827.

beetle

A beetle may be as tiny as a pinhead or as big as your fist. Beetles are insects. They have two pairs of wings, but use only the back wings for flying. Many beetles run on the ground and never fly. Some swim underwater. Many beetles eat only plants. Others are hunters or scavengers that feed on dead animals and plants. Beetles lay eggs which hatch into larvae, or grubs. See **insects**.

▼ The Colorado beetle is a pest because its grubs eat potato crops.

Bible

The Bible is a collection of books. The first part, the Old Testament, is sacred to both Jews and Christians. The second part, the New Testament, tells of the life and teachings of Jesus Christ.

bicycle

The bicycle was invented in the 1800s. The first bicycles had no pedals, and riders pushed themselves along with their feet. Later, pedals were added, driving a chain which turned the back wheel. The high-wheeler had a large front wheel and a tiny back wheel. Modern bicycles are easy to ride.

biology see **science**

birds

Birds are unlike other warm-blooded animals. They have wings, though not all birds can fly. They have feathers, and beaks instead of jaws. Like reptiles and fish, birds lay eggs. But birds have warm blood, like mammals, and most birds care for their young. Scientists think that the first birds developed from flying reptiles who lived millions of years ago.

A bird's body is light, but very strong. Flying takes a lot of energy, so birds spend much of their time eating. Some birds fly amazingly long distances.
A few birds, such as ostriches and penguins, do not fly but run or swim.

Many birds build nests for their eggs. Some are very skillful builders. The parents keep the eggs warm until they hatch. The baby chicks are helpless and must be fed until they can leave the nest and find their own food.

DID YOU KNOW?

Goslings, or baby geese, can run and swim as soon as they hatch. Many birds that nest on the ground can do this. Their parents watch over them and show them how to find food.

BIRDS

Unlike other animals, birds have feathers. Some have as many as 25,000 feathers. Male birds are often more brightly colored than females. All birds have beaks, or bills; the beak's shape tells us what kind of food the bird eats. A bird's feet are also clues to its way of life.

▲ The condor, biggest of the vultures, is the heaviest flying bird.

▲ The kestrel is a bird of prey which hovers in midair, ready to pounce down on small rodents.

◀ The European kingfisher is brilliantly colored. It dives into the water to catch fish.

◀ The ostrich is the largest of all birds. It has wings but cannot fly.

◀ Birds of paradise live in New Guinea. The males display their feathers to attract a mate.

◀ The kiwi is a flightless bird of New Zealand. It wanders around at night, feeding on insects and worms.

◀ The toucan has a massive beak. It lives in the American rain forests.

▶ Penguins can swim as well as fish, using their wings as flippers.

FACTS AND RECORDS

Biggest wingspan: albatross (10–12 ft [nearly 4 m])
Fastest flier: spine-tailed swift (100 mph [160 kph])
Biggest egg: ostrich (up to 8 in [20 cm] long)
Longest migration: Arctic tern (22,400 mi [36,000 km])
Fastest wingbeats: hummingbird (50–75 per minute)

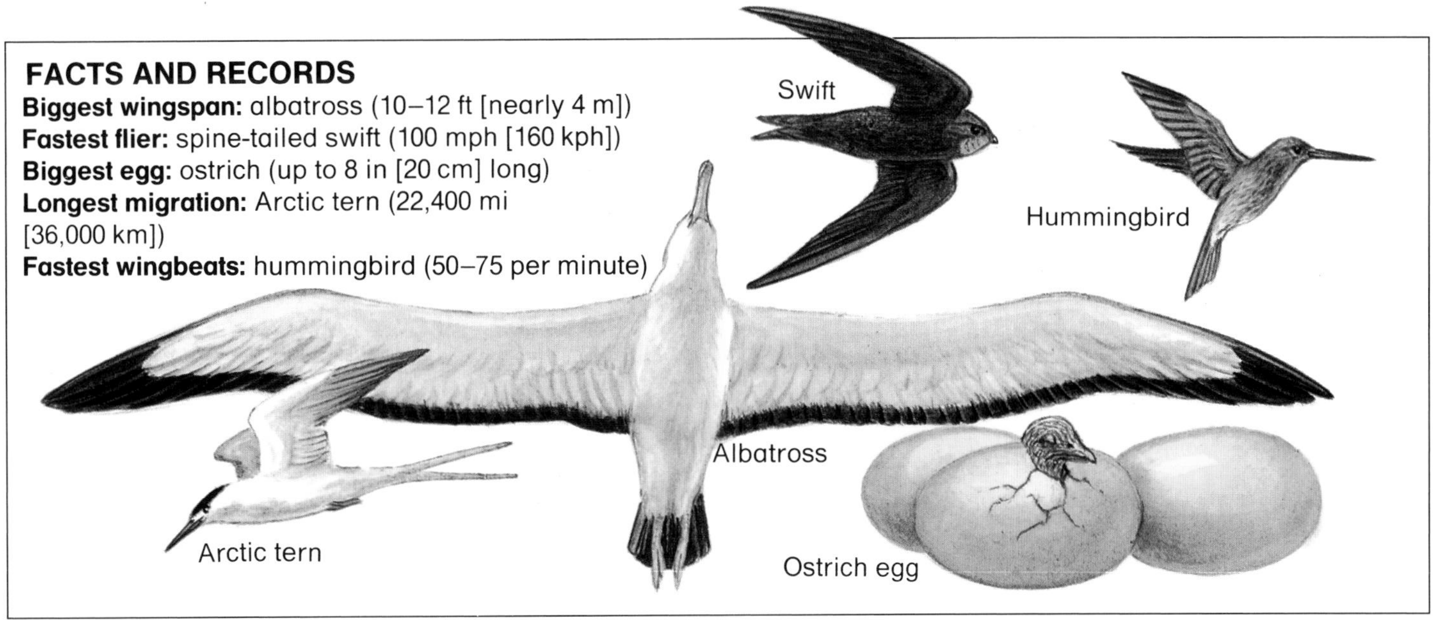

► As a bird flaps its wings, the inner part of the wing beats up and down, while the outer part moves in a circle. The air pressure above the wing is less than the air pressure underneath. This creates lift to keep birds in the air.

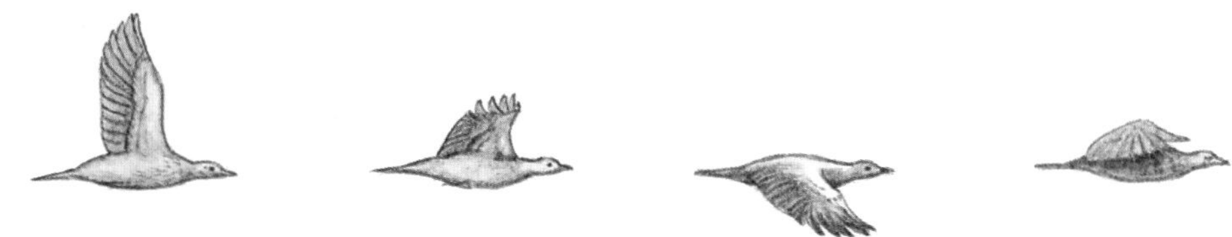

TYPES OF NEST

Most birds make a nest of some kind to protect their eggs and chicks. Some go to great lengths to build homes that are marvels of engineering. Some make nests of twigs, others nest in holes in trees. The house martin's nest is made of mud. The weaverbird twists grasses together for its nest.

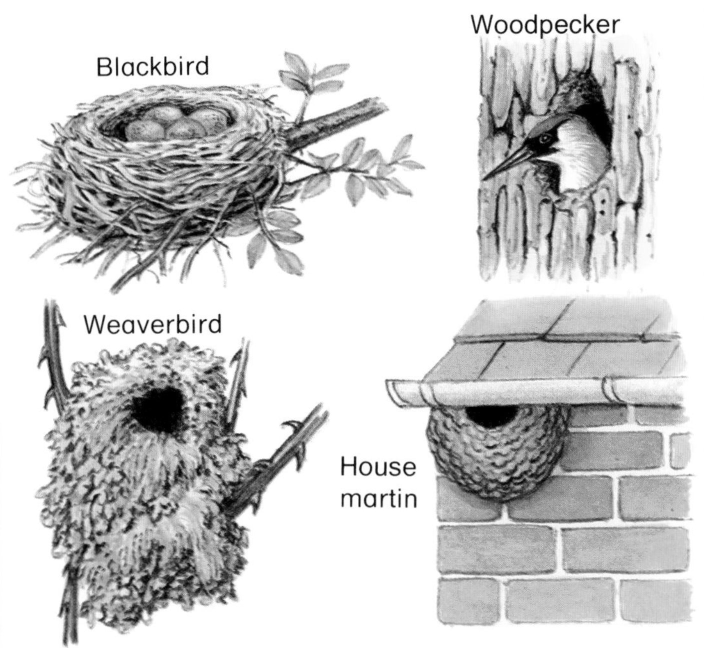

FEET AND BEAKS

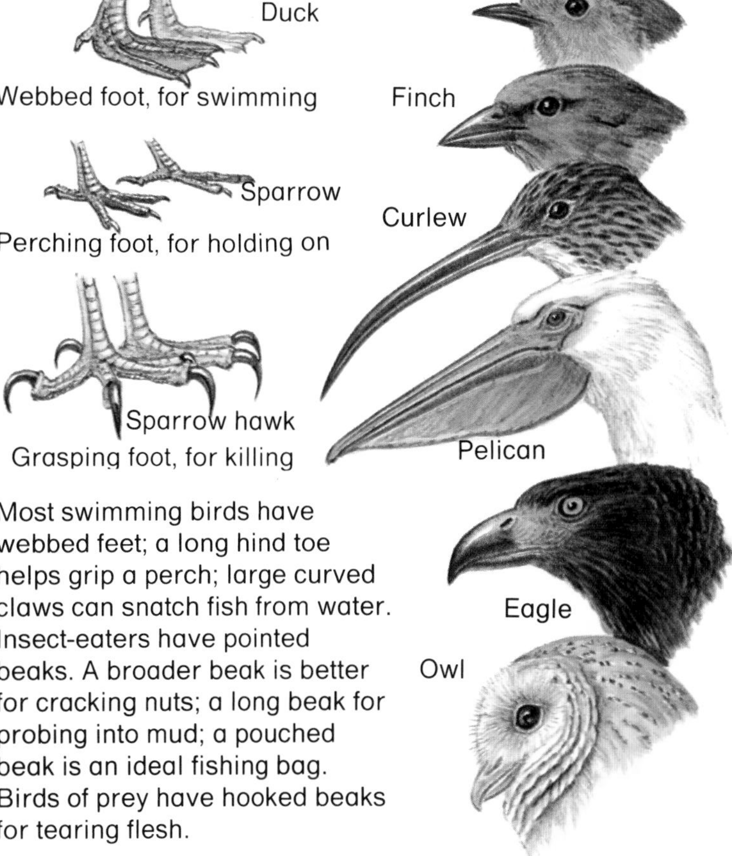

Most swimming birds have webbed feet; a long hind toe helps grip a perch; large curved claws can snatch fish from water. Insect-eaters have pointed beaks. A broader beak is better for cracking nuts; a long beak for probing into mud; a pouched beak is an ideal fishing bag. Birds of prey have hooked beaks for tearing flesh.

B

bison
Bison are wild cattle. They have humped shoulders and short horns. Bison live in America and Europe. Huge herds of bison called buffalo once roamed the North American plains.

blood
Blood is the body's supply and waste removal system. It carries food and oxygen to the body's cells and removes carbon dioxide and water. It also fights germs that carry diseases. Blood is made of red and white cells floating in a liquid called plasma. The heart pumps blood around the body through arteries and veins. See **heart**, **human body**.

boat
A boat is a small ship. The first boats were made thousands of years ago. They were canoes made by hollowing out tree trunks, and rafts made from logs or bundles of reeds tied together. People also made boats from animal skins. Today we use rowboats (boats with oars), canoes, sailboats, and powerboats with engines. See **ships**.

▼ A Viking ship from about A.D. 900. It had a sail and oars.

bones see **human body, skeleton**

brain
The brain is the body's control center. Its message system, the nerves, tell it what is happening all over the body. Each part of the brain has a different job. See **human body**.

Brazil
Brazil is the largest country in South America. The Amazon River and the world's biggest rain forest are in Brazil. Brasilia and Rio de Janeiro are busy cities. See **South America**.

breathing
You breathe through lungs, which are spongy bags inside your chest. They fill with air every time you breathe in. Your lungs take in oxygen from the air. The body needs oxygen to burn the food you eat to make energy. You breathe out carbon dioxide gas. An adult breathes about 15 to 20 times every minute. Many animals have lungs too. Fish breathe through gills, and insects breathe through tiny holes. Plants breathe through their leaves. See **air**.

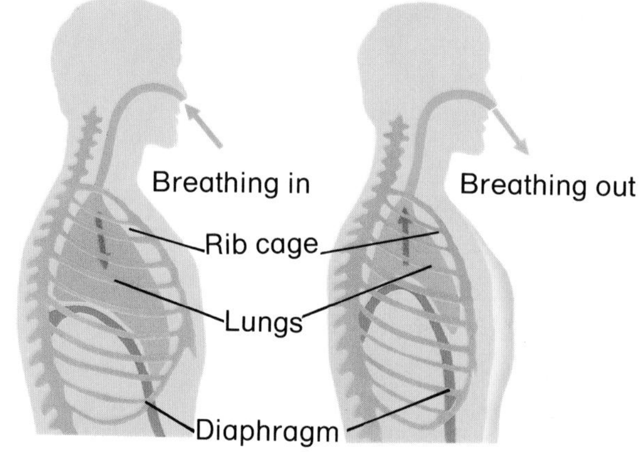

▲ Breathing in sucks fresh air into the lungs. Breathing out pushes out waste air.

BRIDGES

People build bridges to cross a river, road, railway, or gorge. The simplest bridge is a plank of wood across a stream. The ancient Romans built strong stone bridges. Iron bridges were first built in the 1700s. Today, bridges are concrete and steel. The different kinds include girder, arch, cantilever, and suspension bridges.

▼ The beam bridge is an old and simple kind of bridge. It is still used sometimes today. The ends of the beams rest on piers made of wood, stone, or concrete.

▼ A pontoon bridge can be made by laying a bridge across some boats. Early arch bridges were made of stone. Big, modern arch bridges are made of concrete and steel.

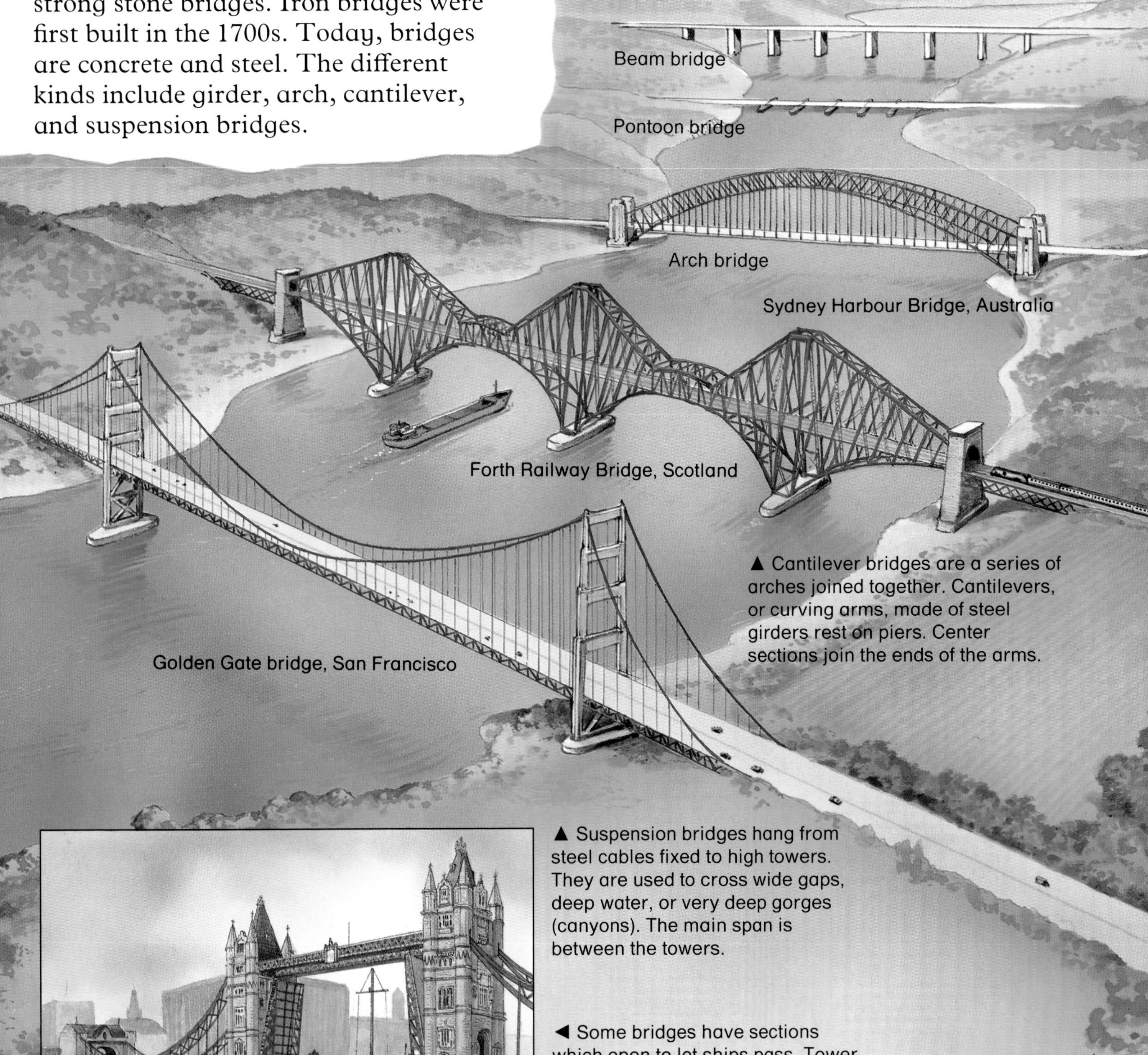

▲ Cantilever bridges are a series of arches joined together. Cantilevers, or curving arms, made of steel girders rest on piers. Center sections join the ends of the arms.

▲ Suspension bridges hang from steel cables fixed to high towers. They are used to cross wide gaps, deep water, or very deep gorges (canyons). The main span is between the towers.

◀ Some bridges have sections which open to let ships pass. Tower Bridge in London is a bascule bridge. Its two halves tilt upward.

B

bronze

Bronze is an alloy, or mixture, of two metals: copper and tin. More than 5,000 years ago people learned how to make bronze for swords, pots, and ornaments. Historians call this time the Bronze Age.

▼ Bronze Age people used bronze to make weapons, pots, and figures. They melted the metal and poured it into molds to harden.

Buddha

Buddha was the founder of the religion Buddhism. He was a prince in India, born about 3,000 years ago. He left his palace to find out why there was unhappiness in the world. He found enlightenment, or truth, while sitting and thinking beneath a tree. Buddha taught that people should be kind to one another and not worry about earthly things. Today millions of Buddhists follow his teachings.

buffalo

Buffalo are wild cattle. The African buffalo is dangerous, with massive horns. The Asian water buffalo can be tamed to pull carts and plows. The American buffalo is really a bison. See **bison**.

buildings

Modern buildings can be very tall. These skyscrapers have a steel frame set in deep concrete foundations. The outside is covered with brick, glass, or plastic. Steel and concrete are the most important materials used in such tall buildings, because they are very strong. Smaller buildings such as houses can be made of other materials, such as brick, stone, wood, or bamboo.

In Europe in the Middle Ages it could take many years to build a huge castle or cathedral. The builders had few machines. Today, a tall office building can go up in a few months, using diggers, cranes, and factory-made parts.

▼ In the late 1700s and early 1800s elegant buildings like this curved terrace were built. Each house is attached to its neighbor.

DID YOU KNOW?

The world's tallest building is the Sears Tower in Chicago, Illinois. It has 110 floors and is 1,454 ft (443 m) high.

The Great Wall of China is the only structure on earth that can be seen from the moon. It is more than 1,500 mi (2,400 km) long.

King Louis XIV of France ordered 30,000 workers to build the Palace of Versailles. It took 50 years, beginning in 1661.

BUTTERFLIES AND MOTHS

Butterflies and moths belong to the same insect family. Butterflies fly in daylight. Many have brightly colored wings. Moths fly mostly in the evening. Butterflies and moths feed on plant nectar and pollen.

Peak white

Holly blue

Painted lady butterfly

Swallowtail butterfly

Tiger moth

Yellow underwing moth

Large emerald moth

Peacock butterfly

▲ Moths have fatter, hairier bodies than butterflies. Their antennae are feathery-looking.

▲ Butterflies have thinner bodies than moths and are not hairy. Their antennae have knobs on the ends.

Many butterflies and some moths have brilliant colors and patterns on their wings.

LIFE CYCLE OF A BUTTERFLY

(1) Butterflies and moths lay eggs, which hatch into hungry caterpillars. After an amazing change, or metamorphosis, they become adult insects.

(2) The caterpillar seldom stops eating. It grows by shedding its skin.

(3) It becomes a dead-looking chrysalis. Inside, its body is changing.

(4) The chrysalis splits and out crawls an adult butterfly. Its wings dry, and it flies away.

Moth at rest

Butterfly at rest

▲ At rest, a butterfly folds its wings above its body to hide the bright colors. A moth, by contrast, rests with its wings spread out flat.

Buff-tip moth caterpillar

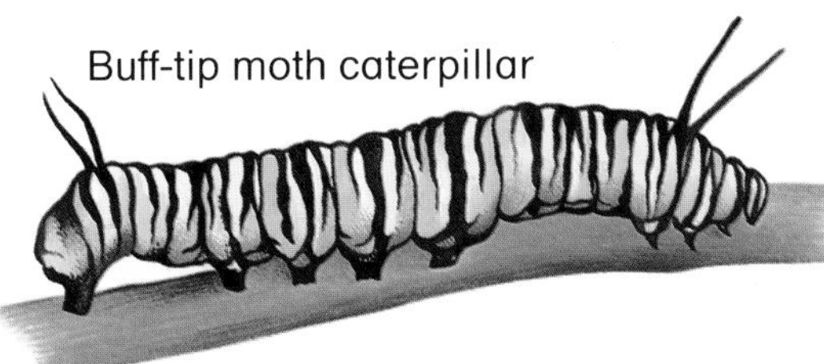

▲ Some caterpillars are green or brown. Others are brightly colored or look spiky or bristly. Their appearance makes caterpillars hard to see or scares off hungry birds.

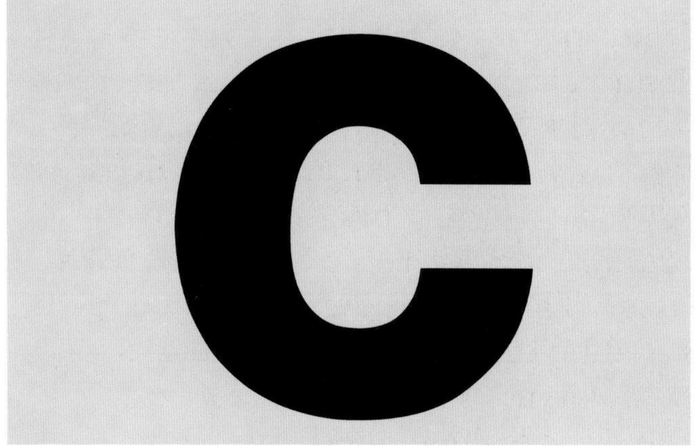

cable car or gondola

A cable car, also called an aerial tramway or a gondola, carries people up mountains. It moves along a wire cable slung between tall towers, pulled by a second moving cable. As one car goes up, another comes down.

cactus

A cactus is a plant that grows in deserts. It has long roots to seek out water, and can store water inside its fleshy stems. Many cacti are covered with sharp spines. These spines are leaves. They keep off hungry animals. Most cacti grow in America. The tallest is the saguaro, which grows 50 ft (15 m) tall.

◀ A cactus has a tough, prickly outside. This stops animals from eating it. The cactus stores water inside.

LIFE STORY

Caesar

Julius Caesar was one of the most famous leaders of ancient Rome. He was born about 100 B.C. of a noble family. At this time Rome had no single powerful leader. Julius Caesar became a brilliant general. He led his army to conquer Gaul (France and Belgium) and parts of Germany. In 55 and 54 B.C. he invaded Britain, but did not attempt to conquer the island. He wrote books about his wars and the people he fought. Later he returned to Rome and defeated his rival, Pompey. He went to Egypt, where he fell in love with Queen Cleopatra. When he came home, victorious after many battles, he was the most powerful man in Rome. His enemies feared he would become king, and in 44 B.C. they murdered him.

calculator see **computer**

calendar

Most of the world uses a calendar with 365 days in a year, plus a leap year every fourth year with 366 days. The Christian calendar starts from the year Jesus Christ was born.

camel

The camel is an animal well suited to desert life. It can go for days without water and stores fat in its hump. The Bactrian camel (see page 59) has two humps. The Arabian camel has one hump. See **animal**.

▼ Arabian camels carry goods and people across the desert.

camera

Cameras take still photographs, moving films, or videos. The first cameras were large and heavy, with a black hood at the back. Light enters the camera through a lens. The film inside is sensitive to light. The light forms an image on the film. When the film is "developed" with chemicals, a picture is made. See **photography**, **television and video**.

Canada

Canada is the second biggest country in the world. Yet only about 26 million people live there. Much of Canada is wilderness, high mountains, thick forests, and wide prairies planted with wheat. There are many rivers and lakes, including the Great Lakes and the St. Lawrence River. Montreal and Toronto are the biggest cities, but Ottawa is the country's capital.

Many Canadians speak either English or French. Their families came to Canada from Europe. People from Asia have also settled in Canada. The native peoples of Canada are the Indians and the Inuit, or Eskimos.

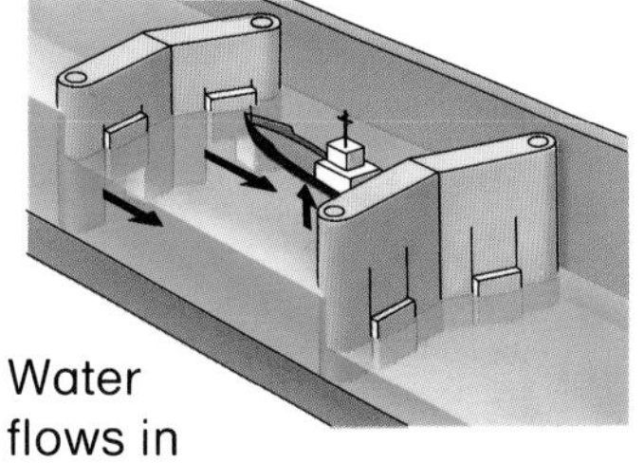

◀ To move from a higher level to a lower level (or the other way around), a canal boat passes through a lock. The water level in the lock is raised or lowered.

canal

Canals are human-made waterways for boats and barges carrying goods. To move to a higher or lower level, boats must pass through locks. The Suez and Panama canals are famous canals.

car

Cars were invented in the 1880s. They were called "horseless carriages," or automobiles. They had gasoline engines. The shape of cars has changed greatly since those days. The first cars were built by hand. Car factories started in the early 1900s, using assembly-line methods. Today, computers and robots help to design and build comfortable and safe cars. See **engines**.

CARS

Steam cars were tried as early as the 1770s. However, it was not until 100 years later that the internal-combustion engine was invented. This engine burned gasoline. It was small but powerful. The first car was built by the German engineer Karl Benz in 1885. Since then, there have been many improvements to car design.

Cugnot's steam gun carriage 1770

Karl Benz's first car 1885

Rolls-Royce Silver Ghost 1911

Ford Model T 1908–1927

Citroen Traction Avant 1934

Volkswagen "Beetle" 1939

Lincoln Continental Cabriolet 1947

Austin Mini 1959

Range Rover Vogue 1988

Peugeot 406, 1987

Most cars burn gasoline or diesel fuel inside the **engine**. The fuel is mixed with air and explodes inside cylinders. The explosion pushes pistons up and down, driving a shaft that turns the wheels.

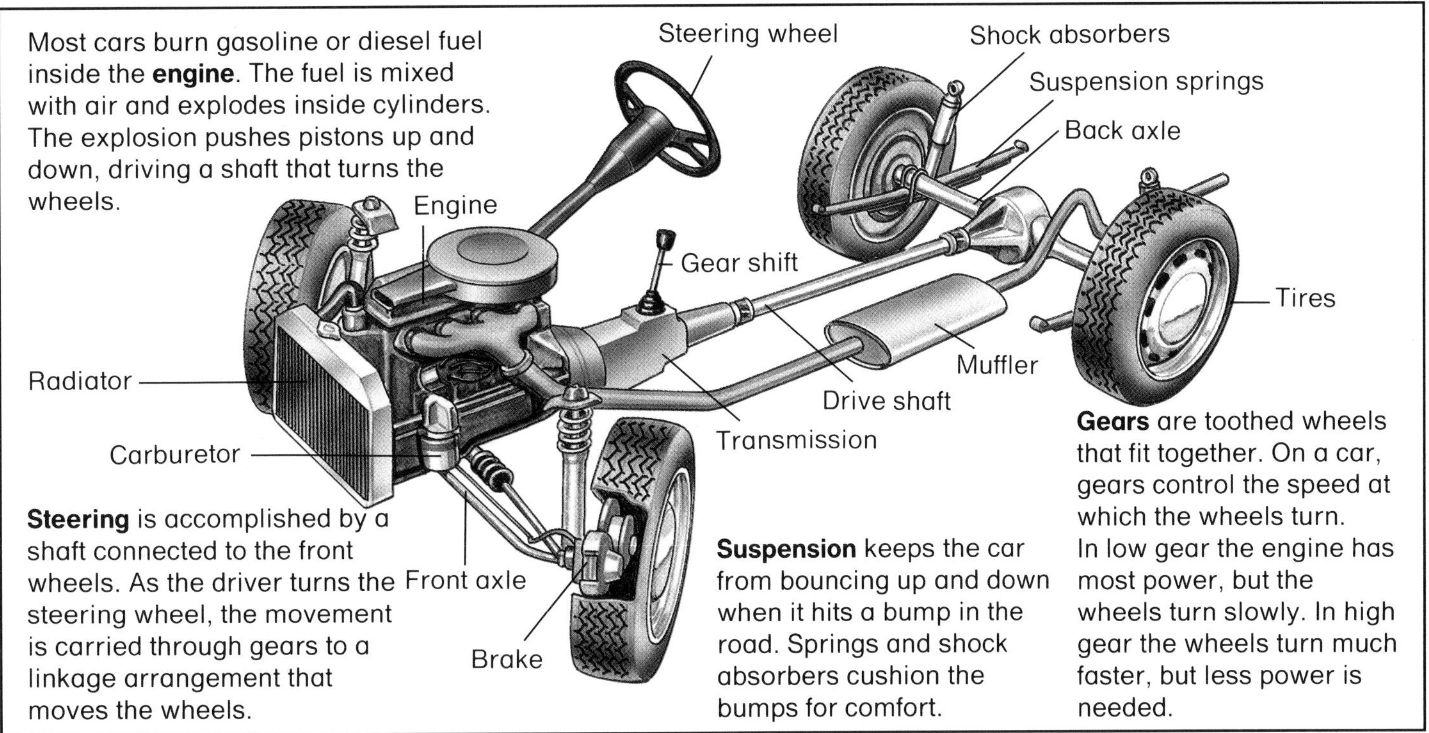

Steering is accomplished by a shaft connected to the front wheels. As the driver turns the steering wheel, the movement is carried through gears to a linkage arrangement that moves the wheels.

Suspension keeps the car from bouncing up and down when it hits a bump in the road. Springs and shock absorbers cushion the bumps for comfort.

Gears are toothed wheels that fit together. On a car, gears control the speed at which the wheels turn. In low gear the engine has most power, but the wheels turn slowly. In high gear the wheels turn much faster, but less power is needed.

Solar-powered car

Gasoline engines give off harmful gases. And someday, all the world's fuel will be used up. So future cars will probably run on batteries or solar energy.

Formula One race car

Fast cars have specially shaped bodies that hug the ground. They are streamlined to cut smoothly through the air.

FASTEST CARS

Year		mph
1898	Jeantaud electric car	39 mph
1899	La Jamais Contente	66 mph
1922	Sunbeam	134 mph
1927	Sunbeam	204 mph
1932	Napier-Campbell	254 mph
1937	Thunderbolt	312 mph
1947	Railton	394 mph
1964	Bluebird	403 mph
1964	Green Monster	537 mph
1965	Spirit of America	614 mph
1970	Blue Flame	631.5 mph
1983	Thrust 2	633.6 mph

In 1985, a steam car was driven at 145 mph (234 km/h) in the U.S.
The fastest road car is probably an Italian Lamborghini Diablo, which was tested at 202 mph (325 km/h) in 1990. It is the most powerful mass-produced car.

Thrust 2, 1983

carbon
Carbon is a chemical element. There is carbon in rocks, air, the sun, and animals and plants. Diamonds, sea shells, coal, and fizzy drinks all have carbon in them. The "lead" in a pencil is really graphite, a form of carbon. See **coal, diamonds**.

cartoon
A cartoon can be a drawing or a film made up of thousands of still pictures. When put together on film and speeded up, the pictures appear to move. The cartoon characters seem to come alive.

▼ This is what a big castle of the Middle Ages looked like. Its massive walls were made of stones.

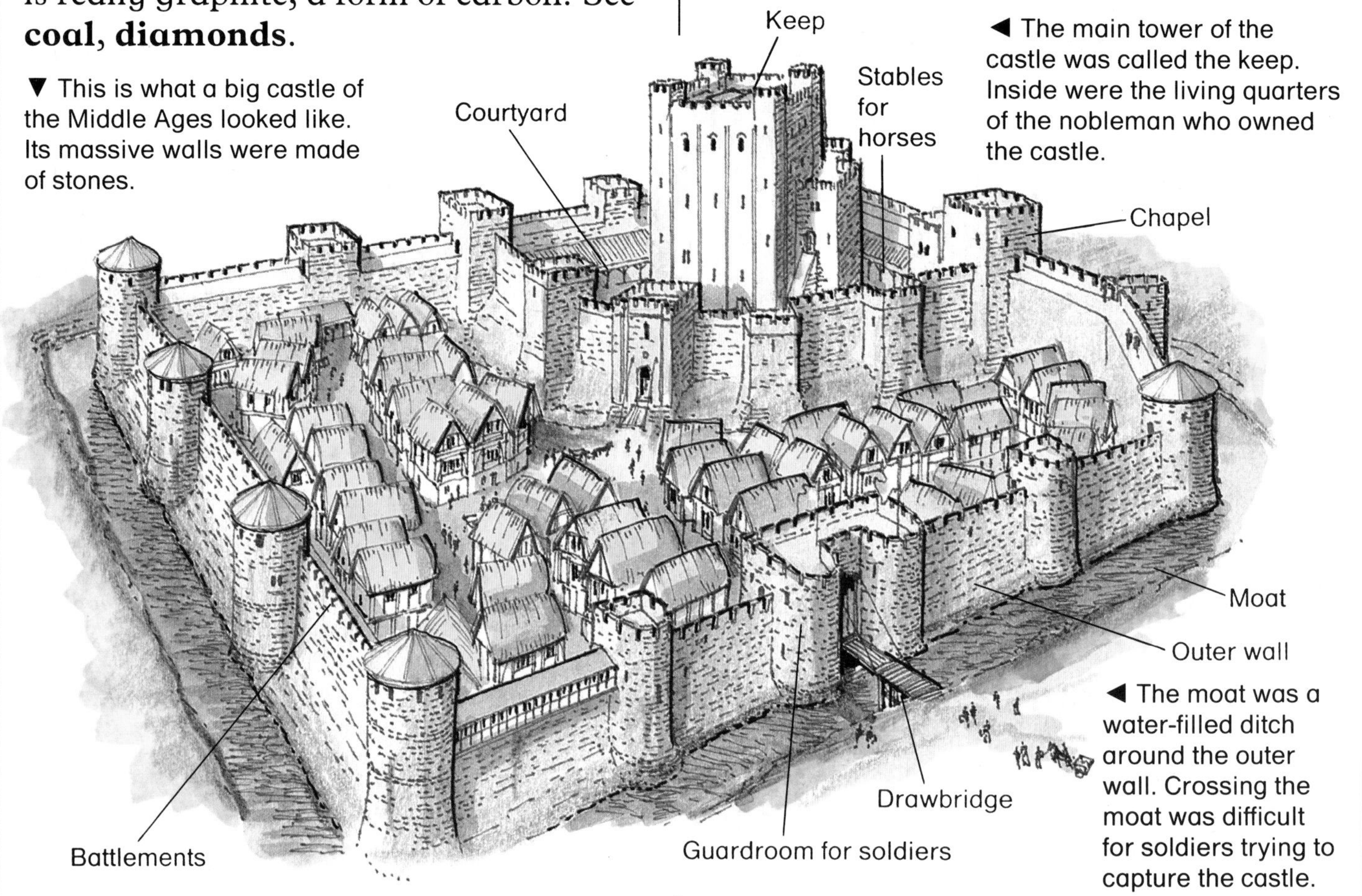

◀ The main tower of the castle was called the keep. Inside were the living quarters of the nobleman who owned the castle.

◀ The moat was a water-filled ditch around the outer wall. Crossing the moat was difficult for soldiers trying to capture the castle.

Caribbean
The Caribbean Sea is really part of the Atlantic Ocean. In the Caribbean are many islands, including the West Indies. The sea is named after the Carib Indians who once lived on the islands.

caribou
Caribou are large deer. They are called reindeer in Europe and Asia. They live in the far north. The Lapp people of Scandinavia keep herds of reindeer. See **deer**.

castle
In the Middle Ages, people built castles to keep out enemies. A good place for a castle was on a hilltop. Around it, the builders dug a moat, or ditch. They made the walls of the castle very high and thick. Inside was a stronghold — a great tower, or keep. Soldiers stood guard around the castle walls. Castles were not much use as fortresses after guns were invented in the 1300s.

caterpillar see **butterflies and moths**

CATS

All cats are hunters, with powerful bodies and sharp teeth and claws. They stalk their prey silently and can climb or leap. Cats usually hunt alone, but lions and cheetahs hunt in pairs or groups. African lions hunt in open grassland; the tiger and leopard hunt alone in jungles and forests. The Siberian tiger is the biggest of all cats.

Leopards often drag a kill into a tree.

◀ Big cats roam over large areas, or territories, to hunt. When not hungry, they rest and sleep. Females teach the cubs how to hunt for themselves.

DID YOU KNOW?

Why does a cat usually land on four feet? Cats have a wonderful sense of balance and climb trees easily. If a cat loses its balance, and falls a short distance, it seldom gets hurt. It twists in midair, using its tail as a rudder, and makes a soft landing on its feet. That's why we say that a cat has nine lives.

Cats are also very good hunters. They can stalk silently, because their claws are pulled back into soft pads and don't make noise the way dogs' claws do. They can see well in poor light and can hear and smell more keenly than humans. Their whiskers are long sensitive hairs. When they touch an object, they send signals to the brain, so the cat can find its way in the dark.

DOMESTIC CATS

People have kept pet cats since about 3500 B.C. African wildcats were the first to be tamed. Cats were useful because they caught mice and rats. Today there are many breeds of pet cats.

C

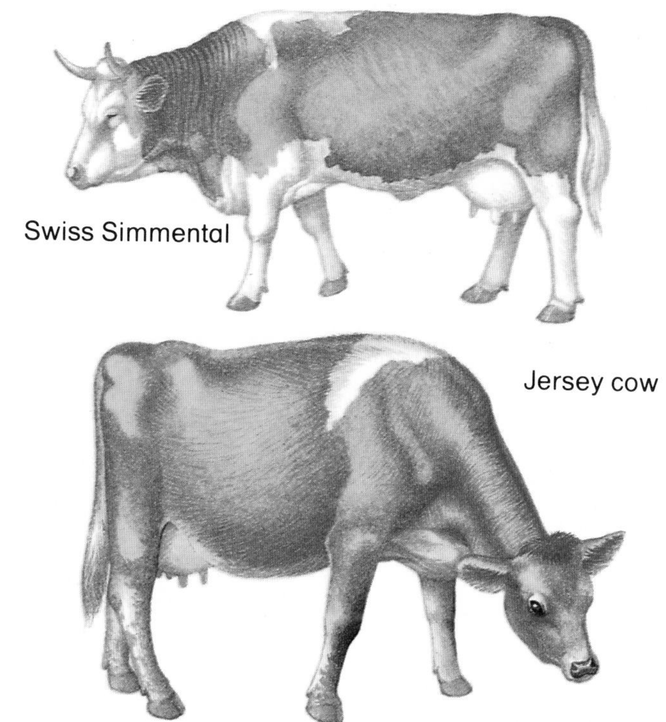

▲ Beef cattle (top) are kept for meat. Dairy cattle (bottom) give milk and other dairy products.

cattle

Cattle are grazing, or grass-eating, mammals. The females (cows) feed their young calves with milk from their bodies. In the wild, a single male (bull) leads a group of cows. Dairy cattle give us milk. Beef cattle are kept for meat. We also get leather from cattles' skins, or hides. Farm cattle are relatives of wild cattle such as bison and buffalo. See **bison**, **buffalo**.

cave

A cave is a hole in the ground. Most caves are made by water flowing or dripping through soft rocks, such as limestone. Acids in the water eat away the rock. Sometimes caverns, or huge caves, are made. Water and dissolved limestone may drip from the roof to form stalagmites and icicle-shaped stalactites.

cave people

Millions of years ago during the Ice Age, people lived in caves. Inside a cave, several families could find shelter from the cold and snow. They lit a fire inside the cave to keep warm and to scare off dangerous wild animals. Cave people made clothes from the skins of animals they hunted. They painted pictures of these animals on the walls of the cave. See **Ice Age**, **Stone Age**.

▼ Stone Age cave people hunted animals for food.

cells

All living things are made of cells. The simplest animals have just one cell. Cells reproduce, or multiply, by dividing. Your body is made of millions of cells. Each body part, such as bone or blood,

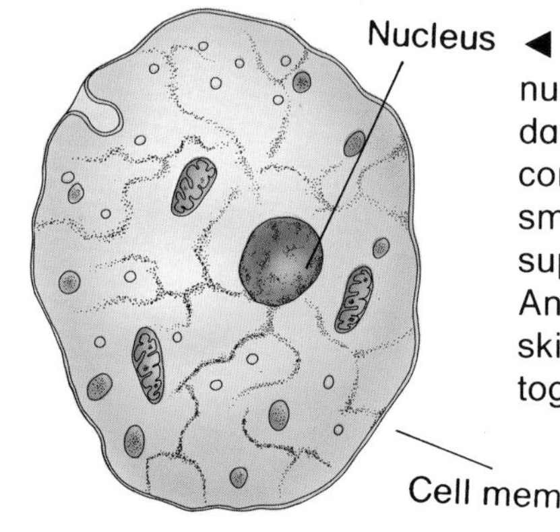

◀ An animal cell: the nucleus is the biggest dark area. It is the cell's control center. The smaller blobs are food supplies and fat droplets. An outer membrane, or skin, holds the cell together.

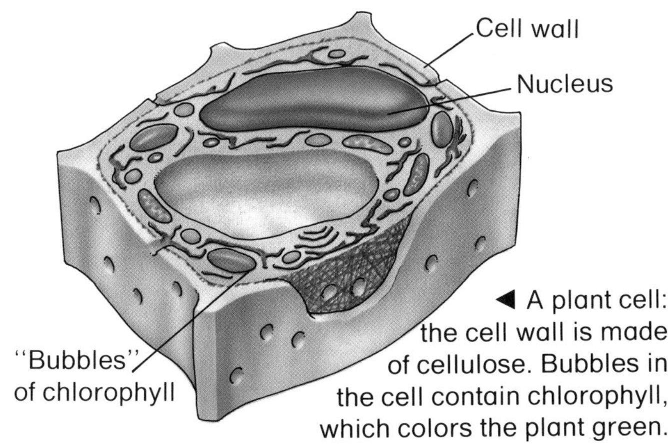

◀ A plant cell: the cell wall is made of cellulose. Bubbles in the cell contain chlorophyll, which colors the plant green.

is made of different cells. In every cell is a substance called DNA. It gives you the features (such as the color of your eyes) that you inherit from your parents. See **genetics**, **medicine**.

cereal
Breakfast cereals are made from plants such as wheat, oats, and rice. Cereal plants are important foods. We eat the seeds or grains, either whole or made into flour. See **rice**, **wheat**.

chameleon
The chameleon is a lizard that moves slowly, but catches insects by shooting out its long tongue. When angry or frightened, it can change its color to match its surroundings.

▼ The chameleon clings to twigs with its feet and tail. Its tongue is almost as long as its body.

LIFE STORY

Charlemagne
Charlemagne means Charles the Great. Born in 742, he was king of the Franks, a people living in what is now Germany. It was a time of war and unrest, but Charles was a good soldier, and soon his kingdom stretched across Europe. He fought the Moors, Muslims from North Africa who had taken over part of Spain. In 800 the pope crowned him emperor of the new Holy Roman Empire. Charles invited scholars and artists to his court at Aachen and founded schools and monasteries. He died in 814, but stories about him were still told throughout the Middle Ages.

Chaucer
Geoffrey Chaucer was an English poet. He lived from about 1341 to 1400. His most famous book is *The Canterbury Tales*, stories told by pilgrims journeying to Canterbury, in England.

CHINA

China is a huge country in Asia. It has more people than any other country (over a billion, or one-fifth of the earth's people). China has a very ancient civilization, over 3,500 years old. The Chinese made many inventions. For most of its history it was an empire, ruled by families or dynasties. In 1949, China became a Communist republic.

▼ The Chinese New Year begins in February. Celebrations last two weeks. Dragons are lucky in China, so a dragon dance is part of the fun.

我要马上找医生
我这里痛上
请别理得太短

◀ The Chinese language is written in characters, or picture signs. There are more than 40,000 characters, but a Chinese person can manage with about 5,000.

▲ Chinese art includes pottery, carving, painting, and casting figures in bronze. This bronze model of a horse and chariot was made in the 2nd century A.D.

▲ In ancient China, most people were poor farmers. Government officials and nobles lived in fine houses with walled courtyards. In the courtyard, people could meet, discuss business, and be entertained.

▶ The Chinese began building the Great Wall about 200 B.C. The wall was meant to keep out invaders. Soldiers kept guard along it. The wall is 1,500 mi (2,400 km) long. Astronauts can see it from the moon.

cheese
Cheese is a food made from the solid part of sour milk from cows, sheep, and goats. There are many different kinds. The blue in some cheese is made by a mold. See **food**.

cheetah see **cat**

chemistry see **science**

chimpanzee see **ape**

Christianity
Christianity is one of the world's major religions. Christians believe that Jesus Christ was the Son of God. They read his teachings in the New Testament of the Bible. The Bible tells of Jesus's life and his death on the cross. See **religion**.

church
A church is a building where Christians worship. It also means a group of Christians with the same beliefs. Large churches called cathedrals were built in Europe, especially in the Middle Ages.

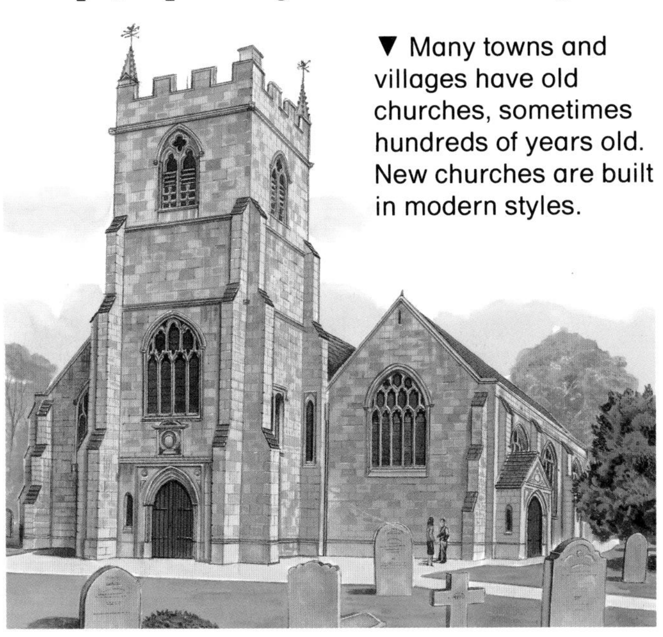

▼ Many towns and villages have old churches, sometimes hundreds of years old. New churches are built in modern styles.

LIFE STORY

Churchill
Winston Churchill led Britain through World War II (1939–1945). He was born in 1874. Young Winston did badly at school. He joined the army, fought in India, and rode in a cavalry charge in the Sudan. During the Boer War in South Africa, he was captured by the enemy, but escaped. In 1900, he was elected as a member of Parliament and held several important jobs in government. In 1940, Britain faced defeat in World War II. Churchill took over as prime minister. He helped plan the Allies' (Britain, U.S., and the Soviet Union) victory. People around the world listened to his speeches on the radio. He was prime minister again after the war and was knighted in 1953. When he died in 1965, he was called "the greatest Englishman of the century."

city

Prehistoric people moved around in groups. About 10,000 years ago people began to settle in villages. These grew bigger into towns. Towns grew into cities. There were cities 5,000 years ago. Today millions of people live in cities.

Civil War

The Civil War was fought between the states of the North and the South from 1861 to 1865. It was caused because the Southern states wanted to keep their slaves and an agricultural way of life. The Northern states felt that slavery was wrong. This led to arguments over whether a state could leave, or "secede" from, the Union. When the war came, it divided the country. The North won because of its industrial strength, but the struggle cost hundreds of thousands of lives. At first the Southern states won several victories. But then the power of the Union began to tell. In 1863, the South was defeated at Gettysburg. After this it became clear that the Union would win.

The Civil War destroyed the prosperity of the South. Many felt, however, that it was more important that slavery be ended and the Union preserved.

▼ New York is the biggest city in the United States and is famous for its many skyscrapers, or tall buildings.

▲ Cleopatra was one of the most famous women in history. She lived in great splendor as queen of Egypt.

Cleopatra

Cleopatra was a famous queen of Egypt. She lived from 69 to 30 B.C. Two Roman generals, Julius Caesar and Marc Antony, fell in love with her. When Antony was defeated in battle, he and Cleopatra killed themselves.

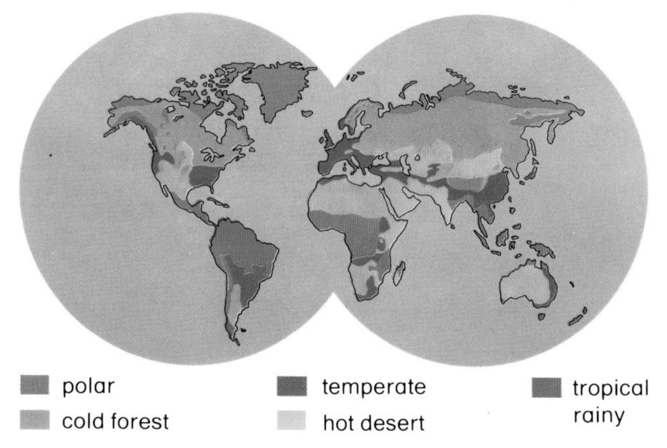

polar
cold forest
temperate
hot desert
tropical rainy

climate

Climate is the average weather of a place on earth. Some places have cold winters and hot summers; others have almost the same temperature all year. The five main climate zones are tropical rainy, dry, mild and damp, snowy forest, and polar. Some scientists believe climate may alter as the earth is warmed by polluting gases. See **weather**.

clock

Ancient peoples measured time by burning threads or candles, or watching sand trickle through hourglasses. Mechanical clocks with no hands, driven by weights, were invented in the 1300s. Bells rang the hours. Pendulum clocks were invented in the 1600s. Modern clocks and watches have electric batteries. Clocks used for scientific research lose only one second in 300 years.

cloud

A cloud is made of millions of tiny water droplets. Have you watched a puddle dry in the sun after a rain? The water turns into a gas called water vapor. It rises into the air. As it rises it cools and turns back to water. The water droplets are so light they float and sometimes form a cloud. When they are too heavy to float they become gray, and the water falls as rain or snow. See **weather**.

▼ Different-shaped clouds are seen at different heights in the sky. Changing clouds bring changes of weather. High cirrus clouds are made of ice. Towering cumulonimbus clouds bring storms and thunder. Puffy white cumulus clouds are a sign of good weather.

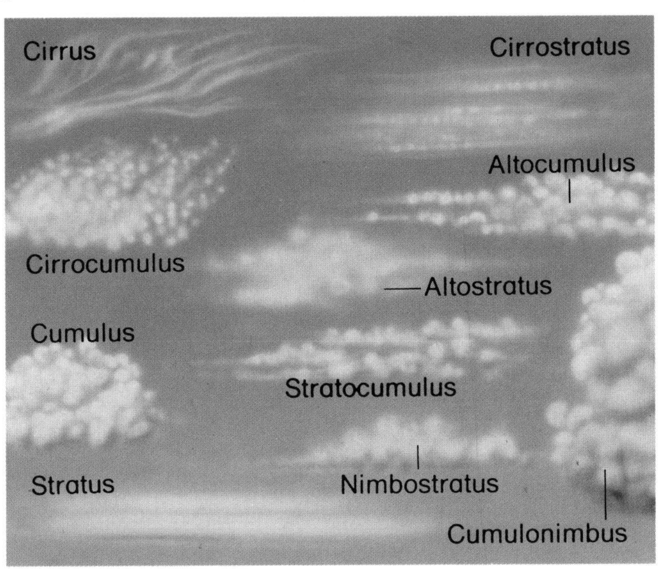

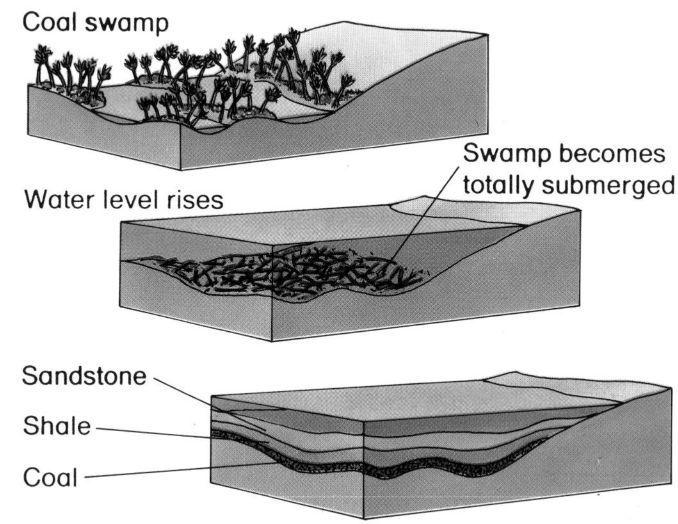

▲ Seams of coal were formed from prehistoric plants. The plants died and were buried under layers of mud and sand. Over millions of years this mud crushed the plants into coal.

coal

Coal looks like black or brown rock, but unlike rock it burns. This is because coal was once wood. The underground seams, or layers, of coal were formed millions of years ago from plants that grew in swamps. The plants died and were covered by mud and sand. These hardened into rocks, squeezing the plant remains into coal. It is an important fuel. See **fuel, minerals and mining**.

coffee

Coffee comes from the beans of the coffee plant, which grows best in warm hilly areas. Brazil and Colombia are the most important coffee-growing areas. The plant has red berries. Inside each berry are two beans. The beans are picked, dried, and roasted. Then they are ground (crushed). Instant coffee is a powder made from dried liquid coffee.

coins see **money**

C

color

Sunlight looks colorless, but it is actually a mixture of colors. We can see the colors when the white light from the sun is split into a rainbow pattern called a spectrum. This happens when light passes through water or glass. There are seven colors in the spectrum: red, orange, yellow, green, blue, indigo, and violet.

You can make a color spinner to show that light is made of different colors. You need a disk of cardboard and a short pencil. Divide one spinner into seven equal sections, and color each section a color from the spectrum. What do you see when you spin the spinner? Make another spinner with three sections: red, green, and blue. What do you see now? Try again with a half red and half blue spinner. See **light**.

▼ A white object reflects all the colors in light. A black object reflects very little light. A red object reflects red, but absorbs, or takes in, most of the other colors.

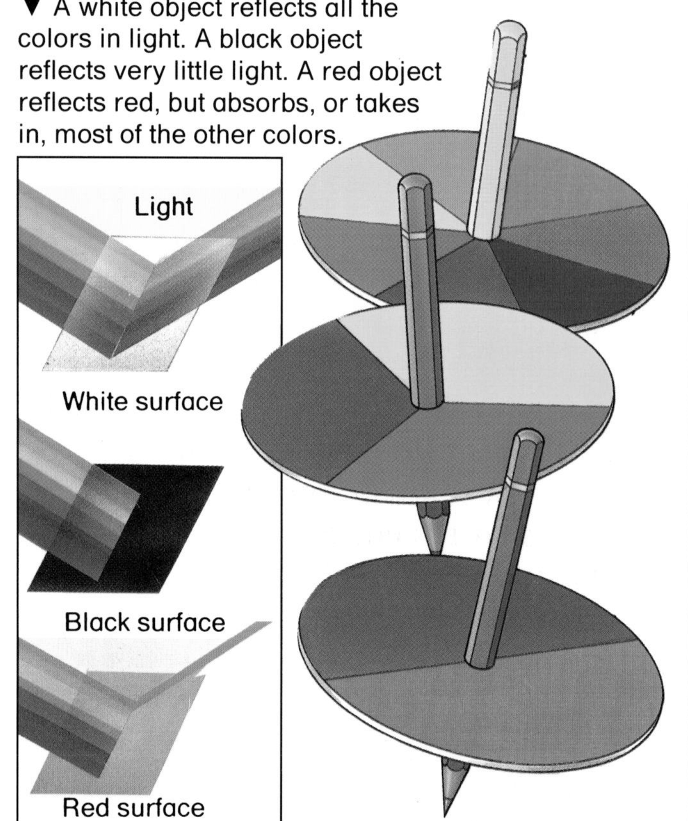

LIFE STORY

Columbus

Christopher Columbus, born in 1451, was the first European since the Vikings to sail across the Atlantic Ocean to America. Columbus was sure that he could sail west to find a new route to the spice ports of the "Indies" (Asia). Finally he persuaded King Ferdinand and Queen Isabella of Spain to pay for a voyage. In 1492, he set sail with three small sailing ships. After 36 days the crew sighted land, in the Bahamas. The local people were amazed to see the strangers. Columbus called the local people Indians, for he believed he had reached the Indies. In fact, he had discovered a New World – America. Columbus died in 1506. See **explorers**.

▼ These navigation instruments were used in the time of Columbus. They are the magnetic compass (left), the astrolabe (center), and the cross staff, for fixing positions by the sun (right). With these instruments, Columbus crossed the uncharted Atlantic.

C

comet

A comet looks like a fuzzy star traveling around the sun. Bright comets have tails up to 93.2 million miles (150 million km) long. The tail always points away from the sun. The head of a comet is a frozen ball of ice, gas, dust, and chunks of rock and metal. You would need a telescope to see most comets, but some pass near enough to the earth to be seen. The most famous comet is Halley's comet, seen by William the Conqueror, which returns close to the earth every 76 or 77 years. It is due to return in 2062.

▲ Comets travel through space, in huge orbits around the sun. They are sometimes very spectacular.

Common Market see **European Community**

Commonwealth of Nations

The Commonwealth is an association of more than 50 countries, some large such as Australia, Canada, India, and Nigeria, others tiny such as the Pacific island of Nauru. The Commonwealth stands for friendship between its peoples, once part of the British Empire.

Guglielmo Marconi, an Italian inventor (above) pioneered radio in the early 1900s. Today we can communicate using desktop computers (below) and can talk to one another by space satellite.

communication

When you speak, write, show someone a picture, or wave your hand, you are communicating, or passing on information. Without communication, there would be no art, science, history, or trade; no films, books, or television shows. We do not know when prehistoric people learned how to communicate by speaking. More than 6,000 years ago people learned how to write. This made it much easier to pass on knowledge. In the 15th century, printing made communication easier. In the 1800s and 1900s came telegraphs, cameras, telephones, radio, and recording. The modern age has brought film and television, communications satellites and computers, videos, and fax machines. Today people can talk to one another at the touch of a button.

C

compass
The compass was first used by sailors to find their way in the 1300s. The earth is a giant magnet. The magnetized compass needle always points toward the north magnetic pole (not the geographic North Pole). See **magnet**.

computer
A computer adds, subtracts, and compares numbers at amazing speed. It can do millions of calculations every second. Computers were invented in the 1940s. Today we use computers at home, school, and work. A computer has a "brain," or central processing unit; an "input" unit, usually linked to a keyboard; and an "output" unit that produces the work. It also has a memory unit where information is stored on magnetic disks. Computers contain tiny electronic chips to make them work. Computer programs, the instructions that tell the computer what to do, are also stored on disks. See **electronics**.

▼ Here are some of the different parts of a computer.

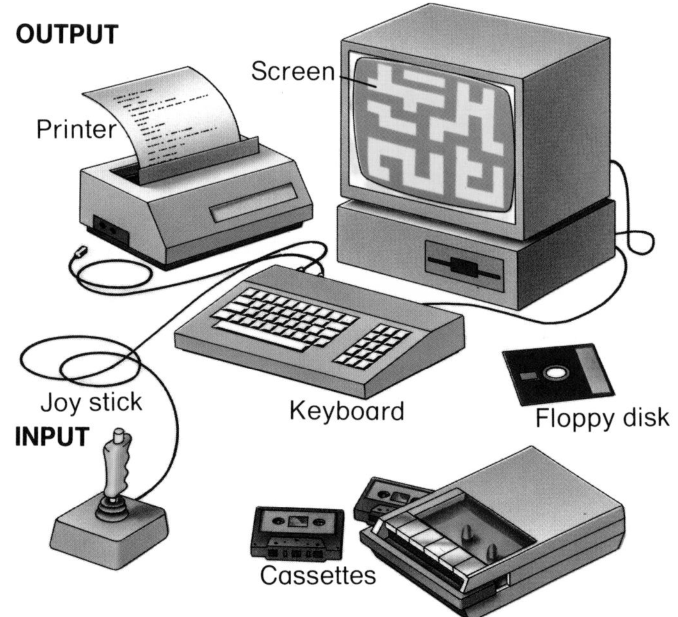

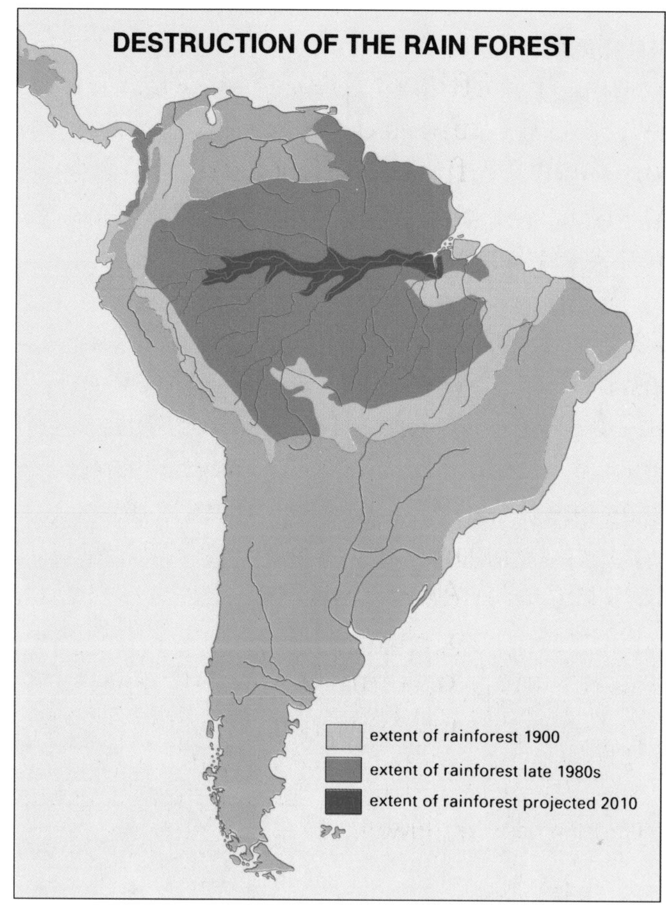

▲ The Amazon rain forest is shrinking as farmers and loggers cut down the trees. Conservationists want to save what remains of the forest and the plants and animals that live in it.

conservation
Conservation means caring for our world. The earth is a treasure store of precious things: animals, plants, minerals, soil, water, and air. People have always used these things. The earth's supply of them seemed endless. Now there are many more people than ever before. We cut down forests to make roads and cities. Some animals and plants no longer have places to live. Animals such as the rhino of Africa have been hunted until very few are left. Conservation means taking care of the earth so that people can continue to enjoy its treasures. See **pollution**.

C

continents

About four fifths of the earth's surface is water. The land is divided into seven continents: Africa, Antarctica, Asia, Australia, Europe, North America, and South America.

Cook

James Cook was one of the greatest of all ocean explorers. He was born in England in 1728. Cook led three long voyages in sailing ships around the world. He explored the coasts of New Zealand and Australia and was the first explorer to cross the Antarctic Circle. Cook made maps and studied the lands and peoples he discovered. He was killed in Hawaii in 1779.

▼ Captain Cook in Hawaii.

Copernicus

Nicolaus Copernicus (1473–1543) was a great Polish scientist. He challenged the ancient belief that the earth was the center of the universe and that the sun moved around the earth. Copernicus realized that the earth and the other planets moved around the sun. It was only because the earth too was spinning that the sun and stars seemed to be moving.

copper

Copper is a metal. It can be mixed with tin to make bronze. About 5,000 years ago people discovered how to make objects from these metals. Electrical wires and water pipes are usually copper.

coral

Coral is found in the sea. It looks like rock but is made by tiny sea animals called polyps. The polyp's soft body has a hard limestone case, which forms coral when the polyp dies.

cotton

Cotton cloth comes from a plant. The fruit of the cotton plant is called a boll. Inside is a mass of white fibers, or hairs. These fibers are removed, washed, and spun to make yarn. See **weaving**.

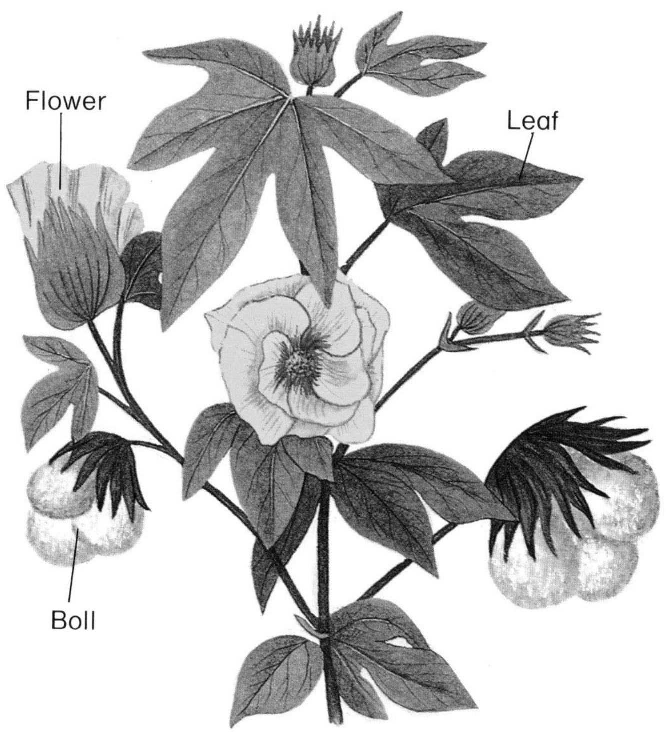

▲ The cotton plant produces a boll, which opens into a white flower. The boll forms as the flower dies. It is about the size of a golf ball.

COUNTRIES

There are more than 5 billion people in the world. They live in more than 160 countries. The Soviet Union, China, India, and the United States are very big countries, which contain many millions of people. Other countries, like Australia and Canada, are big, but have relatively small populations.

ZIMBABWE VENEZUELA USSR USA UK

All countries that govern themselves have their own flag. Often the flag bears a country's national colors, or a symbol, such as a cross or a crescent. Some national flags are shown here.

AFGHANISTAN

ALBANIA

ALGERIA

ARGENTINA

AUSTRALIA

AUSTRIA

BELGIUM

BRAZIL

BOLIVIA

BULGARIA

The United States of America is the world's richest and most powerful country. It is a republic. Its leader is the president. More than 240 million people live in the United States. The U.S. flag is called the Stars and Stripes. Each star represents one of the 50 states. The stripes stand for the 13 original American colonies.

KEY TO COUNTRIES

1 Albania
2 Andorra
3 Austria
4 Bahrain
5 Bangladesh
6 Belgium
7 Benin
8 Burkina Faso
9 Burundi
10 Central African Republic
11 Cote d'Ivoire
12 Congo
13 Czechoslovakia
14 Denmark
15 Equatorial Guinea
16 Gambia
17 Ghana
18 Guinea
19 Guinea-Bissau
20 Israel
21 Jamaica
22 Kuwait
23 Lebanon
24 Liberia
25 Luxembourg
26 Malta
27 Netherlands
28 Portugal
29 Quatar
30 Rwanda
31 Sierra Leone
32 Senegal
33 Switzerland
34 Syria
35 Togo
36 Uganda
37 United Arab Emirates
38 Yugoslavia
39 Zimbabwe
40 Estonia
41 Latvia
42 Lithuania

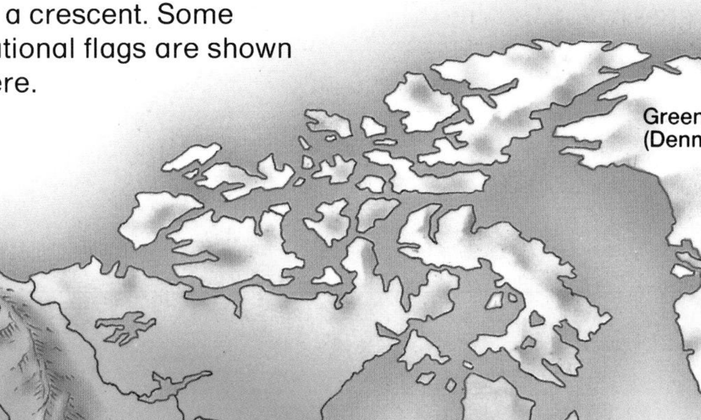

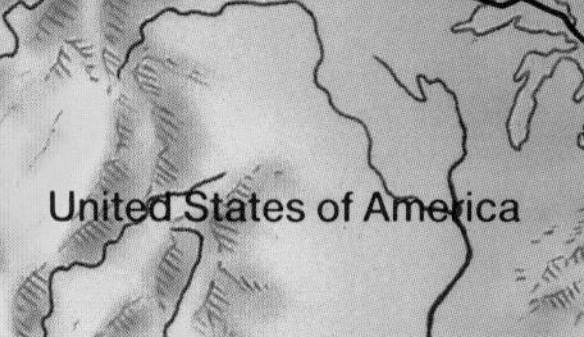

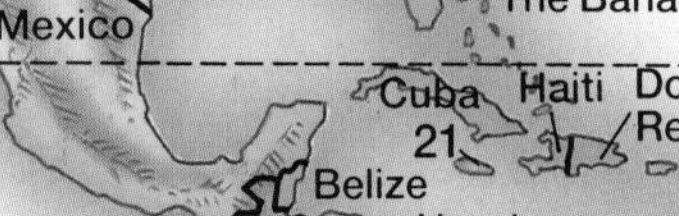

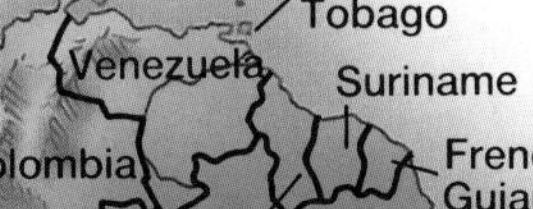

Central America lies between North and South America. Most of its countries are small. Mexico is by far the biggest. The people speak Spanish and American Indian languages.

Brazil is twice as big as any other country in South America. Most Brazilians speak Portuguese.

CANADA

CHILE

CHINA

COLOMBIA

CUBA

CYPRUS

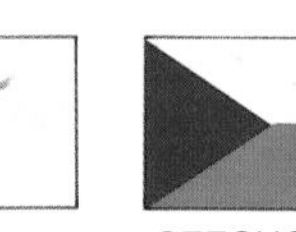

CZECHOSLOVAKIA

DENMARK

Greenland is the world's biggest island. It has its own government but is part of Denmark. Only about 55,000 people live in Greenland.

The world's largest country is the Soviet Union. It covers more than 8.6 million sq mi (22.4 sq km). Three of its 15 republics (the three Baltic States) became independent in 1991.

The country with the most people is China; it has more than a billion. There will be twice as many in 48 years. India will have a billion people by the year 2000.

Africa has more countries than any other continent. It also has the fastest-growing population. Africa's biggest country is Sudan.

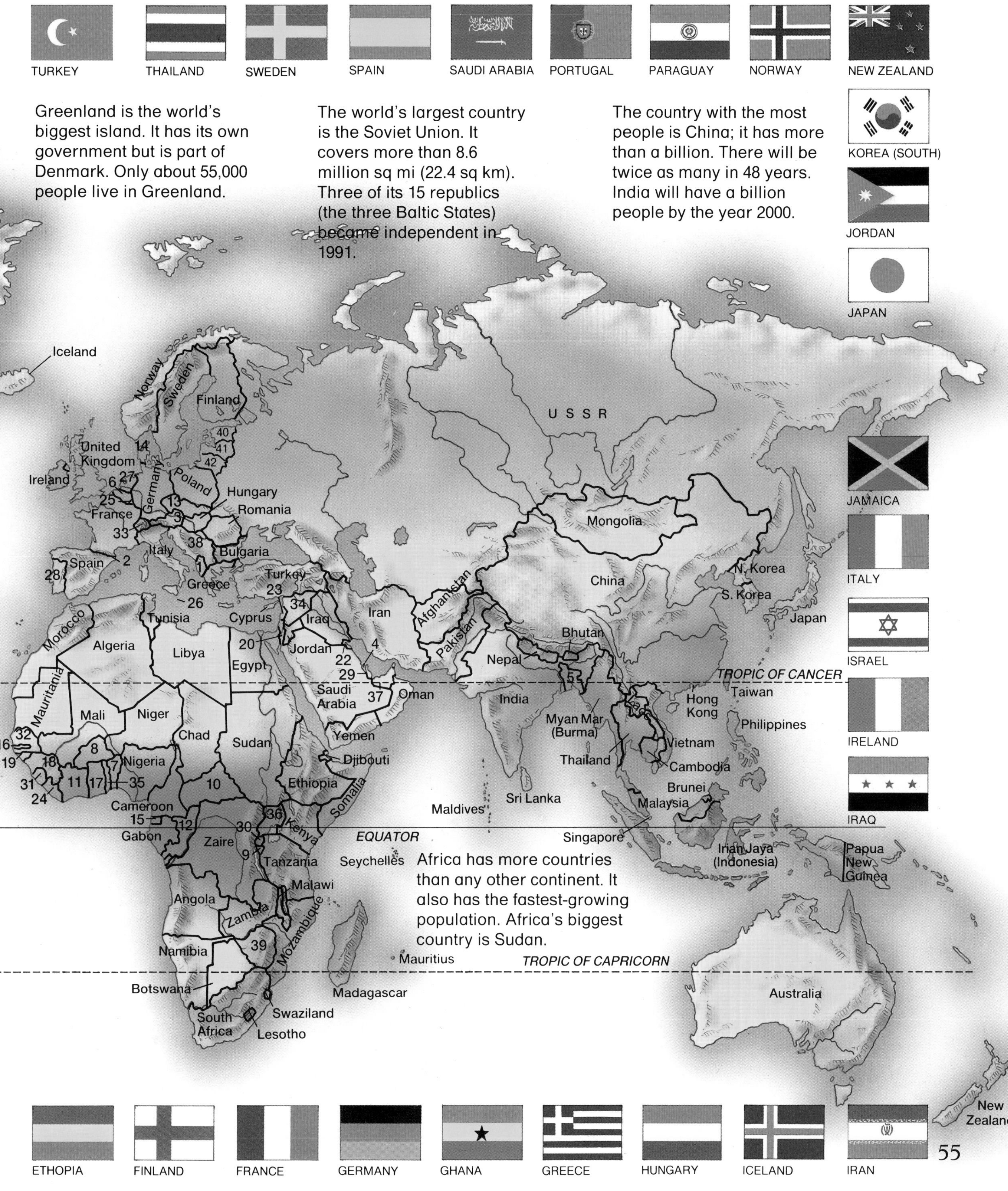

C

court

A law court is where people go for trial if they are accused of breaking the law. Lawyers speak for and against the person on trial, and a judge or jury decides if the person is guilty or not.

► Cowboys of the American West worked mainly on horseback.

cowboy

Cowboys in the Wild West rode horses. They worked on ranches, looking after great herds of cattle. Today cowboys still ride horses, but they also use trucks and helicopters.

crabs and lobsters

Crabs and lobsters are crustaceans, animals with hard shells. They are related to shrimps and prawns. Crabs have rounded shells. Lobsters have longer bodies and tails. These animals live in water, although some crabs live on land and even climb trees. A crab grows by shedding its shell. Crabs use their large front claws as pincers to catch food.

crane

Every big building site has a tall crane at work on it. The crane driver sits high in the air at the controls. Cranes lift steel girders and other large, heavy parts of a building into position. Cranes are also used at docks to lift containers on and off ships.

crocodiles, alligators, and gavials

These large reptiles are fierce hunters with huge jaws and teeth. They live in rivers and swamps, lying in wait for animals to come and drink. They also catch fish. They can lie still in the water like logs, with only their nostrils and eyes showing. They use their powerful tails for swimming and as weapons. When not hungry, they crawl out onto the riverbank and bask in the sun.

▼ The fourth tooth of a crocodile (center) sticks out of its jaw. An alligator's teeth are hidden. The Indian gavial has a long narrow snout.

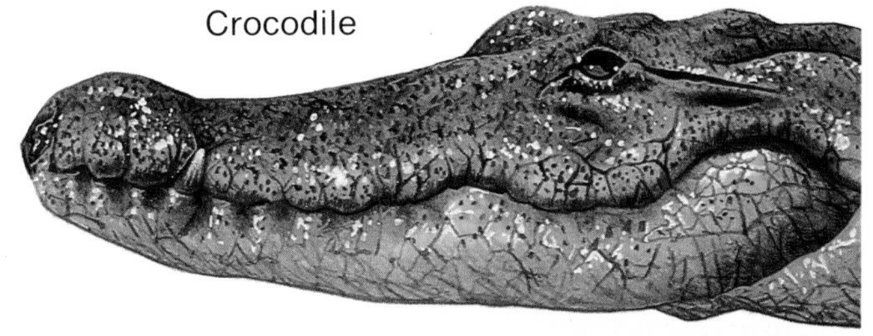

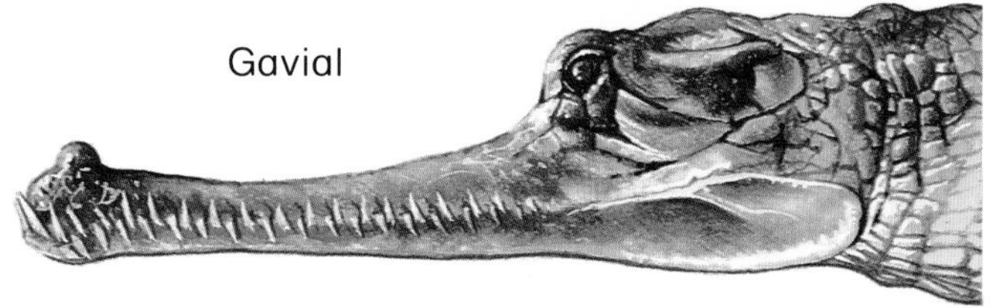

Crusades

In the Middle Ages, Christians and Muslims fought for control of the Holy Land of Palestine. Christian soldiers were called Crusaders, after the cross they wore, and kings and knights journeyed from all over Europe to join the struggle. There were six important Crusades, from 1096 to 1270. Famous castles were built in the Holy Land, such as Krak des Chevaliers in Syria. Both sides won victories, but at the end of the Crusades the Muslims kept Palestine and the city of Jerusalem.

▼ King Richard the Lion-Hearted of England fought in the Third Crusade of 1189. He tried to recapture Jerusalem, but failed. The red cross was the symbol worn by the Crusaders.

crystal

Snowflakes, salt grains, and glittering diamonds are all crystals. In a crystal the atoms or molecules are arranged in regular patterns. Every substance has its own crystal pattern. For example, all snowflakes are six-sided crystals. When you add salt to water, the solid crystals disappear. Heat the water until it turns to steam, and salt crystals will reappear. See **atom**.

LIFE STORY

Curie

Marie Curie was a scientist. She was born in Poland in 1867, as Marie Sklodowska, and in 1895 she married Pierre Curie, a French scientist. They worked together on radioactivity, about which little was known at this time. In 1903 the Curies received the Nobel Prize in physics. Marie Curie was the first woman to win a Nobel Prize. In 1911 she won a second Nobel Prize, this time for her work in chemistry.

The Curies were poor and did a lot of their research in an old shed. They discovered two new elements, named polonium (after Poland) and radium. Pierre Curie was killed in 1903. Marie went on working. She became ill from handling the dangerous radioactive material, but worked until she died in 1934. Her daughter, Irene Joliot-Curie, also won a Nobel Prize in chemistry.

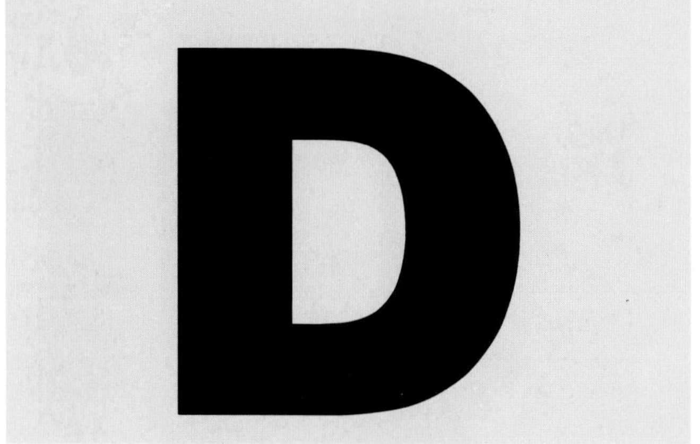

dam

A dam is a wall built across a river. The dam stops the river's flow, and engineers can control how much water is let through. A lake forms on one side of the dam, storing water for drinking, watering crops, or making electricity.

dance

People dance because they like to move their feet and bodies in time to music or rhythm. But in the past people also danced to tell stories, to try to make crops grow, and to make warriors feel brave. Temple dancers danced in honor of gods. There are many kinds of dancing today, including ballet and modern dance, ballroom and disco dance, folk and theater dance. See **ballet**.

▼ There are many styles of dance. Here are three dancers: a ballerina, a temple dancer from Asia, and a dancer in a 1930s-style film or stage show.

LIFE STORY

Darwin

Charles Darwin (1809–1882) was an English naturalist. He believed that animals evolve, or develop, by slow changes from earlier forms.

Darwin sailed around the world on a ship called the *Beagle*. The voyage lasted five years. Darwin discovered the fossils of prehistoric sea animals in rocks on mountains in South America, and he wondered how they had gotten there. He also saw finches (small birds) living on Pacific islands. The birds looked alike, but had different bills. Some ate insects, others seeds or nuts. Darwin believed that the finches all had the same ancestors, and that these changes had come about through evolution. His famous book *On the Origin of Species* caused much argument because some people thought he was challenging the teachings of the Bible. Today most people think Darwin was right. See **evolution**, **fossil**.

Nomads (wandering people) used camels to carry goods across the empty sandy deserts of Africa and Arabia.

day and night

Daytime is when the sun's light shines on our part of the earth. As the earth spins around, the sun's light shines on different parts of its surface, bringing daylight. The part of the earth turned away from the sun has dark night. The earth spins once in 24 hours. See **earth, seasons**.

deer

Deer are hoofed mammals that eat mostly grass and leaves. They have keen eyesight and sense of smell and can run fast. Deer often live in herds. Only the males have antlers, used for fighting in the mating season.

▼ Red deer (below) have branching antlers with long points. The fallow deer's antlers are leaf-shaped. Deer shed and grow new antlers each year.

desert

Some deserts are hot and sandy. Others are cold. Many are rocky. But all deserts are dry. Most are in the middle of continents, and winds carrying moisture from the sea are dry by the time they reach there. With few clouds to keep in the heat, deserts can be very hot by day but cold at night.

DID YOU KNOW?

The Gobi Desert is a vast desert in central Asia. Its Chinese name, Sha-mo, means "sand desert," but there is not much sand. Most of the Gobi is bare rock. In winter it is very cold. The two-humped Bactrian camels that live there have thick fur to keep out the cold. Fossils of dinosaur eggs have been found in the Gobi.

diamonds

Diamonds are crystals made of carbon. They are the hardest of all substances, and only a diamond will cut a diamond. Diamonds are formed deep in the Earth by great heat and squeezing of rocks. They have a brilliant sparkle when cut and polished. See **crystal**.

▼ Miners dig out diamonds from rocks underground with powerful drills.

Dickens

Charles Dickens (1812–1870) was one of the world's great writers. His books are both sad and funny, and they are full of memorable characters. Dickens's poor childhood made him pity those who were badly treated, and to help them he wrote of their hardships. His books include *The Pickwick Papers*, *Oliver Twist*, *David Copperfield*, and *Great Expectations*. They are still popular today.

dinosaurs

Dinosaurs were prehistoric reptiles. Some were plant-eating giants. Others were terrible meat eaters. Some dinosaurs were the size of chickens. Dinosaurs lived from 225 million to 65 million years ago. No one is sure why they died out. See **fossil, prehistoric animals**.

disease

Diseases make our bodies go wrong. Some diseases are passed on from parents to children. Others are caused by bacteria and viruses, or by poisons. Modern medicine has found cures for many diseases. Others can be prevented by vaccination. See **medicine**.

▼ Sneezing spreads germs. Use a handkerchief.

▲ Cockroaches, rats, and flies can spread disease.

► Always wash your hands before touching or cooking food.

◄ Do not leave freshly cooked food uncovered in a warm place.

► Do not share drinks, or use someone else's knife, fork, or spoon.

dodo

The dodo was a flightless bird that lived on an Indian Ocean island. When sailors arrived in the 1600s, they killed dodos for food. Cats and rats from the ships ate their eggs. Soon the last dodo was dead.

DOGS

Dogs were the first animals tamed by people. Prehistoric cave people tamed wild dogs to help hunt deer and other animals. Later, people used dogs to help herd sheep and cattle. The dog family includes many breeds of pet and working dogs, and also wild dogs such as wolves, foxes, jackals, and coyotes. The largest dog is the St. Bernard.

SEEING-EYE DOGS

Dogs help people in many ways. Some guard us. Some sniff out dangerous drugs. Some help rescue people. Seeing-eye dogs are trained to help blind people. The dog becomes the blind person's "eyes." Training begins when the dog is a puppy. It must learn obedience and how to guide its owner.

Some breeds of dog were bred for hunting (greyhound), others for herding work (collie, corgi). Some were bred to be guard dogs (mastiff), or to retrieve birds shot by a hunter (Labrador).

TRAINING A DOG

Many dogs live in busy towns, so it is very important that they are well trained. All dogs should be taught to obey commands and to behave properly when out with their owners. Training should begin when the dog is young; dog-training classes are best. The dog should learn to walk on the leash quietly, beside its owner; to sit and lie down on command; and to "stay" while the owner moves away and not "come" until given the command. Praise your dog every time it does well and it will soon learn.

D

doll see **toys**

dolphin
Dolphins are small whale-like mammals. Like all mammals, dolphins breathe air. Dolphins and porpoises eat fish. They are intelligent and have their own language. See **mammals**.

▼ Dolphins and porpoises look alike, but porpoises have blunt snouts.

donkey
Donkeys carry loads and pull carts in many countries. These hardworking animals are relatives of wild asses. If a female horse is mated with a male donkey, she gives birth to a mule.

dragon
Dragons are make-believe animals, with scaly bodies and long tails. When angry, they breathe fire. European dragons are fierce, but Chinese dragons bring good luck. See **China**.

dragonfly
The dragonfly darts about over water, catching other insects. This marvelous flier spends its early life underwater, as a crawling larva or nymph. See **insects**.

drama
Drama tells a story in words and actions. Actors play out the story in front of an audience. A story written for acting is a play, and the writer is a playwright. The ancient Greeks first performed plays with actors in theaters more than 2,500 years ago. See **Greece**.

▲ In Europe during the Middle Ages there were no theaters. Plays were performed in the town square. They often showed religious stories.

drawing see **painting and drawing**

drugs
Drugs are made from herbs and chemicals to cure disease or ease pain. Antibiotics are drugs that kill harmful bacteria. Some drugs, such as heroin, are dangerous because people cannot stop taking them and become ill.

ducks and geese
Ducks and geese are birds that often live near water. They paddle with their webbed feet. Some eat grass or water plants. Others dig for worms with their beaks or dive underwater for food. Geese are bigger, with longer necks.

eagle

The eagle is a large bird of prey. It soars into the sky on broad wings, then swoops to seize its prey in powerful talons, or claws. Its nest is called an aerie.

▲ All eagles have hooked beaks and strong talons, or claws, to seize their prey. The bald eagle is the emblem of the United States. It lives in Alaska.

ear and hearing

We hear sounds through our ears. The dish-shaped outer part catches vibrations in the air. These travel to the middle ear, where three bones pick up the vibrations and pass them on. Inside the inner ear is a coiled tube full of fluid. The vibrating air makes the fluid vibrate. Nerves send messages about the vibrations to the brain and we "hear" sounds. See **human body**.

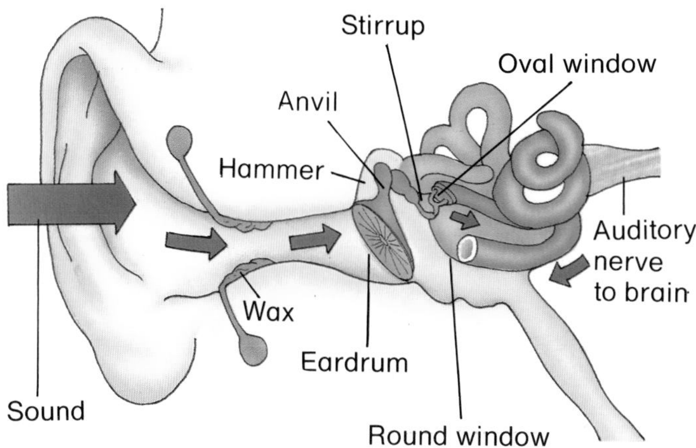

▲ The outer ear picks up air vibrations, which travel through the middle ear to the inner ear. The nervous system translates the signals into sounds.

earth

The earth is the planet on which we live. It is one of nine planets traveling in space around the sun. Only the earth has air, water, and plant and animal life. Water covers four fifths of the earth. The crust, or surface, of the earth is made of rocky plates which carry the continents. These plates move and rub against one another. The rocks bend and fold to form mountains. Below the crust is a thick layer of heavier rocks called the mantle. Below the mantle are more rocks, so hot that they are molten (liquid). The center of the earth is a solid core of nickel and iron.

EARTH

The earth is ball-shaped, but not completely round. It is slightly flatter at the poles, and it bulges at the equator. The equator divides the earth into two hemispheres, or halves. One half is the Northern Hemisphere. The other half is the Southern Hemisphere. Most of the land and people are in the Northern Hemisphere.

Why are the poles colder than the equator? The sun's rays have to pass through the atmosphere before reaching the ground. They must travel farther to get to the poles than to reach the equator; the rays lose more heat on the way, and so the poles are colder.

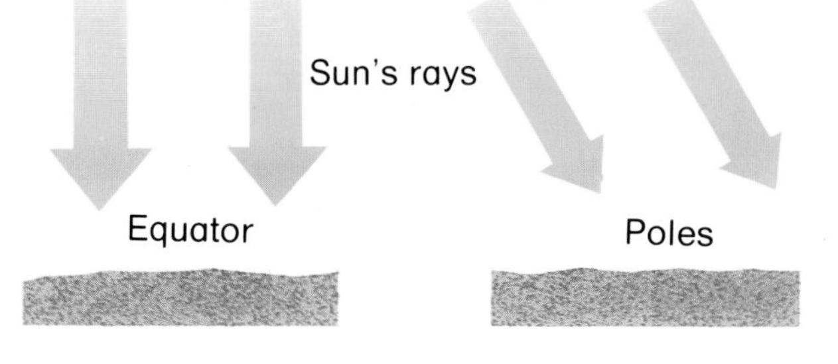

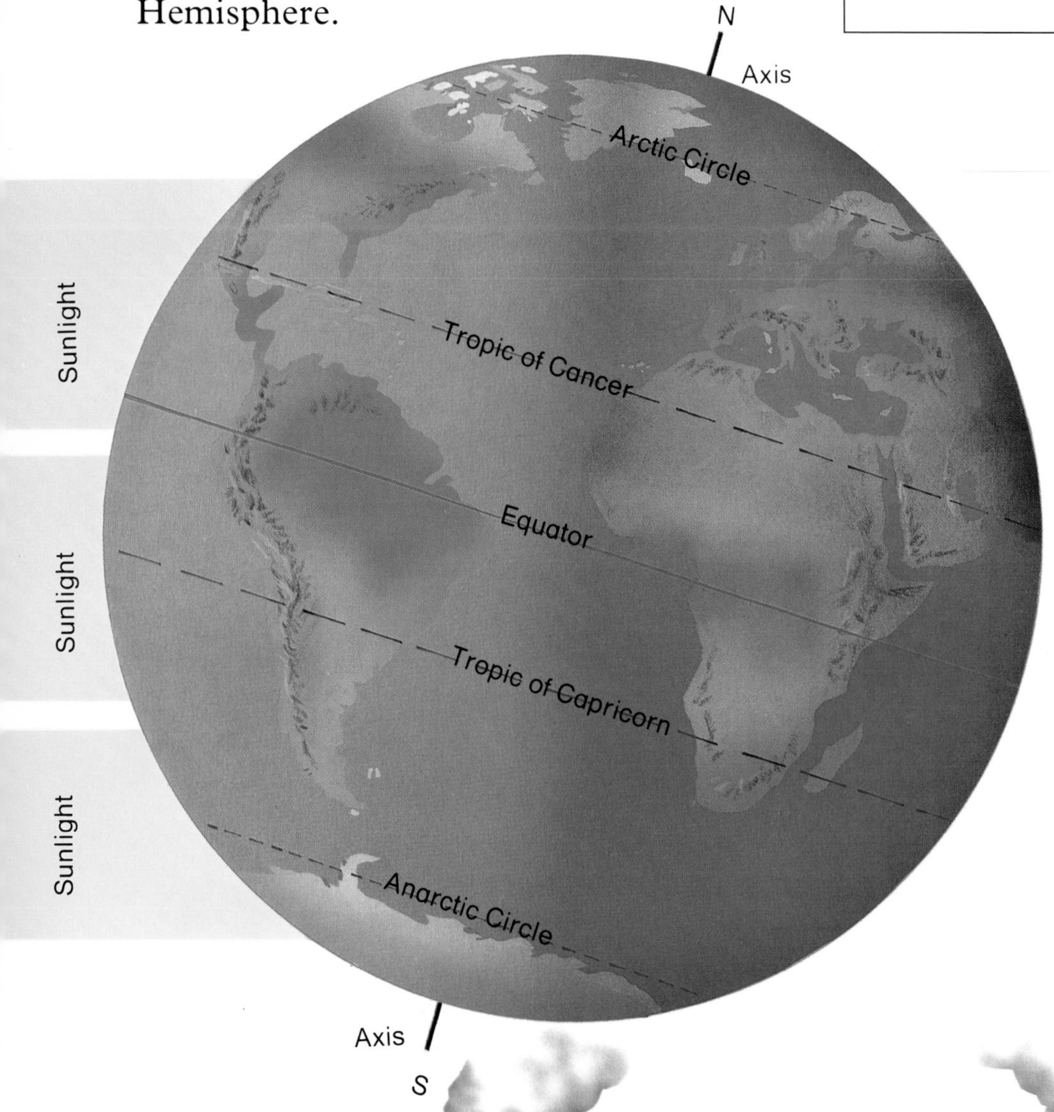

◀ Like a giant ball, the earth is spinning through space. One spin takes 24 hours. The earth tilts to one side. The line around which an object spins is its axis; the earth's axis is an imaginary line from North Pole to South Pole. The sun's rays can only reach the half of the earth facing the sun. This half has day. The half facing away from the sun is in shadow, and there it is night. At the equator day and night last roughly the same time all year round.

EARTHQUAKES AND VOLCANOES

Parts of the world have frequent earthquakes and volcanoes. The plates that make up the earth's crust are always moving. When one plate slides against or underneath another, the strains become so enormous that the rocks move suddenly. This is an earthquake. A volcano is a hole in the earth's crust. Pressure builds up in the rocks beneath until the volcano erupts, or explodes. Hot melted rocks, burning gas, and ash shoot up into the air.

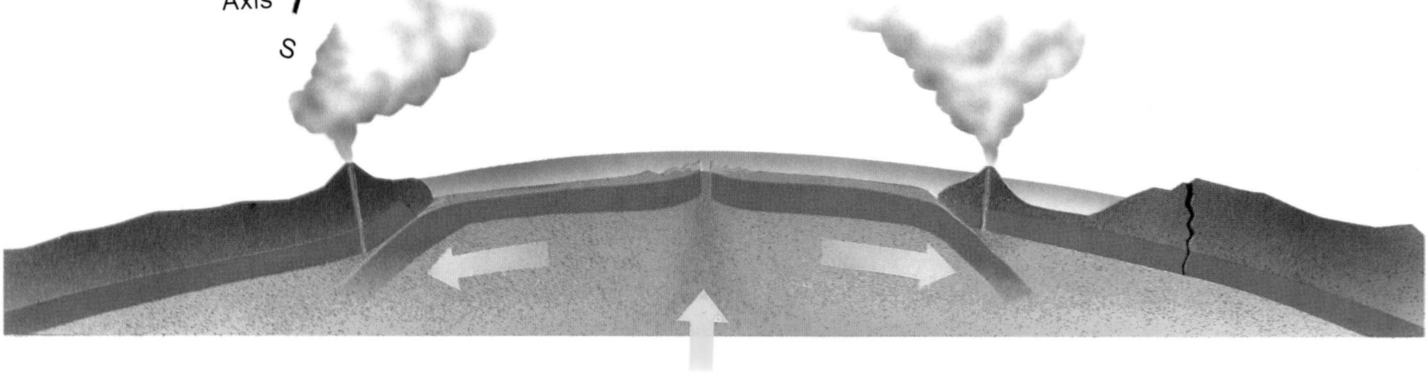

► The earth's axis is an imaginary line from North Pole to South Pole. The equator is an imaginary line around the earth's middle.

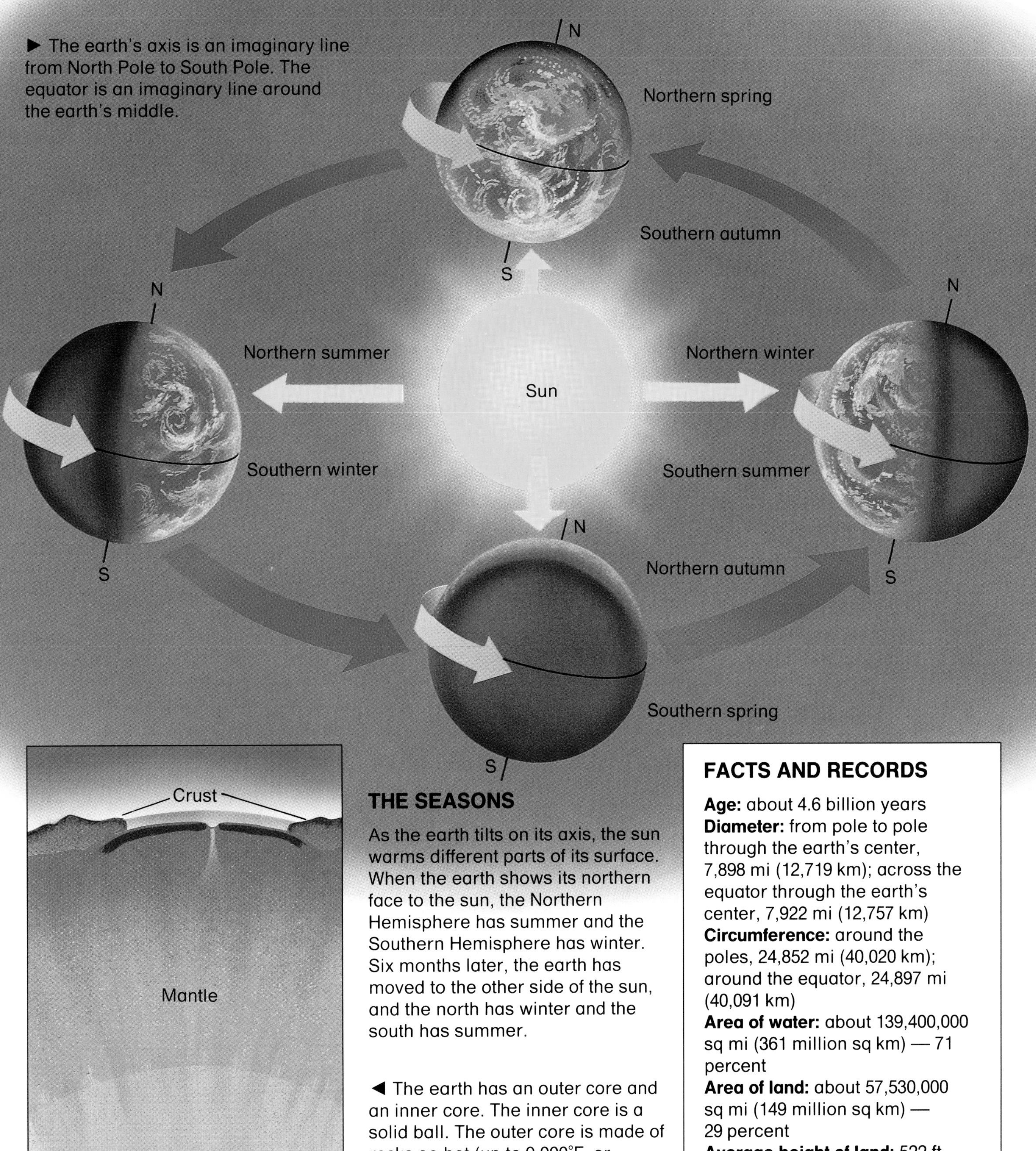

THE SEASONS

As the earth tilts on its axis, the sun warms different parts of its surface. When the earth shows its northern face to the sun, the Northern Hemisphere has summer and the Southern Hemisphere has winter. Six months later, the earth has moved to the other side of the sun, and the north has winter and the south has summer.

◄ The earth has an outer core and an inner core. The inner core is a solid ball. The outer core is made of rocks so hot (up to 9,000°F, or 5,000°C) that they are molten, or melted. Around the cores is a thicker, heavier layer of hot rocks called the mantle. The earth's skin or crust is made up of curved plates of rock, up to 18½ mi (30 km) thick.

FACTS AND RECORDS

Age: about 4.6 billion years
Diameter: from pole to pole through the earth's center, 7,898 mi (12,719 km); across the equator through the earth's center, 7,922 mi (12,757 km)
Circumference: around the poles, 24,852 mi (40,020 km); around the equator, 24,897 mi (40,091 km)
Area of water: about 139,400,000 sq mi (361 million sq km) — 71 percent
Area of land: about 57,530,000 sq mi (149 million sq km) — 29 percent
Average height of land: 522 ft (840 m) above sea level
Deepest part of ocean: Marianas Trench (36,198 ft [11,033 m])
Average depth of ocean: 12,451 ft (3,795 m) below sea level

▲ A strong earthquake makes the ground shake. Buildings collapse, and there is great damage.

▼ Earthquakes happen when two plates of the earth's crust rub against each other at a fault line.

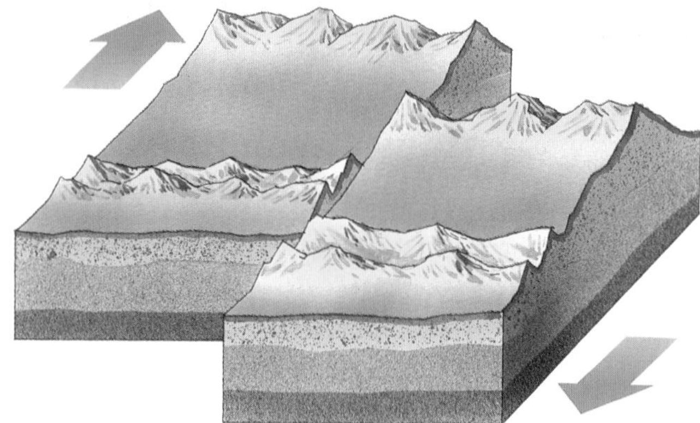

earthquake

The ground under our feet is not as solid as it feels. In an earthquake, the ground shakes and cracks appear. Buildings collapse. The sudden violent shaking is over in seconds. It is caused by movements of the earth's crust, which force the rocks to bend and snap under enormous pressure. There are about 150,000 earthquakes every year, but only about 100 cause serious damage.

echo

An echo is a sound reflected or bounced back from an object. If you shout inside an empty building, your voice comes back as an echo. The sound waves hit the walls and are reflected. Bats use echoes to find their way. See **sound**.

eclipse

A solar eclipse happens when the moon passes between the sun and the earth, blocking out the light. On part of the earth, day becomes night for a few minutes. A lunar eclipse is when the earth's shadow makes the moon seem to disappear. See **solar system**.

▼ The moon is sometimes in direct line between the earth and the sun. The darkest spot is where people see a total eclipse.

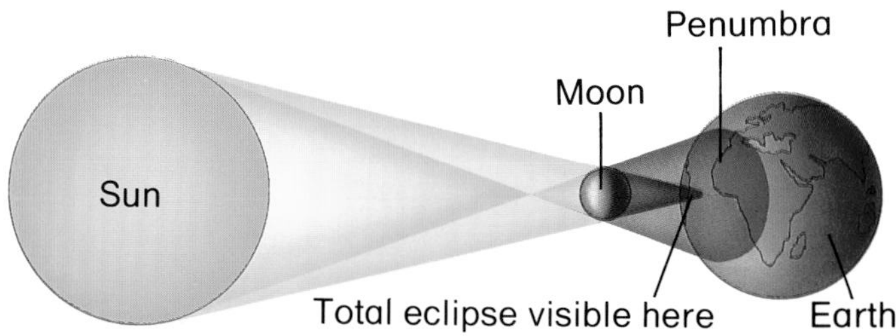

LIFE STORY

Edison

Thomas Alva Edison was born in Ohio in 1847. He was one of the great inventors of all time. He made more than 1,000 inventions, many of which used the new and amazing power of electricity.

Edison's teachers could not teach him, because he asked too many questions. So he finished his schooling at home. At the age of 12 he started a newspaper on board a train. In 1876, Edison set up his own laboratory. He invented a microphone to make the telephone work better. In 1877, he made a phonograph, a kind of record player. His first recording was of himself reciting "Mary had a little lamb." In 1879, he made an electric light bulb. He even designed a power station. By the time he died in 1931, Edison had lived to see a new world of technology, largely brought about by his own brilliant inventions.

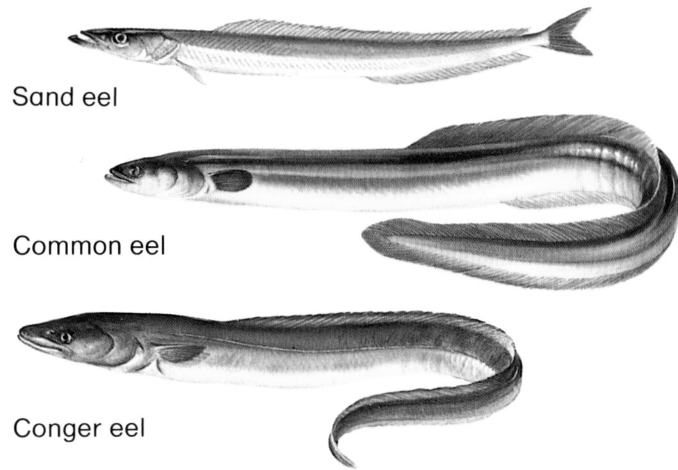

eel

Eels are fish, though they look a lot like snakes. Some eels, such as the little sand eel and the fierce conger eel, spend all their lives in the sea. The common eel lives in rivers, but migrates (journeys) to the sea to breed. It even wriggles overland to reach the sea. The eels lay their eggs far out in the western Atlantic. Then they die. The baby eels swim back to the rivers.

egg

Most animals begin life as an egg, a tiny cell. A female's egg must be joined with a sperm, or male cell, to develop into a new animal. In most creatures, the baby hatches out of the egg. Mammals, including humans, keep their eggs inside their bodies. The baby grows inside its mother until it is born.

► Birds hatch from eggs. The baby, or chick, grows inside the egg. It breaks the shell with its beak. The ostrich lays the biggest egg, weighing about 3.3 lb (1.5 kg).

EGYPT

More than 5,000 years ago the people of ancient Egypt built a great civilization on the banks of the Nile River. The Nile's waters made Egypt's soil fertile. Food was plentiful. Rich families lived in fine houses with beautiful gardens. Boats sailed along the Nile and into the Mediterranean. The pharaohs, or kings, built huge temples and tombs.

▲ The Egyptians built pyramids as tombs for their pharaohs. The oldest are the smaller step pyramids. The Great Pyramid (the biggest in this picture) was built in the 2600s B.C. and is 449 ft (137 m) high. It contains more than 2 million stones.

▲ The pharaoh and his court lived in luxury, waited on by slaves. They enjoyed music and games.

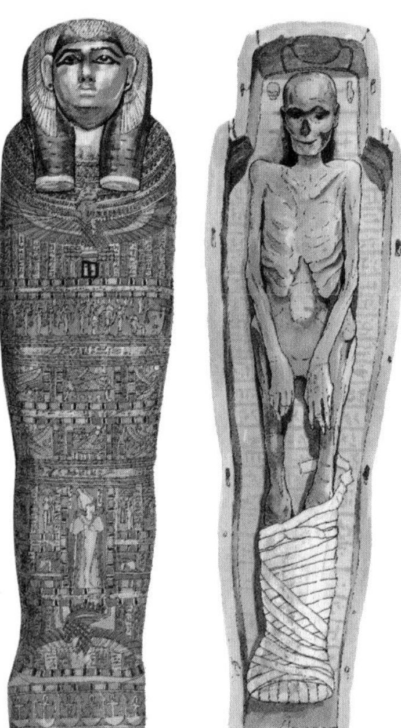

◀ The Egyptians believed in life after death. A dead body was preserved and wrapped in cloth. This "mummy" was put in a coffin or sarcophagus. Beside it in the tomb were food, clothes, jewels, and furniture.

▼ Harvest time on an Egyptian farm. Workers are cutting, threshing, and winnowing the corn to separate the grain. Each basket of grain is counted.

LIFE STORY

Einstein

Albert Einstein (1879–1955) was the greatest modern scientist. He was born in Germany and later lived in the United States. Einstein was fascinated by space, time, and motion. His theory of relativity challenged beliefs held since the 1600s, when Sir Isaac Newton explained why things move. In 1906, Einstein said that Newton's laws are not true for an object moving close to the speed of light: about 186,282 mi (300,000 km) a second. By studying atomic particles, other scientists found that Einstein was correct. Einstein showed that matter and energy are different forms of the same thing. A small piece of matter can be changed into a vast amount of energy. That is the secret of atomic power. See **nuclear energy**.

electricity

Electricity is a form of energy, produced when tiny atomic particles called electrons move from one atom to another. It is hard to imagine a world without electricity, yet before the 1800s people knew little about it. Electricity is found in nature, in lightning. It can travel from one object to another. Metals are good conductors, or carriers, of electricity. Plastic, glass, and rubber are insulators, or poor conductors. Electricity can be stored in a battery. See **battery**, **Faraday**.

electronics

The modern world is full of electronic marvels. Television, computers, digital watches, and videos all work electronically. The valve, a glass tube through which electric current passed, was an early electronic device. It was invented in 1904 and used in early radios. The much smaller transistor was invented in 1948. In 1958, the first integrated circuit was made. This squeezed lots of very tiny transistors onto one piece, or chip, of silicon. Today, thousands of electronic parts can be put on one tiny microchip. The chip works at amazing speed. See **computer**, **electricity**.

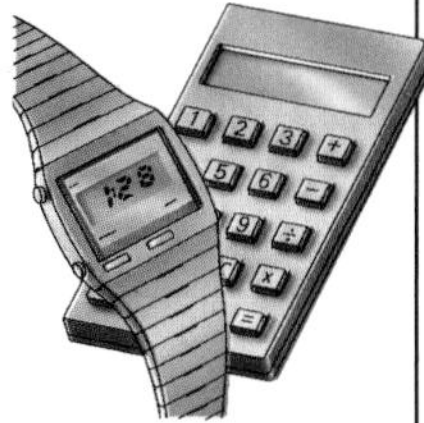

▲ Electronic devices are tiny but very powerful. They can provide a computer with its memory, control a car's systems, and work digital watches and pocket calculators.

ELECTRICITY

Most of the electricity we use is made by turbine generators at power stations. We call it current electricity. It flows through wires. Current flows when electrons jump between the atoms that make up the metal in the wire. Current flows only if a wire makes a complete loop, called a circuit. If there is a gap in the loop, the current stops.

THE TURBINE

A turbine is a fan with many blades. Steam (or sometimes water) pushes the blades so the turbine spins. Several turbines can be joined together. In a power station, turbines drive generators to make electricity.

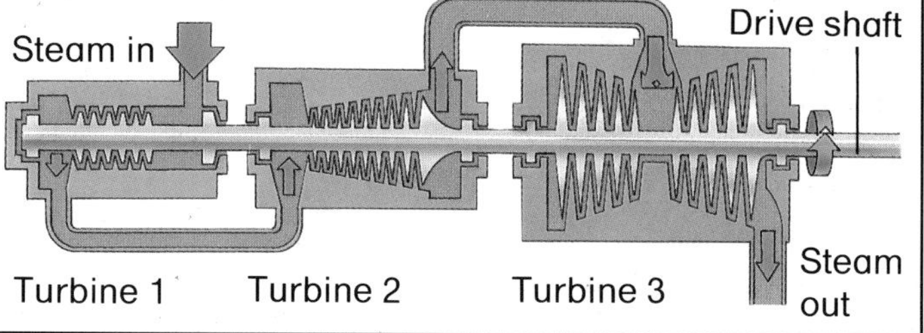

HOW ELECTRICITY REACHES US

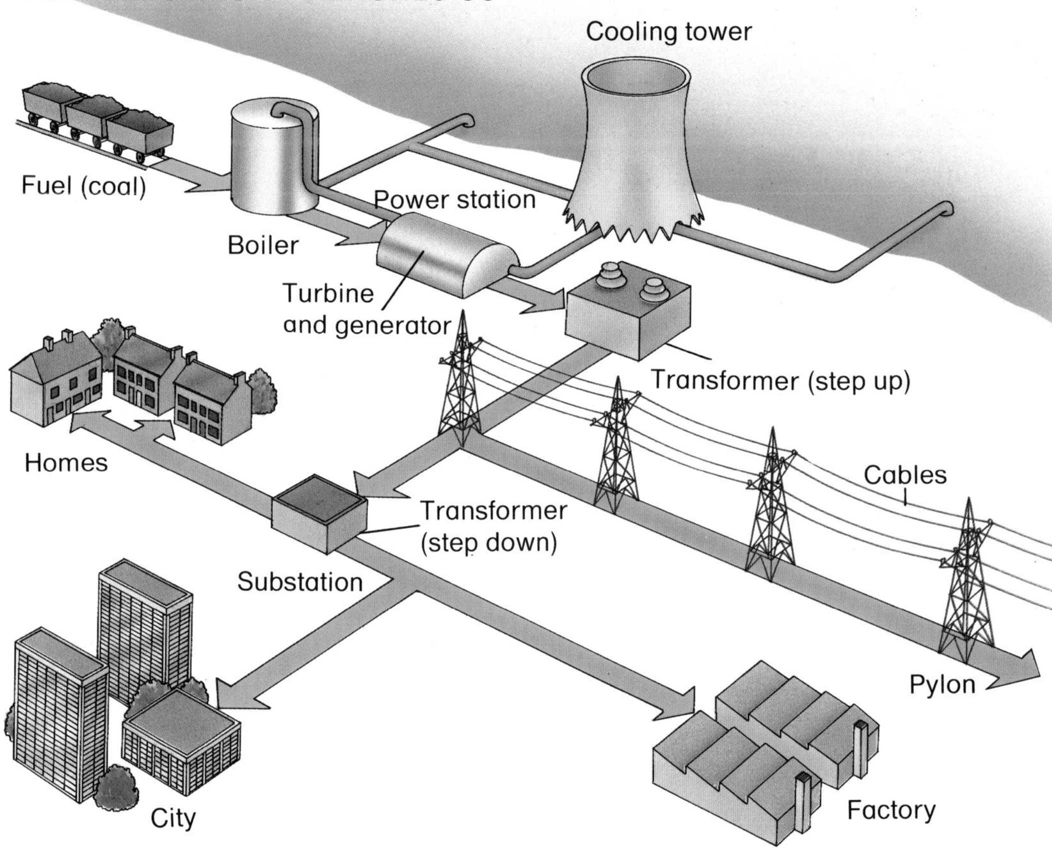

◀ Generators in a power station make electricity. Transformers increase the strength of the current before it travels across country through power cables. Other transformers weaken the current so it is safe for people to use.

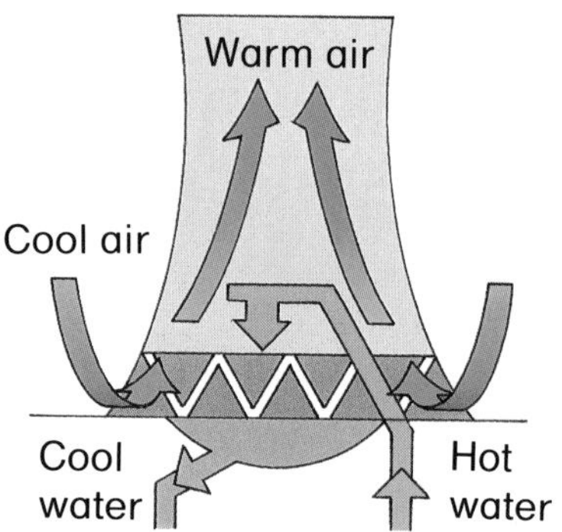

▲ Hot water from power stations is cooled in huge cooling towers. The air takes up most of the heat and the cool water can then be piped safely into a river.

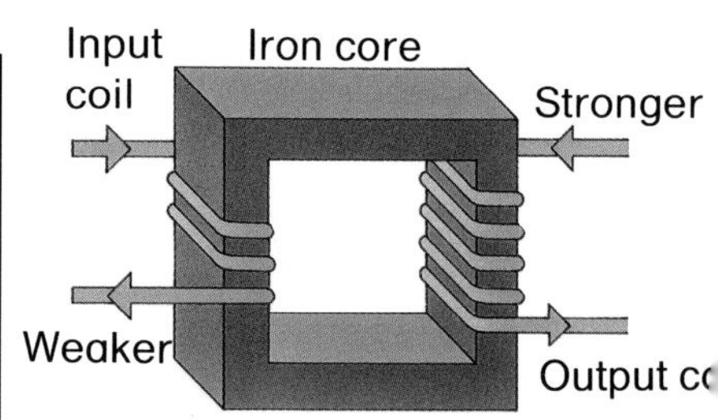

▲ A transformer can step up (increase) or step down (decrease) the strength of a current. It depends which side of the coil (in or out) has the most turns of wire.

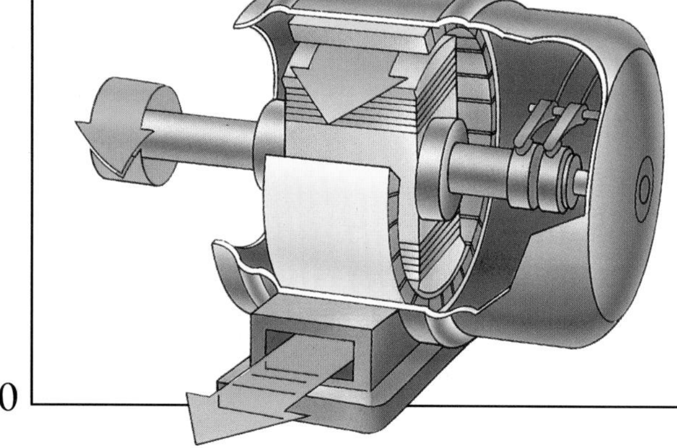

HOW A GENERATOR WORKS

In a power station, turbines drive generators. The turbines provide the energy to work the moving parts of the generator. In the generator are thousands of coils of wire, each of which is made to turn very quickly between powerful magnets. As the coil turns in the magnetic field, the electrons in the wire move and electricity is produced.

NO CURRENT FLOWING

Electrons Wire Atom

− + **CURRENT FLOWING**

▲ Current flows through a wire when electrons from the atoms of the metal move around. A good conductor of electricity is a substance with lots of free electrons.

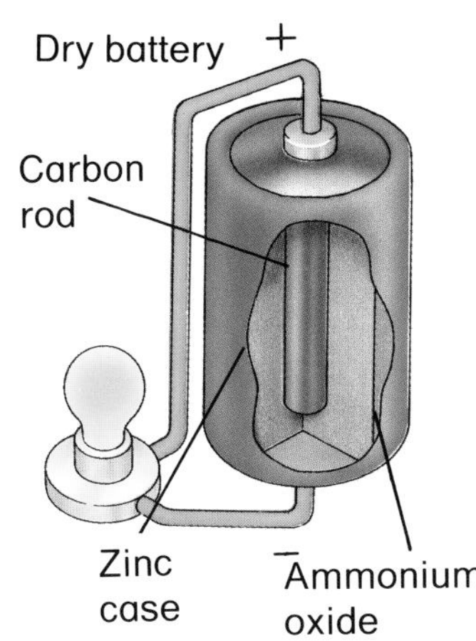

▲ In a dry battery (the kind in a flashlight) a paste-like chemical is packed around a carbon rod inside a zinc case. The three substances react to make electricity.

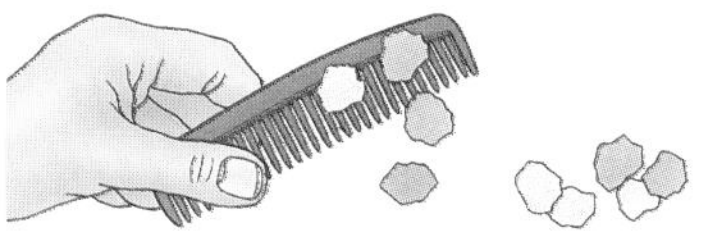

◀ In static electricity, no electrons move. Combing your hair gives the comb an electrical charge. It will pick up bits of paper.

HOW ELECTRIC MOTORS WORK

An electric motor can be small, as in a hair dryer, or large enough to work a factory machine. The simplest motor has a coil held between the poles of a magnet. When an electric current flows through the coil, the coil becomes an electromagnet. The poles of the ordinary magnet repel the electromagnet, making it spin.

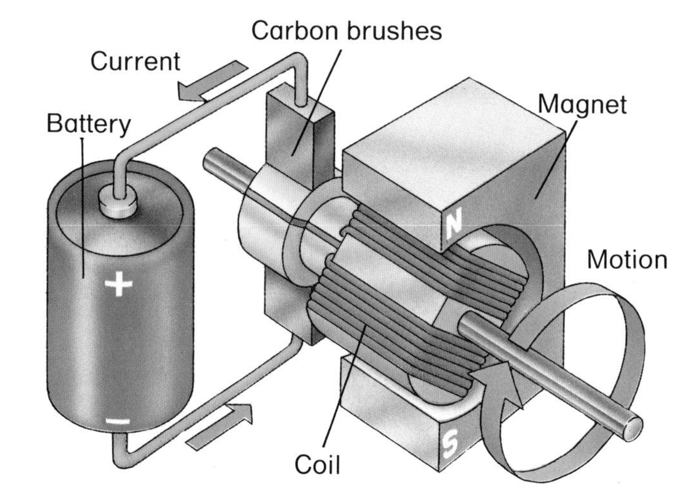

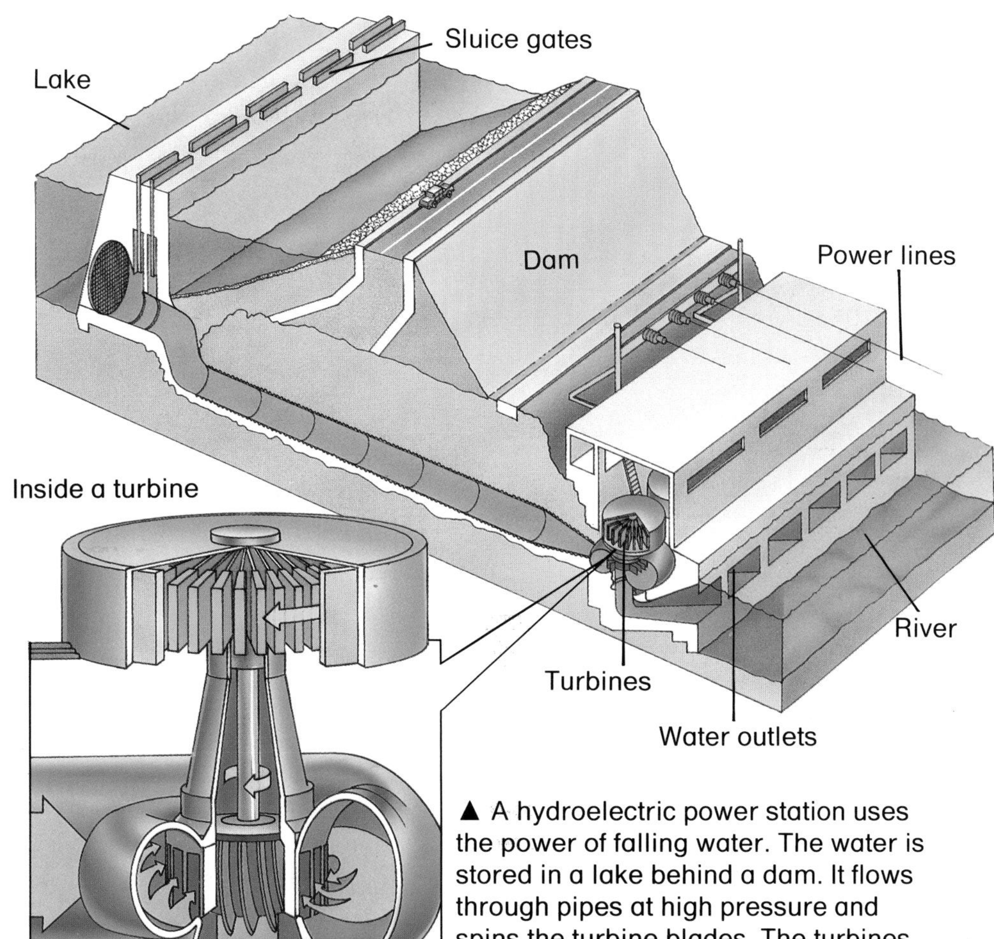

▲ A hydroelectric power station uses the power of falling water. The water is stored in a lake behind a dam. It flows through pipes at high pressure and spins the turbine blades. The turbines drive electrical generators.

FIND OUT FOR YOURSELF

To make a simple circuit with a switch, you need some wire, a battery, a flashlight bulb, a small piece of wood, metal paper clips, and thumbtacks. Look carefully at the picture to see how to wire up your circuit. See if you can use the circuit to turn the bulb on and off.

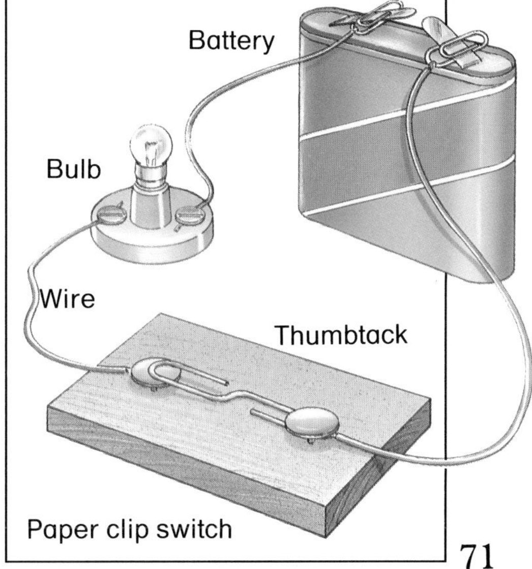

E

An African elephant

elephant

Elephants are the biggest land animal. A male African elephant can be 11.5 ft (3.5 m) tall and weigh almost 8 tons. The Indian elephant is smaller and has smaller ears, too. It can be trained for work, but the African elephant is less easy to tame. Elephants live in herds and eat plants. Their tusks are extra-long teeth, used to dig up food and to fight. The elephant uses its trunk to grab leaves from the treetops. Elephants are now rare in the wild. Hunters still kill African elephants for their tusks. See **animals**.

DID YOU KNOW?

An elephant's trunk is its nose. But it can also use the tip as a delicate "finger" to pick up objects. The elephant uses its trunk to suck up water to drink or to spray for a refreshing shower.

Elizabeth I

The Elizabethan Age in English history is named after Queen Elizabeth I (1533–1603). She became queen in 1558. During her reign the English navy defeated the Spanish Armada, Francis Drake sailed around the world, and William Shakespeare wrote his plays.

emu see **ostrich**

energy

Energy is the ability to do work. When you run, your body is using energy which comes from food. Energy can exist in different forms – as stored energy, energy of motion, electrical energy, heat energy, mechanical energy, and so on. Nuclear energy, or energy from the atom, is the most powerful energy source on earth. The sun and other stars give out massive amounts of energy. Kinetic energy is energy that is

▼ Energy comes from the sun. It is stored by plants and animals. Eating food gives our bodies energy to work and play. When you run, swim, sit, or ride a bike, your body is using energy.

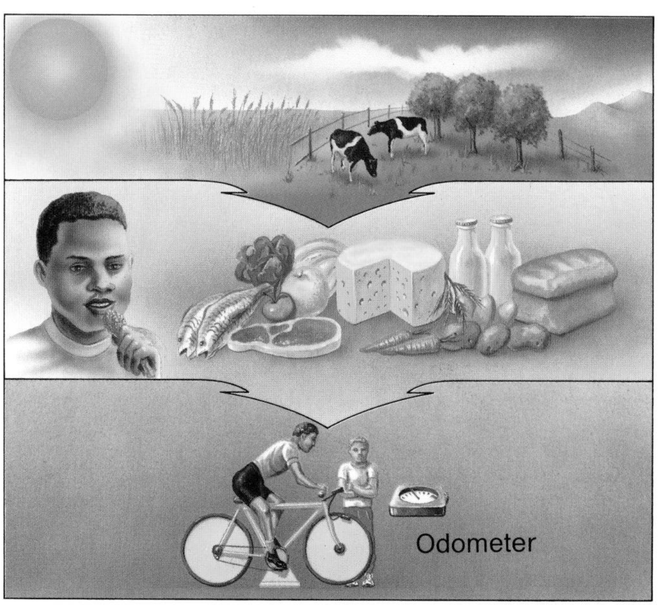

E

► The energy in a jack-in-the-box is potential energy until the catch is released. Then it becomes kinetic energy, or energy of motion. As the catch is released, the jack jumps out of the box.

used for movement. Potential energy is stored-up energy. A spring has potential energy. See **nuclear energy, sun**.

FIND OUT FOR YOURSELF

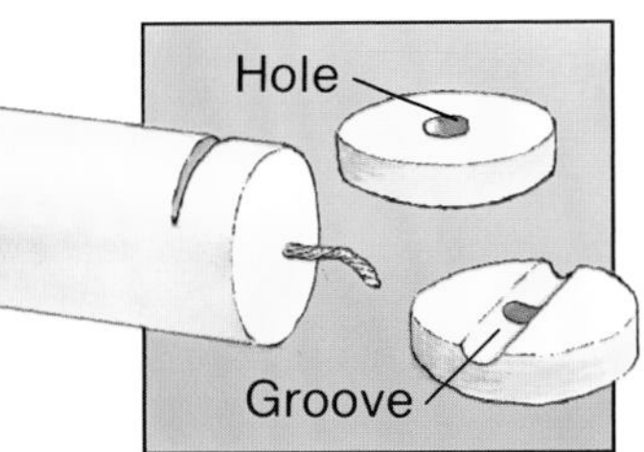

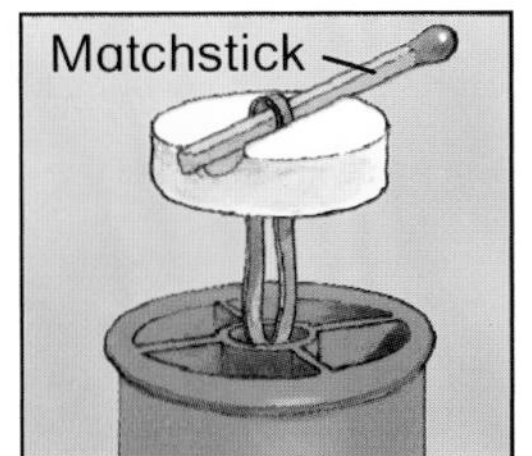

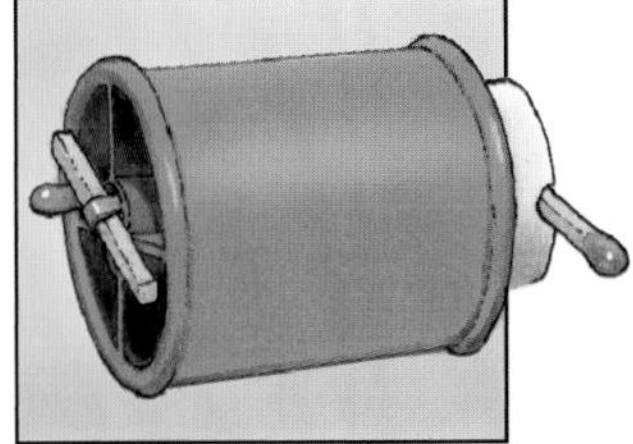

You need an empty thread spool, a slice of candle with a hole in it, matchsticks, and a small rubber band. Turn the matchstick to wind up the rubber-band motor. As the band unwinds, it releases stored energy to make the crawler move.

engines

Engines or motors drive machines in planes, ships, cars, and trains. They drive factory machinery and home appliances such as washing machines. An engine needs energy to make it work. It gets this energy from fuel. A car engine burns gasoline or diesel fuel. Steam engines, such as turbines, are driven by steam made by heating water until it boils. See **car, fuel**.

HOW A CAR ENGINE WORKS

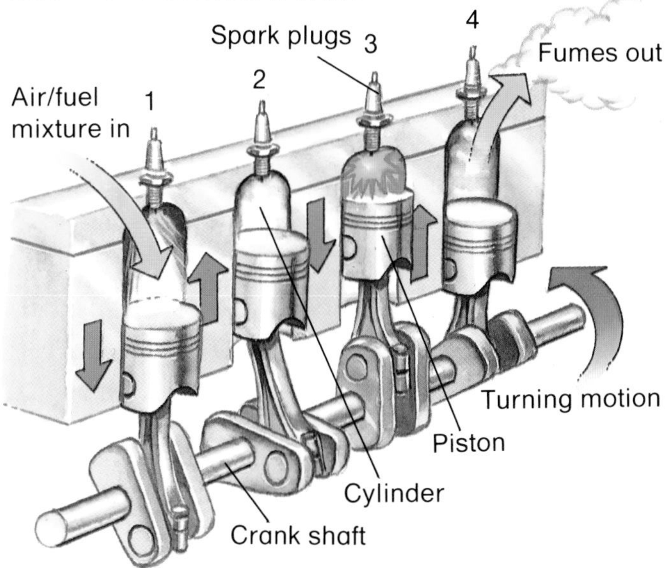

▲ Most car engines work on a four-stroke cycle. (1) Fuel and air are sucked into the cylinder. (2) The piston compresses, or squashes, the mixture. (3) A spark makes the mixture explode. (4) A valve opens to release waste gases.

▼ In a steam engine, steam is made by heating water in a boiler. The steam pushes the pistons backward and forward.

HOW A STEAM ENGINE WORKS

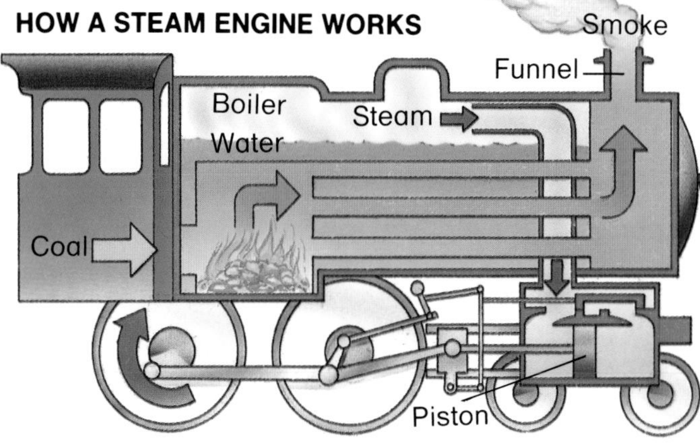

EUROPE

Europe is the sixth-biggest continent, but is second in population. Most of Europe has a mild climate and fertile soil. There are some high mountains, including the Alps and the Urals. In its long history, Europe has been home to many peoples. Europeans have settled in other parts of the world, taking their customs and knowledge with them.

FACTS AND RECORDS

Area: 4,066,000 sq mi (10,531,000 sq km). This includes 25 percent of the U.S.S.R. and 3 percent of Turkey.
Number of countries: 32 (excluding Baltic states)
Population: 786,000,000
Largest country: U.S.S.R. 8,649,489 sq mi (22,402,200 sq km*) (total area)
Country with most people: U.S.S.R. (total 288,000,000)
Largest city: Moscow (U.S.S.R.) 10,367,000
Highest mountain: Mt. Elbrus (U.S.S.R.)
Longest rivers: Volga, Danube, Ural
Largest lakes: Caspian Sea, Lake Ladoga

**The U.S.S.R. is partly in Europe and partly in Asia.*

▲ Europe has many old and beautiful cities. This is the city of Budapest, on the banks of the Danube River in Hungary.

Eastern Europe was Communist-ruled until 1989–1990. It is less industrialized and wealthy than Western Europe.

▲ Europe has no large deserts, and most of the continent has a mild climate. In the north winters are cold. Among the snow-covered mountains of the Alps, people can enjoy winter sports such as skiing. Switzerland is famous for its mountain scenery.

▲ The British Isles lie off the northwest coast of Europe. They include Great Britain (England, Scotland, and Wales) and Ireland. Here can be found quiet country villages not far from large, busy industrial cities.

◀ The Mediterranean lands of Europe are warm and sunny. Many people earn their living from farming or fishing. Tourists from other parts of Europe come to enjoy the sun.

Europe has many different landscapes and peoples. It is rich in farmland and in raw materials, such as coal. Almost every country has its great cities. Roads, railroads, and air routes cross the continent.

The three Baltic republics of the U.S.S.R. (Lithuania, Estonia and Latvia) have recently been recognized as independent from the Soviet Union.

E

Ramapithecus: 15 million years ago. Africa, Asia

Australopithecus: 4 to 1 million years ago. Africa

Homo habilis: 2 to 1.5 million years ago. Africa

Homo erectus: 1.5 to 0.1 million years ago. Africa, Asia, Europe

Neanderthal: 100,000 to 35,000 years ago. Europe

Modern human: From 100,000 years ago. Worldwide

▲ Most scientists believe that human beings, like animals, evolved from earlier human-like beings. Six stages in human evolution are shown here.

European Community

This is a group of 12 countries in western Europe. They work together in trade and other matters. The Community has its own form of government, a parliament and laws. But each country still controls much of its own affairs. The Community began in the 1950s with France, West Germany, Holland, Belgium, Luxembourg and Italy. Great Britain, Ireland, and Denmark joined in 1971. Greece became a member in 1981, followed in 1986 by Spain and Portugal. Other countries want to join, as the Community is an important world trading power. See **Europe**.

Everest

Mount Everest is the earth's highest mountain. It is in the Himalayas, on the border of Nepal and Tibet. Everest is 29,028 ft (8,848 m) high. Edmund Hillary and Tenzing Norgay first climbed it in 1953. See **mountains**.

evolution

Evolution is the process by which living things change over millions of years. From fossil remains, we know that many prehistoric animals were unlike modern animals. Their modern relatives evolved by changing or adapting to new conditions on earth. See **Darwin**.

explorers

People have explored since ancient times. Bold travelers like Marco Polo went to find new land or treasure or simply to find out more. Explorers did not know what dangers they might face. Some such as Christopher Columbus and Vasco da Gama went across wide oceans in tiny ships. Others crossed jungles, mountains, and deserts, as David Livingstone did in Africa. By 1900 most of the earth had been explored.

EXPLORERS

The great age of exploration by Europeans began in the 1400s, when navigators such as Columbus braved the wide oceans. Many early explorers were looking for trade and treasure. Later explorers such as the Americans Lewis and Clark, and Livingstone in Africa, were more interested in discovering new lands.

◀ Amundsen of Norway was the first to reach the South Pole. He just beat Captain Scott, a British explorer. Amundsen used dogs to pull sleds.

▼ Livingstone walked across central Africa, helped by African guides.

▼ When Columbus sighted the islands of the Caribbean, he thought they were the East Indies.

▶ Lewis and Clark explored the American West. They traveled by boat, on horseback, and on foot.

TIME CHART

Vasco Nunez de Balboa (1475–1519) from Spain crossed the Isthmus of Panama and was the first European to see the Pacific Ocean.

Robert O'Hara Burke (1820–1861) of Ireland was the first explorer to cross Australia from south to north.

James Cook (1728–1779) of Britain explored the Pacific, mapping the coasts of Australia and New Zealand.

Vasco da Gama (1469–1525) of Portugal sailed to India in 1497–1498.

Ferdinand Magellan (1480–1521) from Portugal led the first voyage around the world (1519–1522), but was killed before the only surviving ship reached home.

Robert E. Peary (1856–1920) claimed to be first to the North Pole in 1909. (Some experts are not sure he got there.)

Marco Polo (1254–1324) from Venice traveled overland to China and stayed for 17 years.

Abel Janszoon Tasman (1603–1659) of Holland sailed around Australia and discovered New Zealand.

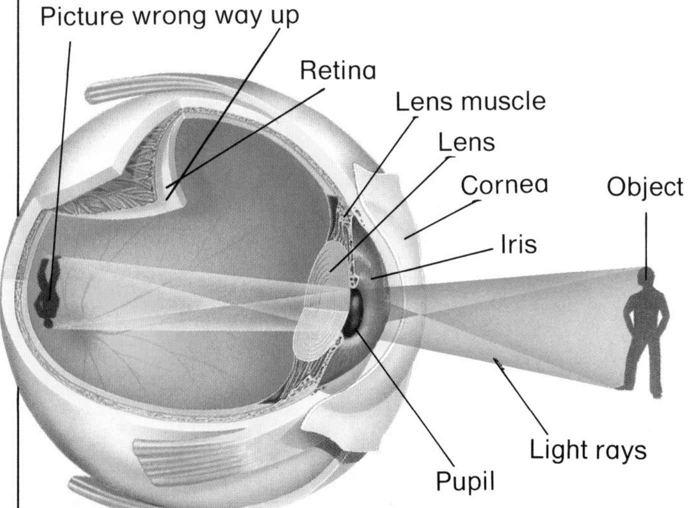

▲ The human eye works much like a camera. Light rays are reflected off objects we see. The rays hit our eyes and bend to form a picture of the object inside the eye. The picture is upside-down. The brain turns it right side up.

eye

For many living things, eyesight is the most important sense. Your eyes receive information about the world as rays of light reflected from objects we see. The eye is a ball filled with liquid. The outer layer is the white of your eye. At the front is a transparent part called the cornea. The middle part is colored; the part of it you can see is called the iris. The black dot in the middle of the iris is the pupil. Behind it is a lens. The lens focuses an image of whatever you are looking at on a screen called the retina. It contains over 120 million light-sensitive cells. The image is upside-down because the light rays are bent as they pass through the cornea. A nerve sends electrical signals to the brain, which turns the signals into a right-side-up picture. Blind people learn to live without sight. They read books printed in Braille, an alphabet of raised dots that can be read with the fingertips. See **human body**.

famine

A famine is when people starve, or go very hungry, from lack of food. Famines happen when crops fail because of disease or drought.

LIFE STORY

Faraday

Michael Faraday made important discoveries about electricity and magnetism. He made the first dynamo, a simple generator, and made possible the generators and electric motors of today.

Faraday was born near London, England, in 1791. He taught himself science and listened to talks given by Sir Humphry Davy, a famous scientist. He wrote to Davy, who made Faraday his assistant. Faraday became a famous professor of chemistry. He died in 1867.

FARMING

About 12,000 years ago people learned how to farm. They planted seeds to grow crops of wheat and vegetables. They learned how to herd tame animals such as sheep and cattle. On a modern farm, jobs such as plowing and reaping can be done by machines. However, in Africa and Asia many people still use older farming methods.

▲ Rice is the main food in Asia. The young rice plants are planted in flooded fields.

▲ Combine harvesters cut a huge field of wheat. Farmers in North America grow much of the grain we use to make flour.

▲ On a dairy farm, cows are milked by machines. Milk is used to make butter and cheese.

◀ Australia has more sheep than people. Sheep farms are called stations and are fenced off into huge paddocks.

▲ Tea pickers at work. Tea is made from the leaves of the tea bush, grown on hillside plantations in Asia.

◀ Farmers keep some animals and plants indoors. These tomatoes are being grown in a heated greenhouse.

FEASTS AND FESTIVALS

People all over the world have special days called feasts and special periods called festivals. They mark important events, some solemn, some joyful. People may observe a solemn festival by fasting (going without food) and saying prayers. They celebrate a happy festival with special foods, presents, parties, and processions.

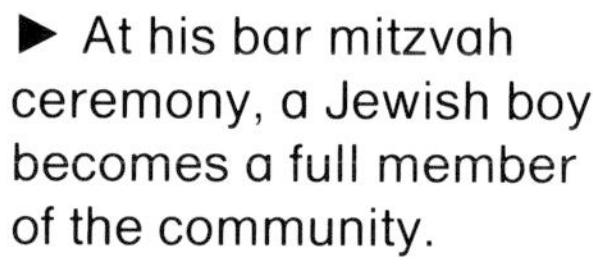

► At his bar mitzvah ceremony, a Jewish boy becomes a full member of the community.

▼ Muslim pilgrims visiting the holy city of Mecca observe the Great Festival.

▼ On Halloween (October 31) children dress up and go trick-or-treating. Halloween began 2,000 years ago as a pagan festival connected with darkness, year's end, and death.

▲ Mardi Gras, or Carnival, is held on Shrove Tuesday, the day before the Christian fasting season of Lent. In some countries people parade through the streets in colorful costumes.

► The Hindu festival of Holi marks the coming of spring. People sing and dance, and throw colored water or powder over one another.

◄ Christians celebrate the birth of Jesus at Christmas. They sing songs or carols. Christmas trees are hung with lights and decorations.

F

fern

Ferns are some of the oldest plants. Some look like mosses, others like palm trees. Most grow in damp, shady places. They have no flowers or seeds, but scatter tiny spores. See **plants**.

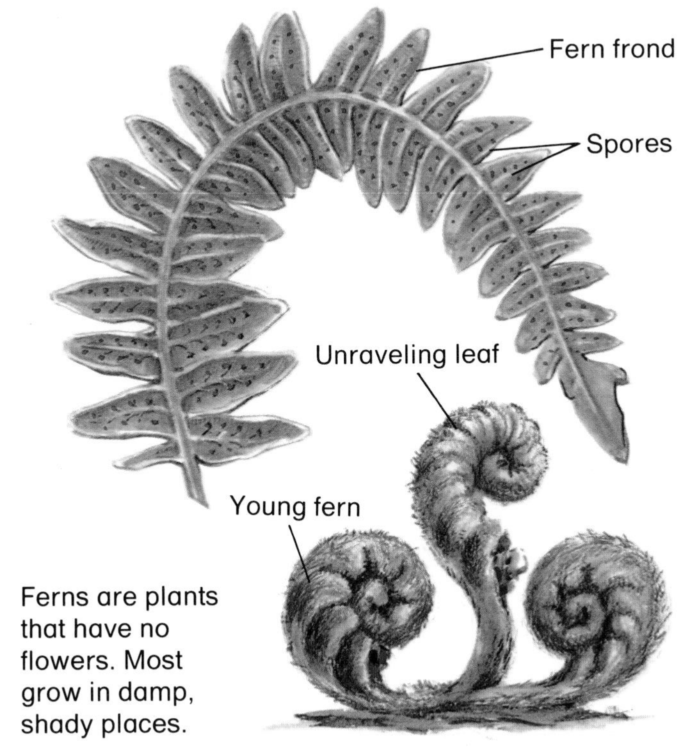

Ferns are plants that have no flowers. Most grow in damp, shady places.

fertilizer

Farmers and gardeners add fertilizers to the soil to help plants grow. Fertilizers are rich in plant foods. Some are made from rotted plants or animal manure. Others are chemicals.

film see **motion picture**

fire

People use fire to keep warm, to cook food, and to make things. Fire is the heat and light from something that is burning. All fires need a fuel (something to burn), enough heat to start the burning, and oxygen from the air to keep the fire going. See **air**.

▲ Special fire-fighting trucks are used to put out oil and chemical fires at factories or airports. The fire fighters wear protective suits.

fire fighting

When a building catches fire, fire fighters rush to put out the flames. They travel in a fire engine, which has hoses and pumps to spread water or flame-killing chemical foam on the fire. Fire fighters climb ladders to rescue people from tall buildings.

fireworks

Fireworks were first made in China. They are tubes filled with gunpowder and chemicals to make sparks, smoke, and bright colors. Some make a loud bang. Rockets shoot high into the sky.

fish

Fish are cold-blooded animals that spend all their lives in water. They breathe through gills. Some also breathe through their skin, and a few have lungs. Some fish live in lakes and rivers, but many more are in the oceans. Fish can be all shapes and sizes. Some are covered with lumps or spines. The largest fish, the whale shark, weighs twice as much as an elephant. All fish swim by using their tails and fins for power and steering. Most fish have bony skeletons. A few, including sharks, have gristly skeletons. All fish lay eggs. Out of millions of eggs only a few survive.

FISH

Fish live in cold and warm water, from the poles to the tropics. Fish that live in salt water are called marine, or sea, fish. Fish that live in lakes and rivers are called freshwater fish. Some fish, such as salmon, spend part of their lives in fresh water and part in the sea. Lungfishes are unusual because they can live on land and breathe air.

Salmon

Herring

Eel

Cod

Sea trout

Sole

HOW DO FISH BREATHE?

Like all animals, a fish needs oxygen. It breathes through gills at the sides of its head. Water flows into its mouth and over the gills, which transfer oxygen from the water into the fish's blood. The water then passes out through the gills. With it goes carbon dioxide gas, a waste product.

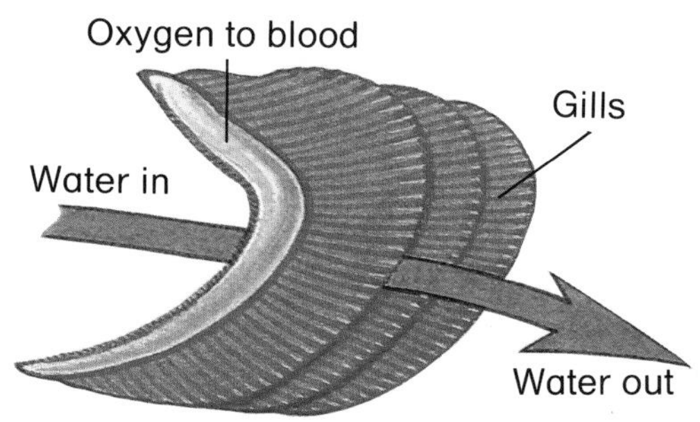

FRESHWATER FISH

The fish shown here live in rivers and lakes. The male stickleback builds a nest for its eggs and guards it. The piranha of South America is feared for its ferocity, despite its small size. Nearly half of the world's fishes (about four out of ten) live in fresh water.

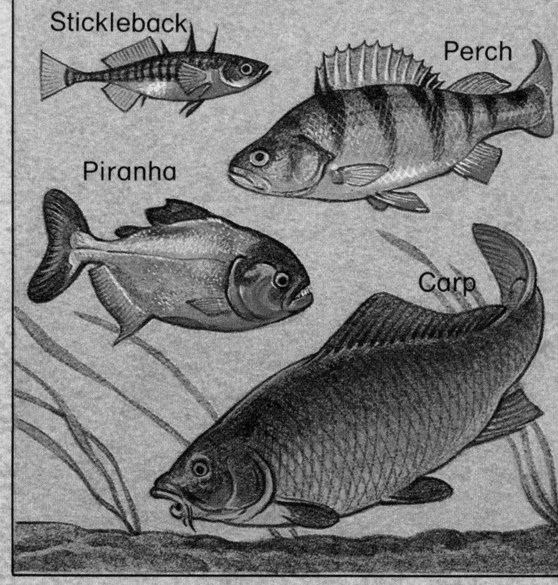

DID YOU KNOW?
The sea horse swims upright and can hold onto seaweed with its tail. The male sea horse is an attentive parent. After his mate lays eggs, he takes them and carries them in a pouch on his stomach until they hatch.
Hammerhead shark
Thresher shark
Tuna
Manta ray
Grouper
Long-snouted coral fish
Trumpet fish
Moorish idols
Angelfish
Clown fish
Squirrel fish
Flat-bodied coral fish
Moray eel
Deep-sea angler fish

F

fishing

Most of the fish we eat today comes from the sea. Large fishing boats use radar to find fish in the open sea. They scoop them up in huge nets and freeze their catch to keep it fresh. Small boats catch fish near the shore and in lakes. Japan is the leading fishing country. Some fish are reared in ponds on fish farms. Anglers catch fish for sport, using rods and lines with baited hooks.

flag

A flag is a piece of colored cloth hung on a pole. Flags are important because they represent countries, people, or organizations. Every country has its own flag. Flags were once used in battle as rallying points for soldiers. Flags can also be used to send messages.

▼ Signal flags were used to send messages from ships at sea in the days before radio. Each flag represents a letter.

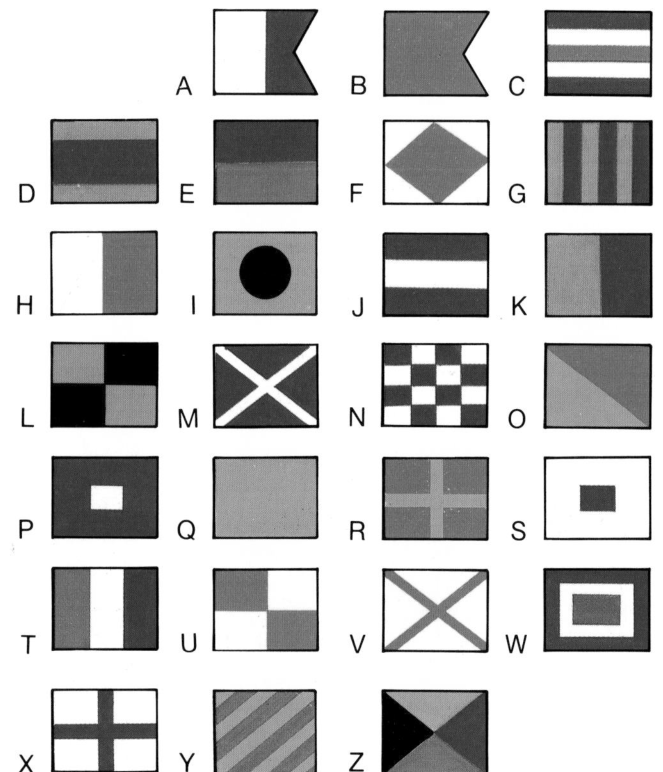

◀ A housefly. Like all true flies, it has two wings. Behind the wings are small knobs, used for balance and steering.

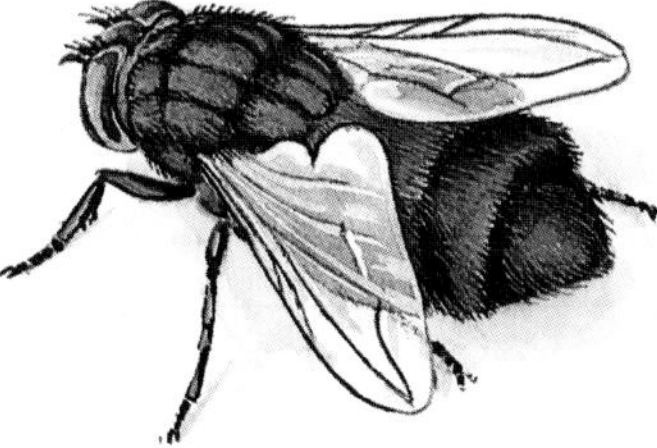

▶ A bluebottle fly. These flies lay their eggs on dead animals, whose bodies provide food for the maggots.

flies

Flies have two wings and can fly faster than other insects. There are about 100,000 kinds of flies. Some are harmless, but many carry germs and spread disease. Houseflies lay eggs on animal dung or on rotting food. The eggs hatch into wriggly maggots. The maggot becomes a dead-looking pupa. In time, an adult fly crawls out of the pupa case. See **insects**.

flowers

Most plants have flowers. Flowers are where the plant's seeds will grow, from which new plants can develop. Flowers appear when the plant is fully grown. They have male and female parts. The male parts make pollen. Pollen from one flower must touch the female parts of another flower to make seeds. Insects visit flowers to feed on the nectar, and then carry away pollen dust on their bodies. When an insect takes pollen to another flower of the same kind, the flower can then make seeds. Flowering plants grow all over the world. Some plants, such as mosses, have no flowers.

FLOWERS

There are more than 250,000 kinds of flowering plants. Garden flowers and wildflowers make up only part of this plant family. Grasses have flowers. So do trees, potatoes, peas, vines, and herbs. Flowers come in an amazing variety of shapes, sizes, and colors. Some are bright and showy. Others are so small you would hardly notice them.

THE PARTS OF A FLOWER

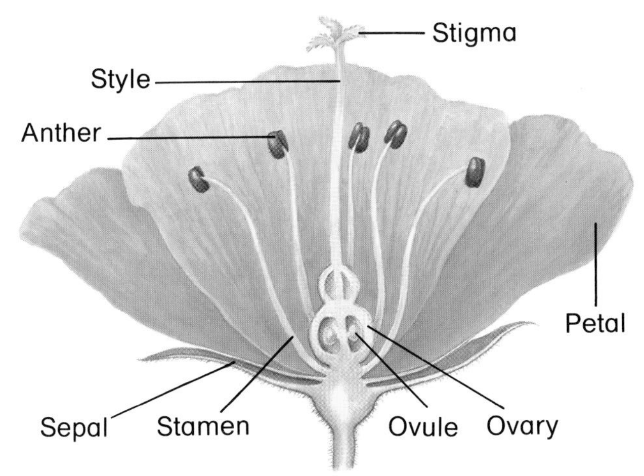

The flower of a plant has one important job — to help the plant reproduce itself by making seeds, which can grow into new plants. The picture above shows a typical flower cut away to show its parts. Pollen from the anther must unite with an ovule in the ovary for the ovule to become a seed.

The shape, smell, and colors of many flowers make them attractive to birds, insects, and other small animals. No two flowers are exactly alike.

HOW DO FLOWERS SPREAD POLLEN?

Flowers spread their pollen in several ways. Some rely on the wind to shake their pollen loose and carry it away. Other flowers attract insects to feed on their sweet nectar. When an insect, such as a bee, pushes its way into the flower, pollen dust sticks to its body. The bee flies away, carrying the pollen with it to fertilize other flowers.

Catkin

Bee

FOOD

Food gives our bodies the energy we need. We need nourishment from food to grow, to work and play, and to repair body damage. Plants make their own food from the air and sunlight. Our food comes from plants or from the animals that eat plants. A balanced diet is important for good health.

TYPES OF FOOD

Proteins come from lean meat, fish, cheese, grains, nuts, and dried beans.
Carbohydrates are fuel foods, to give us energy. Sugar and starch are carbohydrates. We eat them in potatoes, bread, and rice.
Fats also give us energy. Cream, butter, eggs, and nuts contain fats.
Minerals help build our bodies, especially bones and teeth. Milk contains plenty of minerals.
Vitamins help the body to grow and fight disease. Foods have various vitamins. Milk and carrots contain vitamin A, oranges and lemons vitamin C.

FOOD FROM ANIMALS

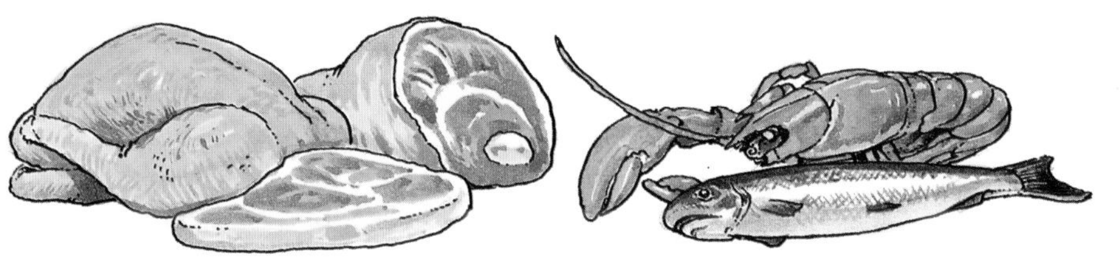

Meat: beef from cattle; lamb and mutton from sheep; ham, bacon, and pork from pigs.

Seafood: fish (including freshwater fish), crab, lobster, shrimps, squid, shellfish (oysters, clams, mussels).

Dairy foods: mostly from cows' milk, such as butter, cheese, milk, yogurt. Also eggs from chickens.

FOOD FROM PLANTS

Fruit: such as apples, lemons, cherries, oranges, grapefruits.

Vegetables: such as potatoes, squash, cauliflower, cabbages, carrots.

Cereals: bread and pasta (from wheat), rice, oats, corn.

Liquids: coffee, tea, cocoa, fruit juices, water.

Other foods: such as nuts, vegetable oils and margarine, sugar and syrups.

CANNING FOOD

Much of the food we eat comes from a factory. It is processed by being dried, frozen, or boiled in cans. Processing kills the bacteria that make food go bad, so the food keeps for longer. When you buy baked beans in a supermarket, have you ever thought about how the beans got into the can?

football, soccer, and rugby

Hundreds of years ago people played a rough football game, which had few rules. In the 1800s players made rules for different forms of football. In American football, Australian Rules football, and rugby, players throw, kick, and run with the ball. In soccer only the goalkeeper may handle the ball — the other players must use their feet and legs.

Soccer

American Football

Australian Rules

LIFE STORY

Ford

Henry Ford was born in Michigan, in 1863. He became an engineer, and in the 1880s he heard of the new gasoline-engine automobile. The first cars were made in Europe. Ford wanted to build cars in America. He made a gasoline engine in 1893 and his first car three years later. In 1903, Ford started his own firm. Cars were expensive because they were built one at a time by hand. Ford decided to use an assembly line to make his Model T car. The first was completed in 1908. Each worker added a part as the car moved by on the assembly line. Ford cars were cheap enough for ordinary families, which made driving more popular. Ford died in 1947. See **car**.

forest

A forest is land covered with trees. Bushes and flowers grow among the trees. Different kinds of forests grow around the world. About a third of the earth is forested. See **plants**, **trees**.

FOREST

In a tropical rain forest, most of the trees are evergreen; they keep their leaves all year round. In cooler climates, forest trees are a mixture of deciduous trees (which shed their leaves in fall) and evergreen conifer trees. Conifer trees grow in the forests of cold northern lands. Many forest trees are valuable for their timber.

◀ A deciduous forest is a mixture of trees. Most have broad leaves that fall in autumn. Some forest trees, like the oak, have wide spreading branches.

▲ Many kinds of trees grow in a rain forest. The tallest trees form a layer, or canopy, over 150 ft (45 m) high. Little sunlight reaches the forest floor.

THE VANISHING FORESTS

Forests are being cut down for timber (we need wood for fuel, building, paper, and other products), and to clear land for farming. It takes years to grow a tree, but only minutes to cut it down. We must protect forests, by planting new trees to replace those cut down for timber and by recycling, or reusing, paper.

▼ Conifer forests include pines, spruces, and firs. These trees are hardy. Snow slides off their sloping branches. Their trunks grow tall and straight.

fossil

Fossils are remains of long-dead animals and plants, found in rocks. Leaves, shells, skeletons, and footprints have been found as fossils. When an animal died, its body was buried by mud. The mud hardened to rock, preserving the animal in stone.

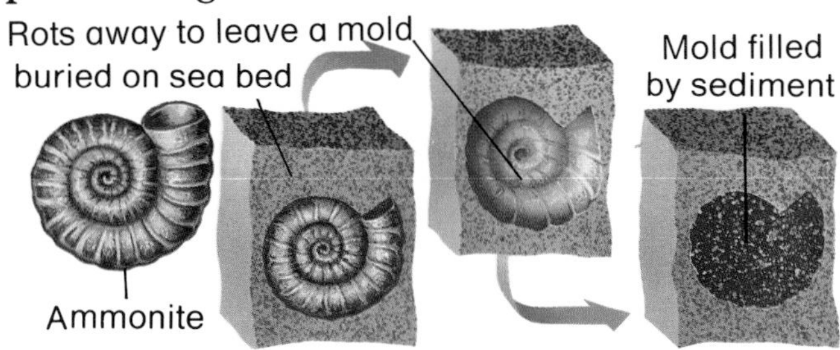

▲ This is how the shell of a dead sea creature became a fossil. It took millions of years.

fox

The fox is a cunning hunter. It is a member of the dog family, with pointed ears and a bushy tail. The female, or vixen, rears her young cubs in an underground den. See **animals**.

► A red fox. Foxes hunt mostly at night. In towns they come into gardens and take food from trash cans.

France

France is the largest country in western Europe. Most French people live in the countryside. It is a rich country, with many farms and factories. The capital and biggest city is Paris. France is famous for art and learning, food and wine. It has always played an important part in Europe's affairs. Today it is a republic and a leader of the European Community. See **Europe**.

LIFE STORY

Franklin

Benjamin Franklin was born in Boston in 1706. He had 16 brothers and sisters, and his family could not afford to send him to school after he was 10. So young Ben taught himself, from books. He was interested in everything.

He worked as a printer. He also published a newspaper and a yearly almanac, a book full of wit and wisdom. He helped to set up a postal system in America. He did scientific experiments, including a dangerous one with a kite in a thunderstorm to prove that lightning was electricity. He invented the lightning rod and bifocal (two-lens) spectacles. He helped write the Declaration of Independence and signed the Constitution. Franklin went to France as the United States ambassador. He died in 1790.

F

▲ In Paris the crowd attacked the Bastille prison. Bastille Day (July 14) is now a national holiday in France.

French Revolution

In 1789 the French people began a revolution to overthrow the king. The people wanted a fairer government and equality for all. The revolution caused much suffering, but its ideas were copied throughout the world.

fruit

The fruit of a plant protects the seed inside and helps to spread it. See **plants**.

fuel

We burn fuel to give us energy. Fuels heat and cool our homes, drive our trains and cars, and power our machines. Coal, natural gas, and oil are the most-used fuels, sometimes called fossil fuels. (They are the remains of dead plants and animals.) Wood and peat (moss) are also fuels. Rocket engines burn chemical fuel. A small lump of uranium fuels a nuclear submarine.

furniture

We use chairs, tables, desks, beds, and other pieces of furniture in various ways – to sit on, work at, or keep things in. Furniture makes our lives more comfortable. It can be made from wood, metal, plastic, or other materials. The ancient Egyptians had fine furniture 5,000 years ago. The style of a piece of furniture (the way it looks) tells an expert when it was made.

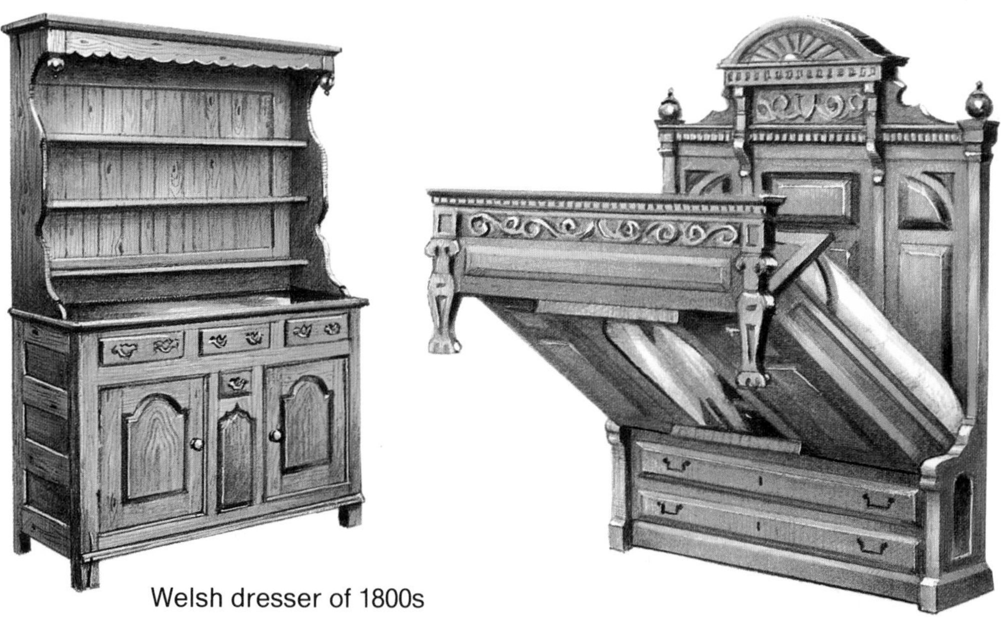

Welsh dresser of 1800s

American parlor bed 1891

▲ Good furniture is useful and pleasing to look at. Antiques, like this wooden furniture, are valued for the skill of the craftspeople who made them.

Light, elegant chair *c.*1900

galaxy
A galaxy is a huge group of stars. Our own galaxy, the Milky Way, may have 100,000 million stars in it. Our sun is just one star in the Milky Way galaxy. See **solar system**, **star**.

Galileo
Galileo (1564–1642) was an Italian scientist. He was the first to use a telescope to study the moon and planets. He also showed that objects of different weights fall at the same rate. See **inventions and discoveries**, **moon**.

games
Games test our wits and skill, usually against other players. Outdoor games are often called sports. Indoor games such as playing cards and chess are very old. Target games such as darts, word games, and computer games are also popular. See **sport**.

LIFE STORY

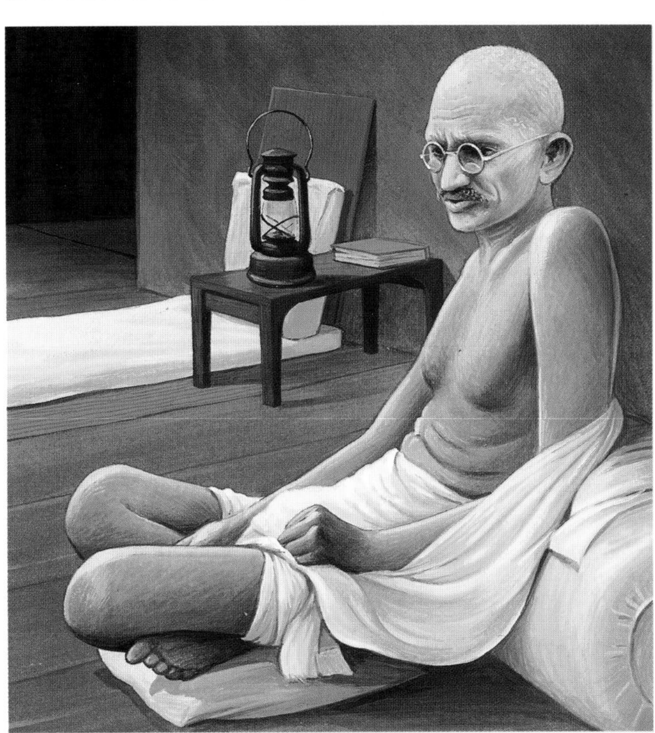

Gandhi
Mohandas Gandhi was India's greatest modern leader. He was born in 1869, when India was still part of the British Empire. In 1888, Gandhi went to London to study law. He later lived in South Africa and set up a farm community where people grew their own food. He became a leader of Indian people in South Africa and was well known when he returned to India in 1915. Gandhi led the Indian people in their struggle for independence from British rule. He called for peaceful protest because he hated fighting. He was sent to prison several times but never gave up his beliefs. In 1947, India became independent. Gandhi was called Mahatma, meaning "great soul." People everywhere mourned when he was murdered in 1948.

G

gas
Things can exist in three states: as liquid (such as water), solids (ice), or gas (water vapor). Gases are different from liquids and solids because they have no shape. A gas fills any container it is in. Air is a mixture of gases. Natural gas is used for fuel. See **air**.

genetics
Genetics is a science that explains why we inherit our looks and so much else from our parents. This process is called heredity. Inside every cell of our bodies are chemical messengers called genes. They carry all the information to make a new plant or animal. See **medicine**.

Genghis Khan
Genghis Khan (1167–1227) conquered the biggest land empire of all time. He was a Mongol, from central Asia. Genghis Khan led his Mongol armies into China, Russia, and Persia (Iran).

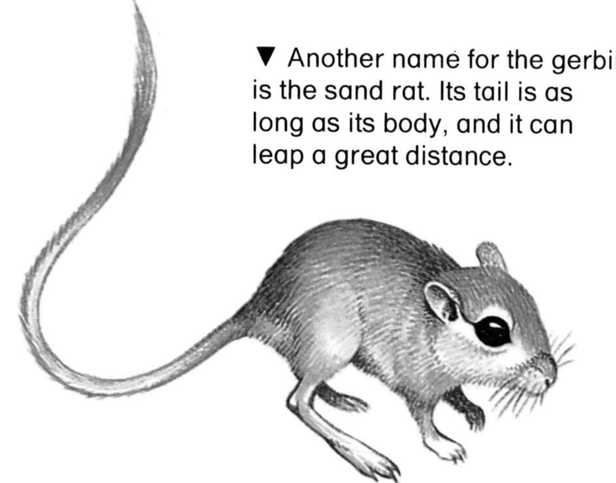

▼ Another name for the gerbil is the sand rat. Its tail is as long as its body, and it can leap a great distance.

gerbils and hamsters
Many people keep these little rodents as pets. In the wild, they live in burrows and eat fruit, vegetables, and seeds. Gerbils have longer tails than hamsters. See **rodents**.

Germany
Germany is a country in northern Europe. It was made up of many small states until the 1800s. Germany was defeated in World War I (1914–1918). In the 1930s, the Nazi leader Adolf Hitler gained power. After defeat in World War II (1939–1945), it was divided into West and East Germany. West Germany grew prosperous in the European Community. East Germany had Communist rule until 1990, when Germany became one country again.

germs see **disease, medicine**

giraffe
Giraffes are the tallest land animals. They live in Africa. With their long necks, they reach to eat leaves from treetops. See **animals**.

glacier
Ice sliding slowly downhill forms a glacier, which looks like a river of ice. It flows until it melts in warm lowland air or breaks up in the sea. Ice chunks float away as icebergs. See **iceberg**.

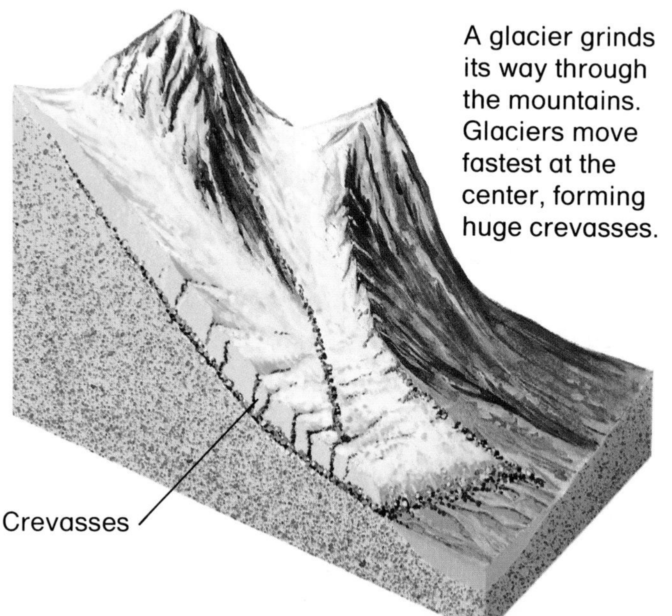

A glacier grinds its way through the mountains. Glaciers move fastest at the center, forming huge crevasses.

▲ These pictures show how a glass jar is made by hand. A blob of melted glass is blown, twisted, and shaped while it is still hot.

glass
We use glass for windows, lenses, and bottles. See-through glass is especially useful. Glass is made from sand, limestone, and soda ash, heated until they melt. Glass hardens when cool.

glider see **aircraft**

goat
People keep goats for their milk, meat, and wool. Goats need less care than sheep. They can find food even in near-deserts. Wild goats live on mountain slopes. See **Asia**, **Europe**.

gods see **religion**

gold and silver
For thousands of years people have dug for gold and silver. These metals are scarce. They are shiny and easy to shape by craftspeople. Coins and jewelry are made from gold and silver.

government
Countries have governments to make laws. In a democracy, people choose who governs them by voting in an election. The United States is a democratic republic, led by an elected president. In Canada and other countries, members of Parliament make the laws, and ministers run the government.

See **kings and queens**.

grass
Grasses are plants. Lawn grass is short, but bamboo is a grass as tall as a tree. Wheat, rice, sugar cane, and maize (corn) are grasses that are grown as food crops. See **food, plants**.

grasshopper
A grasshopper is an insect with long legs, for jumping. It can jump 20 times its body length. Grasshoppers "sing" by rubbing their legs. See **insects**.

gravity
Everything has gravity. Gravity is a force that attracts all objects to each other. A pebble thrown in the air falls because it is pulled by gravity. Gravity keeps the earth circling the sun.

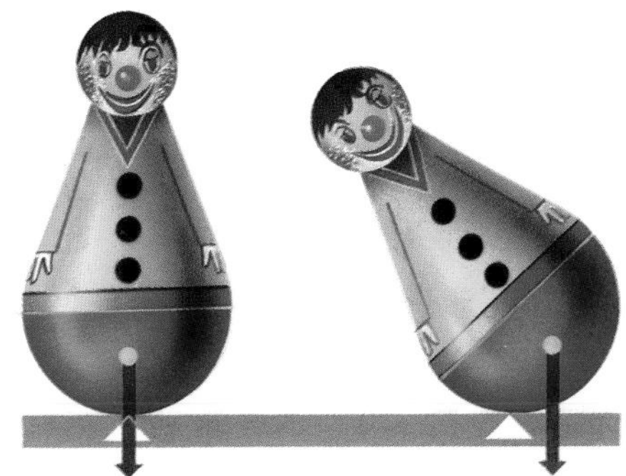

◀ Every object has a center of gravity. This toy figure always springs upright, because its center of gravity is so low. Gravity pulls it back upright.

GREECE

The people of Greece built a great civilization about 2,500 years ago. In the city of Athens they set up a new form of government, called democracy. They developed arts and sciences. They built beautiful buildings. They loved sports, dance, and theater. Modern civilization owes much to the ideas of the ancient Greeks.

◄ The Greeks were warriors and sailors. Greek soldiers fought on foot. They had armor, round shields, and long spears.

► A Greek doctor treating a boy. The most famous Greek doctor is Hippocrates, known as the Father of Medicine. There were many Greek scientists and thinkers.

◄ The Greeks loved theater. Actors performed plays in open-air theaters, as part of a festival.

▲ In ancient Greece, people believed that the gods lived on Mount Olympus. Above is a bronze head of the goddess Aphrodite. The temple of the Parthenon (right) was built on the Acropolis, a hill in Athens, to honor the city's patron goddess, Athena.

guinea pig

The guinea pig comes from the Andes Mountains, in South America. It is a rodent with short legs and no tail. Wild guinea pigs are brown, but pet ones can be other colors. See **rodents**.

gun

A gun is a weapon that fires bullets or shells. An explosive charge set off at one end of the gun sends the bullet shooting out of the open end. Guns were first used in war in the 1300s. The first guns

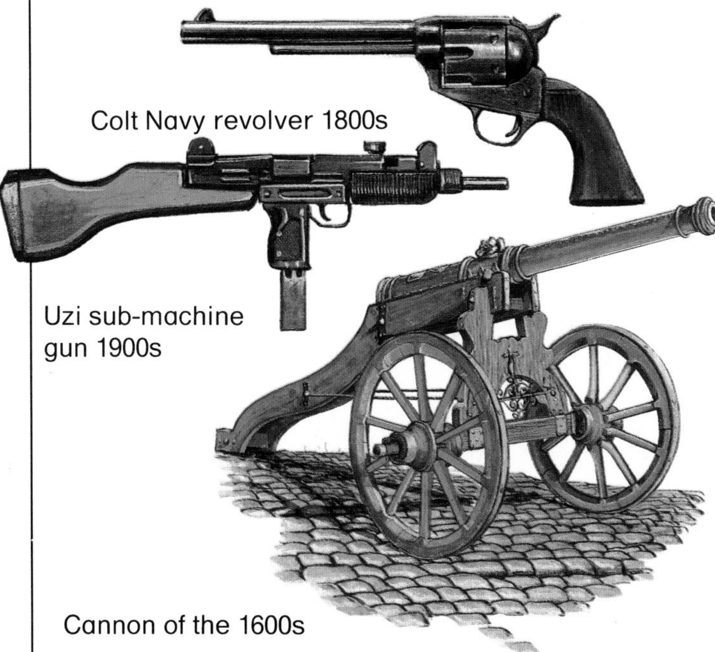

included cannons and muskets. They fired solid balls of metal or stone. In the 1800s, rifles were invented. Grooves cut inside the gun barrel made the bullet spin as it flew. Rifles fired farther and more accurately. Some modern guns can fire thousands of bullets each minute.

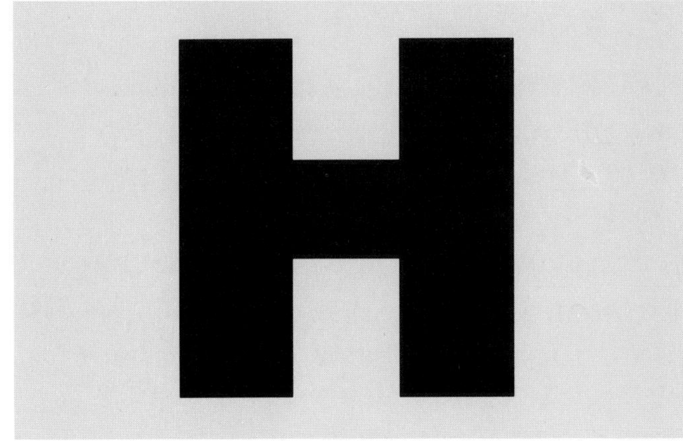

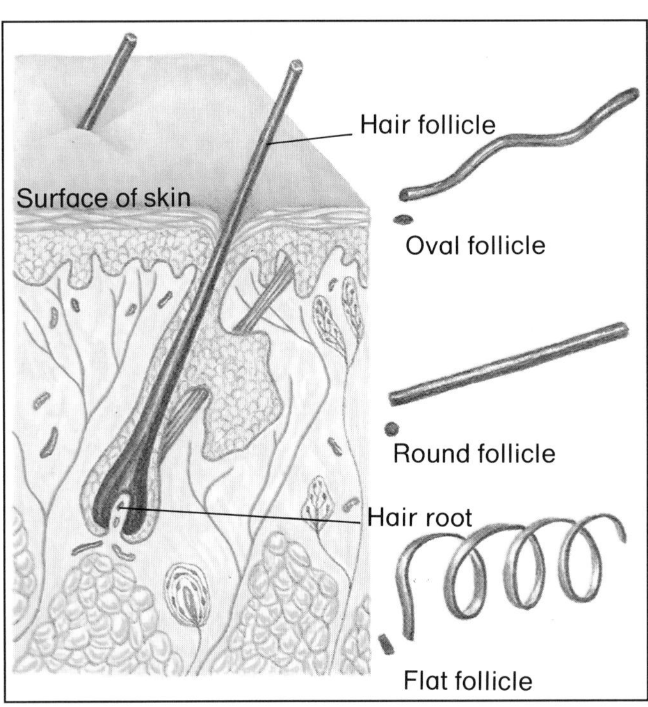

▲ Each hair grows from a follicle. Oval follicles make wavy hair. Round follicles make straight hair. Flat follicles make curly hair.

hair

Hair grows on the bodies of many mammals. Some have thick fur to keep them warm. A cat's whiskers are long, sensitive hairs. On a human, hair grows thickest on the head. There is hair all over the human body, except on the palms of the hands and the soles of the feet. See **human body**.

hearing see **ear and hearing**

H

heart

The heart is a hollow muscle that pumps blood. Blood carries oxygen to the brain and other parts of the body. Without oxygen the body would die. Your heart is about as big as your fist. It beats about 70 times a minute. In that time it pumps roughly 5.25 qt (5 liters) of blood. The right side of the heart takes blood from the body and pumps it to the lungs to collect oxygen. The left side collects blood from the lungs and pumps it to the body. See **blood**, **human body**.

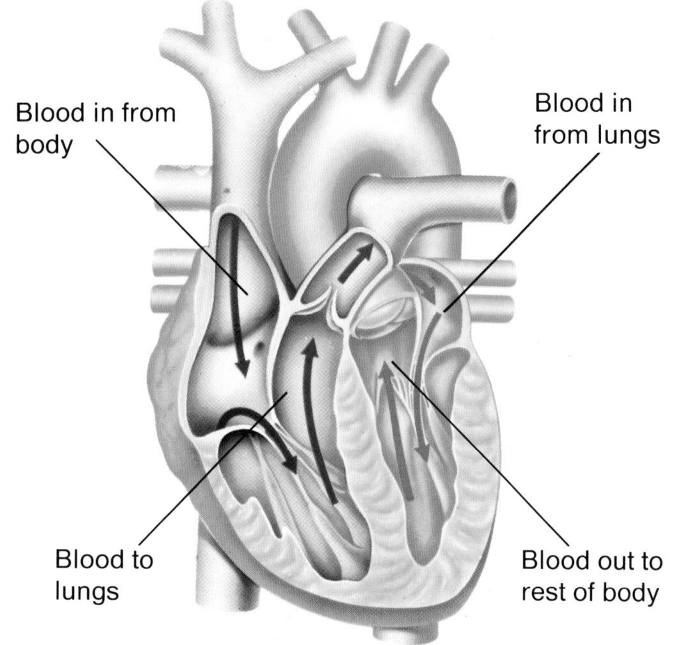

▲ Blood from the lungs carries oxygen. The heart pumps this oxygen-rich blood to all parts of the body through the arteries. The blood comes back to the heart through veins.

hedgehog

A hedgehog is a prickly animal, and when it rolls into a ball it is safe from most enemies. Hedgehogs snuffle about at night, hunting insects, frogs, and worms. In winter, hedgehogs sleep in a nest of leaves.

▲ A small tail rotor keeps the helicopter from spinning around and around in the air.

helicopter

A helicopter can fly up, down, sideways, and backward. It can also hover. Instead of fixed wings like an airplane's, it has spinning rotors. Some helicopters have two big rotors. Most have one big rotor and a small side-facing rotor on the tail. The helicopter's engine spins the rotor blades, which "bite" into the air. By changing the angle of the blades, the pilot controls the direction of flight. Helicopters are useful for rescue work and are also used in war.

hibernation

In cold countries, some animals sleep through winter when food is scarce. This sleep is called hibernation. Bats, hedgehogs, snakes, tortoises, frogs, and butterflies all hibernate. They find snug shelters, often underground, to sleep in. They wake up when warm weather returns. Squirrels only sleep for part of the winter. On sunny days, they wake up and look for food.

Himalaya

The Himalaya are the highest mountains on earth. These towering mountains separate India from northern Asia. Mount Everest is the world's highest peak. See **Everest**, **mountains**.

Hinduism

Hinduism is an ancient religion that began in India. Hindus worship many gods and goddesses and study sacred books such as the Vedas. They worship at home and in temples. They hold festivals to honor their gods. Hindus believe the Ganges River in India is sacred. Hinduism teaches that the soul never dies, but is born over and over again. See **religion**.

▲ Hindus believe in many gods, which each take different forms. Here are three of them.

▲ The rare pygmy hippo lives in the forests of West Africa. It is a shy animal and does not spend as much time in water as its relative the river hippo does.

hippopotamus

The river hippopotamus of Africa is a big, heavy animal with short legs. It has enormous jaws, but eats only plants. Hippos live in herds. They swim well and walk around on the riverbed. At night, they come ashore to feed. A river hippo can weigh five tons (4,500 kg). The rare pygmy hippo is much smaller.

history

History is the study of our past. A person who studies history is called a historian. History records the rise and fall of empires, and also the everyday lives of ordinary people. Most historians divide time into periods, such as the Middle Ages. They call the time before the birth of Jesus Christ B.C. ("before Christ"), and the time after his birth A.D. (Latin *anno domini*, "in the year of our Lord"). If a person's dates are given in a book as (50 B.C.–A.D. 17), he or she was born in 50 B.C. and died in A.D. 17. So that person lived for about 67 years. See **Middle Ages**.

HISTORY

History is the story of the past. People who write history are called historians. They may be interested in things that happened thousands of years ago, or in the events of modern times. Historians write about important events such as wars and revolutions, and also about the way people lived at different times and in different places.

▲ This is a boat from Ancient Egypt, as pictured in a tomb. In Egypt, historians recorded the reigns of the pharaohs (kings) in picture-writing carved in stone.

▲ Through history we learn about vanished civilizations, like that of the Aztecs of Mexico. This strange-looking figure is an Aztec god.

EUROPE

BC	
*c.*6500	Farming begins in Greece and the Aegean
*c.*2000	Bronze Age in Northern Europe
*c.*2000–1200	Minoan and Mycenean civilization in Crete and Greece
509	Roman republic founded
*c.*380–300	Work of Plato, Euclid, and Aristotle
27	Augustus made Roman emperor
A.D.	
101–107	Roman Empire at peak
300–500	Barbarians invade Europe,
476	Roman Empire collapses
711	Muslims invade Spain
800	Charlemagne crowned
1066	Battle of Hastings
1215	Magna Carta
1337–1453	Hundred Years' War in France
1347–50	Black Death
1400s	Renaissance (rebirth of learning)
1453	Constantinople falls to Turks
1455–85	Wars of the Roses in England
1521	The Reformation: Martin Luther, Protestantism
1588	Spanish Armada
*c.*1600–1650	Scientific work of Kepler, Galileo and Descartes
1618–48	Thirty Years' War
1642–48	Civil war in England
1707	Union of England and Scotland
1756–63	Seven Years' War
1789	French Revolution begins
1799	Napoleon seizes power in France
1815	Battle of Waterloo Congress of Vienna
1848	Revolutions throughout Europe
1854–56	Crimean War
1870–71	Franco-Prussian War
1914–18	World War I
1917	Bolshevik Revolution in Russia
1922	Mussolini takes power in Italy
1933	Hitler becomes German Chancellor
1936–39	Spanish Civil War
1939–45	World War II
1945	United Nations formed
1957	Treaty of Rome: formation of European Community
1961	Berlin Wall built
1961	Yuri Gagarin is first astronaut
1968	Soviet troops invade Czechoslovakia
1987	Mikhail Gorbachev begins changes in USSR
1989	Berlin Wall dismantled Political change throughout Eastern Europe
1990	Re-unification of Germany
1991	Internal disputes in Yugoslavia Attempt to overthrow President Gorbachev fails in USSR; Soviet Communist Party dissolved; Baltic States granted independence

AMERICA AND AUSTRALASIA

BC	
3372	First date in Mayan calendar
*c.*3000	Agriculture in Tehuacan Valley in Mexico First pottery in Mexico
*c.*900–100	Olmec culture in Middle America
*c.*400	Navigation among Pacific islands
*c.*300	Maya civilization in Yucatán and Central America
AD	
*c.*800	Classic Maya civilization
1002	Leif Ericsson explores North American coast
1100	Polynesian islands colonized
*c.*1325–1520	Aztec civilization in Mexico
*c.*1400–1525	Inca civilization in Andes
1492	Columbus reaches America
1513	Vasco Nuñez de Balboa discovers Pacific Ocean
1521	Hernán Cortés conquers Aztecs
1522	First circumnavigation of the world by Magellan
1533	Pizarro conquers Peru
1607	English found Virginia
1608	French found Quebec
1619	First black African slaves arrive in Virginia
1620	*Mayflower* puritans (Pilgrim Fathers) settle in New England
1645	Tasman discovers New Zealand
1768	James Cook explores east coast of Australia
1775–83	American War of Independence
1776	American Declaration of Independence
1788	First convicts transported from Britain to Australia
1817–30	Bolivar and San Martin liberate South America
1848	California Gold Rush
1861–65	American Civil War
1867	US purchases Alaska from Russia Dominion of Canada formed
1895–98	Spanish–American War
1901	Commonwealth of Australia
1907	Dominion of New Zealand
1911	Mexican Revolution
1914	Panama Canal opened
1929	Great Depression
1941	US enters World War II
1959	Communist Revolution in Cuba
1965–75	Vietnam War
1969	US astronauts land on Moon
1970–73	Chinlean Revolution
1975	Papua New Guinea independent
1980s	US ends 'Cold War' with USSR
1982	Argentina invades Falkland Islands
1991	Gulf War between US (and Allies) and Iraq

AFRICA AND THE NEAR EAST

BC	
*c.*9000	Farming begins
*c.*4000–3500	Invention of wheel, plough and sail in Mesopotamia and Egypt
*c.*3500	Early writing in Mesopotamia and Egypt
*c.*2780	First pyramid built in Egypt
334–323	Campaigns of Alexander the Great
*c.*6	Birth of Christ
AD	
*c.*30	Crucifixion of Christ
226–636	Sassanid Empire in Persia
527–565	Justinian emperor of Byzantium
570	Birth of Muhammad
636–700	Arab conquest of most of Middle East and North Africa
1055	Seljuk Turks capture Baghdad
1096–99	First Crusade
1258	Mongols sack Baghdad
*c.*1300	Ottoman Turkish expansion
1308–1405	Career and conquests of Timur (Tamerlane)
1453	Fall of Constantinople to the Turks End of Byzantine Empire
1485	Bartolomeu Dias rounds Cape of Good Hope
*c.*1500–1870	African slave trade
1652	Cape Town founded by Dutch
1795	British take Cape of Good Hope from Dutch
1818	Zulu Empire founded in South Africa
1822	Liberia in West Africa founded as colony for freed US slaves
1830	French rule Algeria
1835	Great Trek of Boers in South Africa
1869	Suez canal opened
1899–1902	Anglo-Boer War
1920	Palestine under British rule
1948	State of Israel founded
1956	War in Middle East between Israel and Arabs
1960	17 African states independent
1967	War in Middle East between Israel and Arabs
1967–70	Nigerian Civil War
1979	Shah of Iran deposed Peace Treaty between Egypt and Israel
1980	Zimbabwe (Rhodesia) independent
1980–88	Iran-Iraq War
1980s	Civil wars in Angola, Mozambique and Ethiopia Lebanon in turmoil
1990	Nelson Mandela released from prison in South Africa Namibia gains independence Iraq invades Kuwait
1991	Gulf War

ASIA

BC	
*c.*2500	Indus Valley civilization
*c.*2350	First dynasty in China
*c.*1766–1000	Shang dynasty in China
*c.*1000–500	Zhou dynasty in China
*c.*600	Early cities in Ganges Valley
563	Birth of Buddha
321–184	Mauryan dynasty in India
*c.*200BC–*c.*220AD	Han dynasty in China
AD	
*c.*320	Gupta Empire: 'Golden Age' of Hindu culture
618–906	T'ang dynasty in China
960–1280	'Golden Age' of arts in Japan
1206–80	Genghis Khan and Mongol conquests
1363	Tamerlane moves into Asia
1368–1644	Mung dynasty in China Mongol Empire disintegrates
1467–1500s	Civil wars in Japan
1498	Vasco da Gama sails to India
1522–1680	Mughal Empire in India
1557	Portuguese settle in China Akbar, Mughal emperor, unifies northern India
1590	Hideyoshi unifies Japan
1600	East India Company founded
1603	Tokugawa appointed shogun
1644–1912	Manchu dynasty rules China
1707	End of Mughal Empire in India
1757	British rule in India
1839–42	Opium War Britain takes Hong Kong
1857–59	Rebellion in India against the British fails
1868–1912	Meiji period in Japan
1895	Korea gains independence
1904–5	Japan at war with Russia
1910	Japan annexes Korea
1912	China becomes a republic
1927	Civil war in China
1945	Japan defeated in World War II
1946	Civil War in Indochina
1947	India, Pakistan, Burma and Indonesia independent
1949	Communists rule China
1950–53	Korean War
1959	Uprising in Tibet
1965	India and Pakistan at war
1965–75	Vietnam War
1966–68	China's 'Cultural Revolution'
1971	Bangladesh independent
1979–88	Soviet forces occupy Afghanistan
1987	Civil War in Sri Lanka
1989	Chinese government suppresses democracy movement in Beijing.

▲ Queen Elizabeth I and her court. In the 1500s England began to build an overseas empire.

◀ In the 1800s in Britain came the first railways, and an Industrial Revolution which changed people's lives.

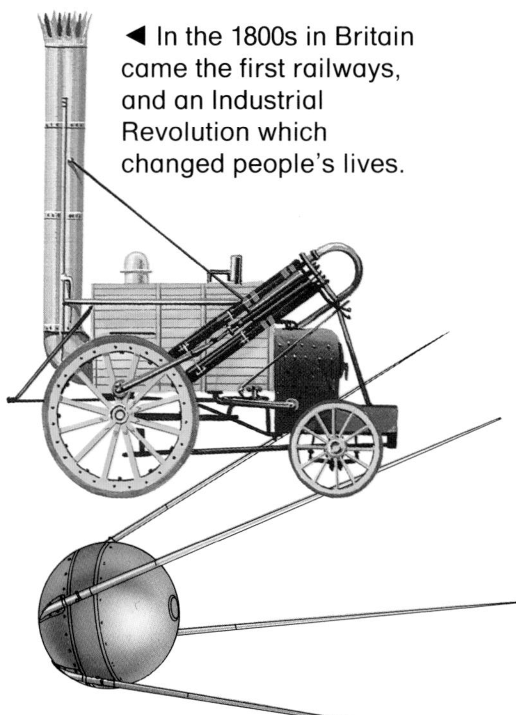

▲ The USA and the Soviet Union were rivals in a 'Cold War'. In 1957 the Soviet Union launched *Sputnik 1*, to begin the Space Age.

▲The 'Cold War' ended in the late 1980s, but in 1991 Iraq's invasion of Kuwait caused a war between the USA (and its Allies) and Iraq.

HORSES

The horse was one of the first animals to be tamed by people. Prehistoric hunters killed horses for food. Later, people learned to ride horses and to harness them to pull wagons and plows. The modern horse is the descendant of small, shy woodland animals that lived millions of years ago. Today, only a few truly wild horses are left.

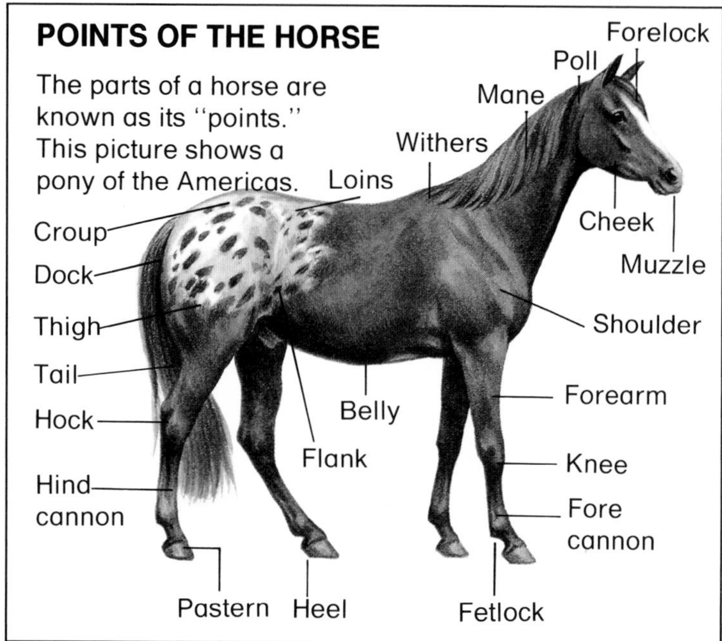

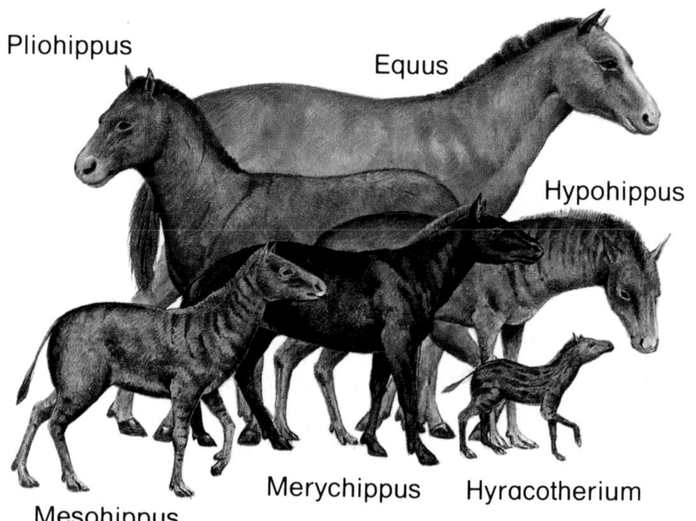

◀ Modern horses (Latin name *Equus*) are bigger than their ancestors. The early horses have died out. The first horse-like animals had short legs, and four toes on each foot. Later horses had longer legs and fewer toes, and ran faster. The modern horse has one toe; its toenail is a hoof.

▼ Horses have been bred in different colors and sizes. The biggest is the Shire. The smallest is the Falabella. Ponies are small horses. The finest riding horse is the Thoroughbred. All Thoroughbreds are descended from three Arabian stallions (males) brought to England over 300 years ago.

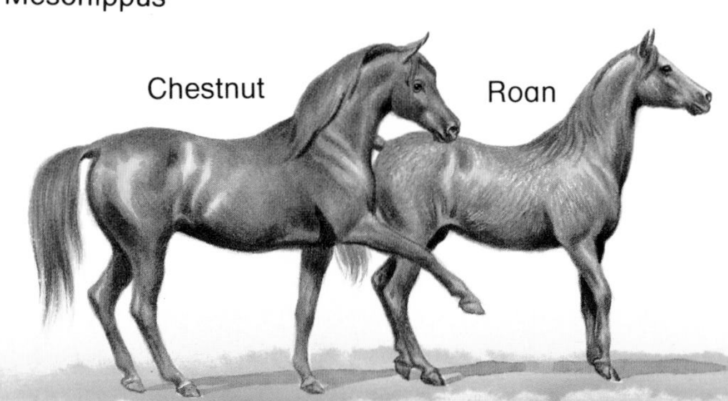

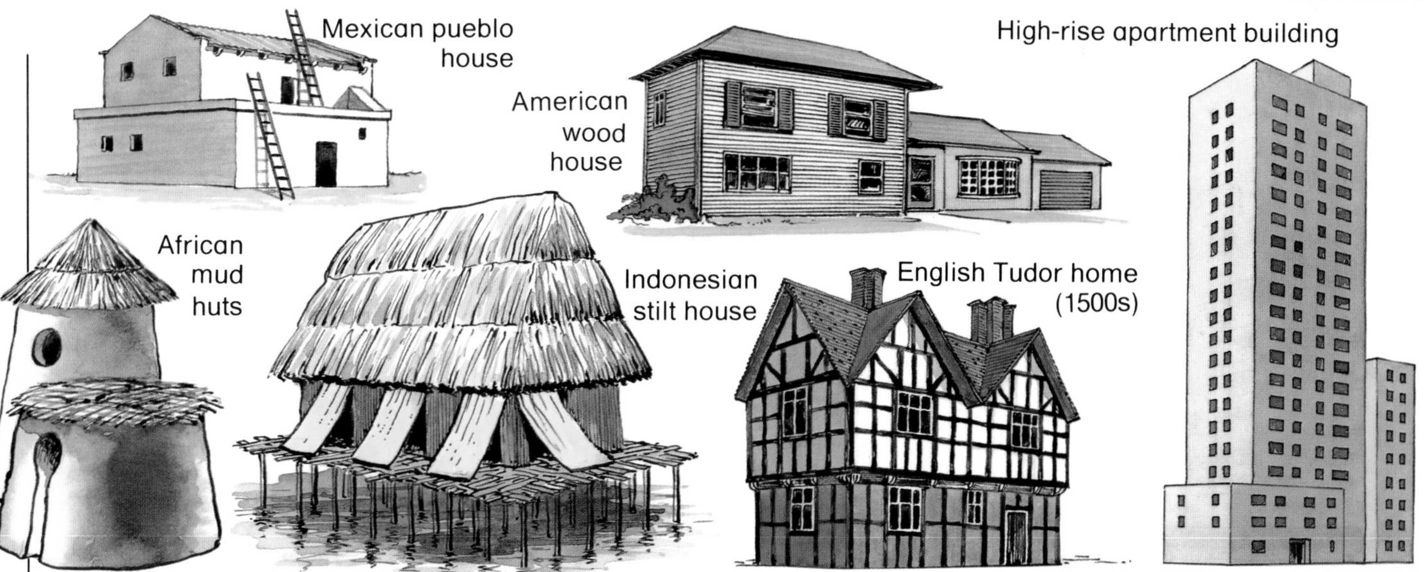

hospital

The first hospitals were run by religious people, such as monks and nuns. Doctors knew little about the causes of disease, and hospitals were often dirty and overcrowded. In the late 1800s hospitals became cleaner and better-run. Today, a hospital has rooms for sick people, laboratories, X-ray and scanning rooms, and special rooms where surgery is done. See **medicine**.

houses

The simplest house is a hut made from mud and sticks. In some countries, people still build their own houses, but usually a builder does the work. In hot, dry lands houses often have flat roofs. In rainy or snowy lands, sloping roofs are best. In cities, houses are often built in rows along streets. Tall apartment buildings tower into the sky. A house may be home to one family or to several. In Borneo, all the people of a village may live in one building called a longhouse. See **architecture**, **buildings**.

Hovercraft (air cushion vehicle)

A Hovercraft rides on a cushion of air. The air is blown downward by fans and held in by a skirt. The air pressure lifts the craft off the ground. Hovercraft can travel over land or water.

▼ A Hovercraft rides on a cushion of air blown downward by fans. Propellers drive the craft forward.

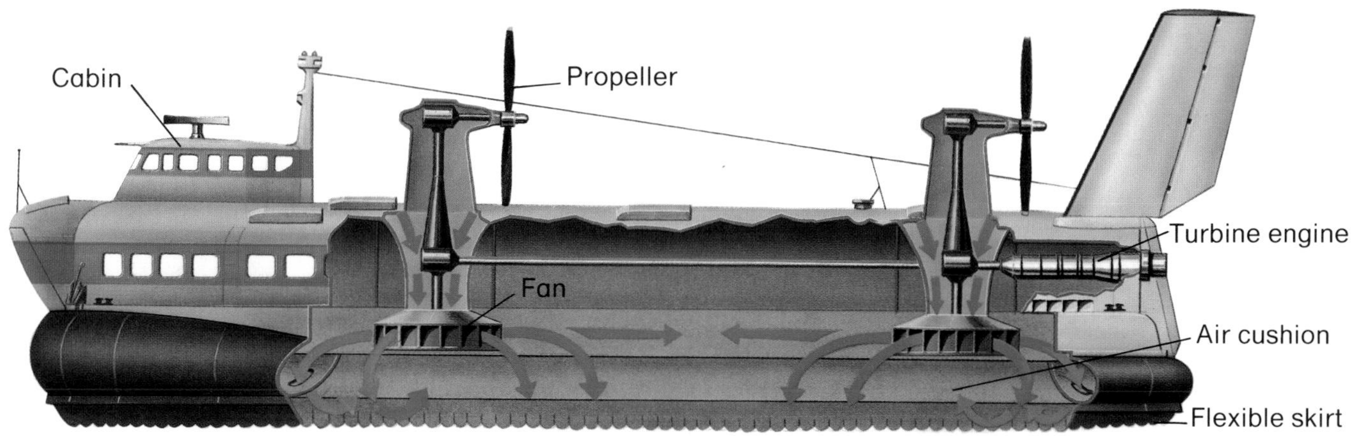

HUMAN BODY

Your body needs energy to keep alive and healthy. The food you eat is fuel, and the oxygen you breathe helps turn the food into energy. Your body is made of millions of tiny cells. There are many different kinds of cells. A group of cells together is called a tissue. Tissues that work together make organs, such as the heart, liver, lungs, and stomach.

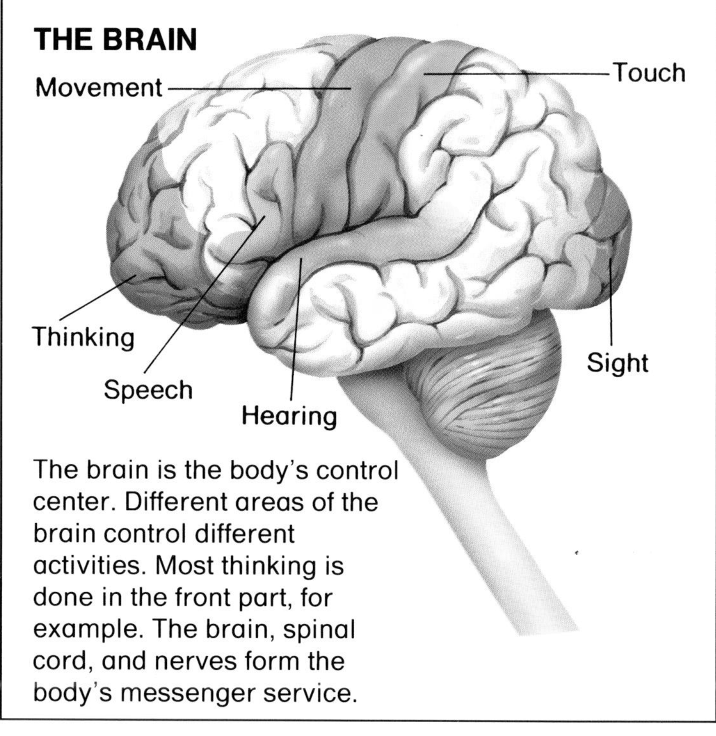

The brain is the body's control center. Different areas of the brain control different activities. Most thinking is done in the front part, for example. The brain, spinal cord, and nerves form the body's messenger service.

▶ The body has a special system to fight off disease. It is called the lymph, or immune, system. It releases disease-fighting chemicals into the blood when a person is ill. These chemicals, called antibodies, attack and destroy harmful bacteria and viruses.

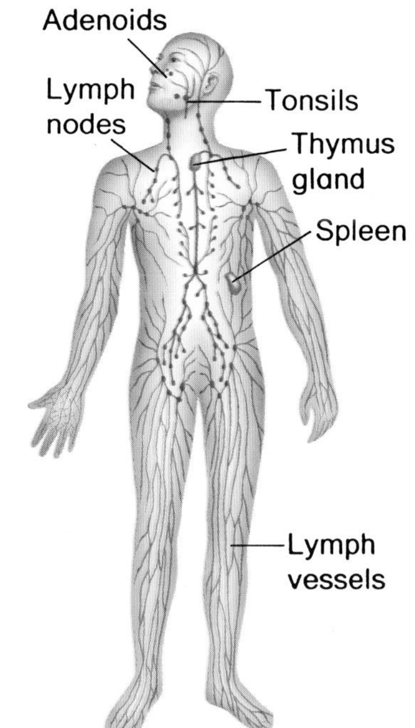

▼ Organs that work together are called systems. The digestive system, for example, is your mouth, stomach, and intestines. The pictures below show the body's main systems.

▶ Skin covers the outside of your body. It is thickest on the soles of your feet. It is very thin on the eyelids. Skin has two layers. The top layer is the epidermis. A chemical in this layer gives skin its color. The inner layer of skin is called the dermis. It contains nerves, blood vessels, sweat glands, and hair roots.

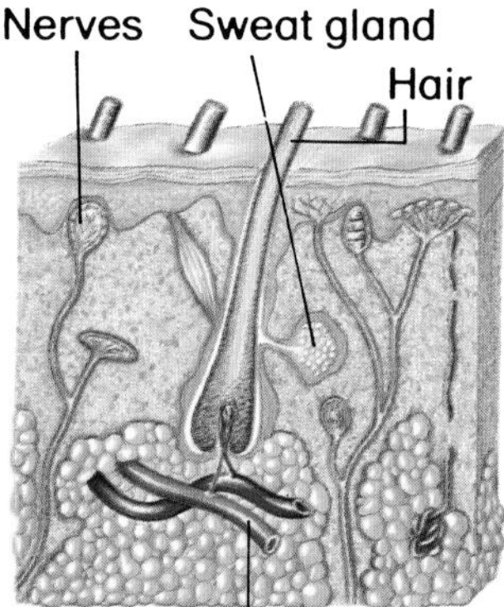

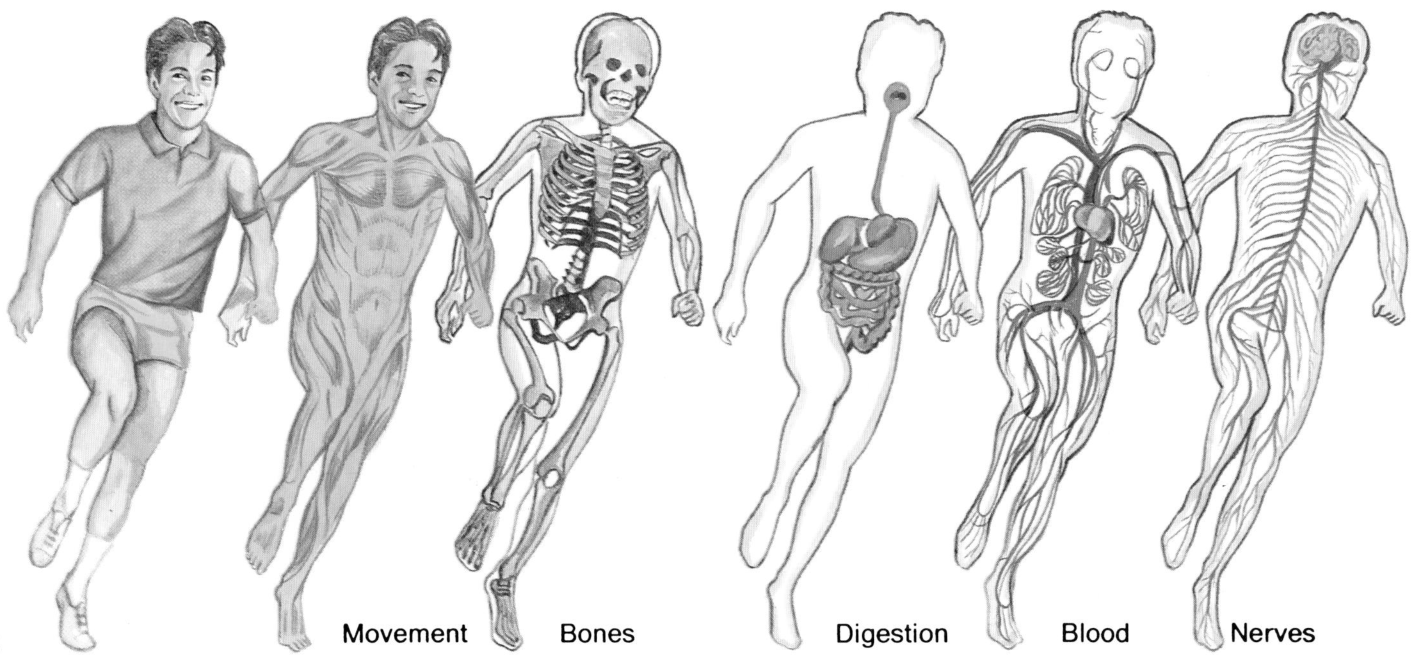

▲ A hummingbird can hover in front of a flower. It sucks up nectar with its long tongue.

hummingbird

Hummingbirds are the world's smallest birds. Some of these brightly colored birds are only bee-sized. They fly so fast their wings hum, and they hover before a flower to feed on its nectar. See **birds**.

hurricane

A hurricane is a whirling windstorm. It builds up over the sea, and does great damage when blown over the land. Pacific hurricanes are called typhoons.

hydrogen

Hydrogen is the lightest of all the gases. The sun and stars are mostly made of hydrogen. Water is made of hydrogen and oxygen. See **oxygen**.

hyena

Hyenas are scavenging animals. They eat whatever is left of a dead animal. They also hunt and kill their own prey.

ice

Ice is frozen water. Pure water freezes at a temperature of 32°F (0°C). Ice is slightly lighter than water and takes up more space, which is why frozen water pipes sometimes burst in winter.

Ice Age

During the earth's history, it has sometimes been colder than today. These cold periods are called Ice Ages. The last one ended about 11,000 years ago. Ice sheets spread across northern Europe, Asia, and America. People sheltered in caves. See **cave people**.

▼ Much of Britain and North America was covered by ice during the last Ice Age, as this map shows.

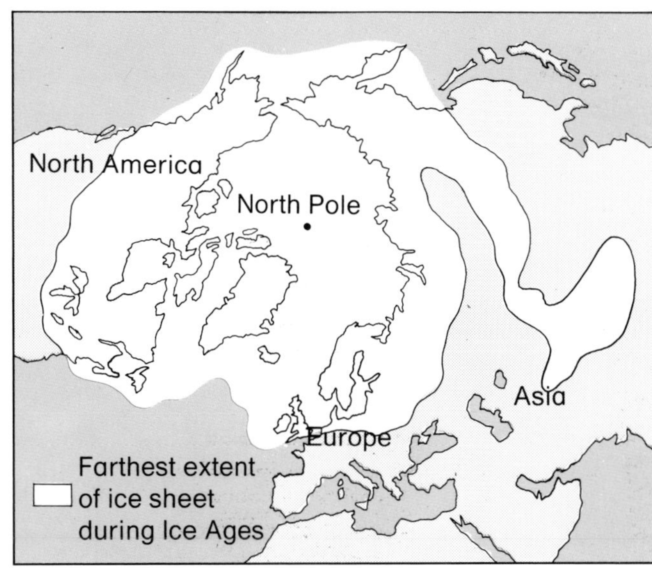

iceberg

An iceberg is a chunk of ice that splits from a glacier or ice sheet and drifts out to sea. Only the tip shows above water. About nine times as much ice is hidden below the sea's surface. Icebergs are found in the Arctic and Antarctic.

Incas and Aztecs

The Incas ruled an empire in the Andes Mountains of South America. The Aztecs lived in Mexico. They were conquered by the Spanish, who came seeking treasure in the 1500s.

▼ The wealth of the Incas amazed the Spanish soldiers, who loaded their ships with Inca gold.

India

India is a big country in south Asia. It has more people than any country except China. Most Indian people are farmers. They live in villages close to rivers such as the Ganges and Brahmaputra. Others live in busy cities, such as Bombay and Calcutta. India has an ancient history. Modern India became a republic in 1947, after 200 years of British rule. See **Gandhi**.

▲ A city street in India. Indian people enjoy the cinema and many films are made in India.

DID YOU KNOW?

In India, elephants are tamed to work in the forests. The rider sits on the elephant's neck as the animal moves huge tree trunks.

I

Industrial Revolution

The Industrial Revolution is the period in history when factories and modern machines became common. It led to all the technology, such as television and automobiles, that we take for granted. The Industrial Revolution began in England in the 1700s and spread to the U.S. in the early 1800s. Most people then lived in villages, growing their own food and making goods at home. The invention of the steam engine made it possible to make goods faster in factories. People went to live and work in towns.

industry

Industries make goods, such as clothes and cars. They also provide services, such as electricity and entertainment. Goods are made in factories and sold in stores. The people who make the goods are paid wages. Labor unions try to make sure workers are treated fairly.

▼ Modern industry uses huge amounts of oil and gas as fuels. Oil is also used to make goods, such as plastics. Tankers carry oil and gas to factories.

insects

Insects are the most numerous of all animals. They first appeared on earth about 400 million years ago. Now there are four times as many insects as all the other animals put together, and they are found in every part of the world. All insects have six legs. Many insects have wings and can fly. Others live underground. Some spend part of their lives in water.

Many insects are harmful to humans because they carry diseases or eat farmers' crops. However, many insects are useful. They pollinate flowers and eat other insects that do harm. Bigger animals, such as many birds and reptiles, eat insects.

Although insects have many enemies, they breed very quickly. They can live in hot and cold places. They eat almost any food. They can hide in places too small for other animals to get into. Social insects, such as bees and ants, live in large groups called colonies. See **ant**, **bee**.

INSECTS

There are at least 850,000 different kinds of insects. The smallest insects can be seen only through a microscope; the largest is a beetle as big as your hand. Among the most interesting insects are the social insects, such as ants, bees, and termites. Insects may look very different, but they all have the same basic body shape.

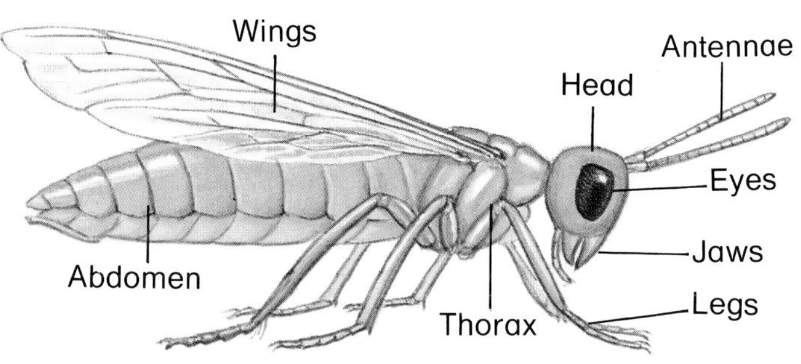

▲ An insect's body has three parts. The head has eyes, jaws, and feelers (antennae). The thorax has the legs and wings. The abdomen contains the stomach and other organs.

LIFE CYCLE OF AN INSECT

Dragonflies have a three-stage life cycle. (1) The adult lays eggs in water. Each egg hatches into a larva called a nymph. (2) The nymph lives in water for at least a year. (3) Then it crawls up a reed, its skin splits and (4) out comes an adult dragonfly.

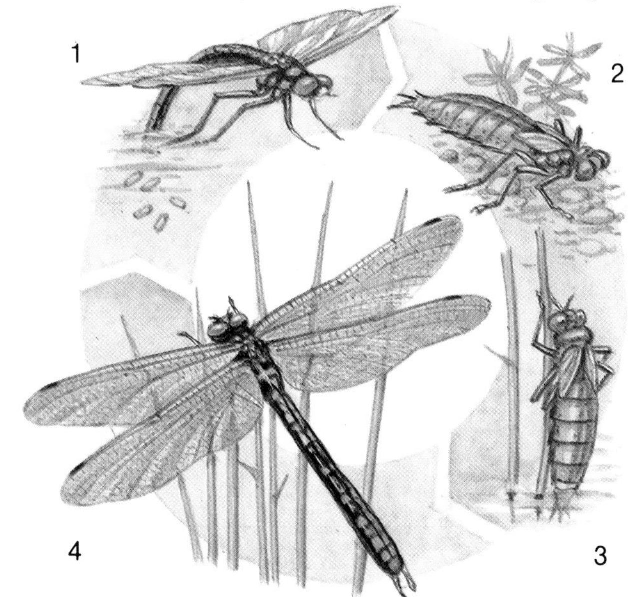

HARMFUL INSECTS

Harmful insects carry disease and destroy our food. They include locusts, cockroaches, flies, lice, fleas, and other pests. The anopheles mosquito carries the disease malaria. The female mosquito bites people to suck their blood. As the mosquito feeds, juices in its tube-like mouth spread the malaria germs.

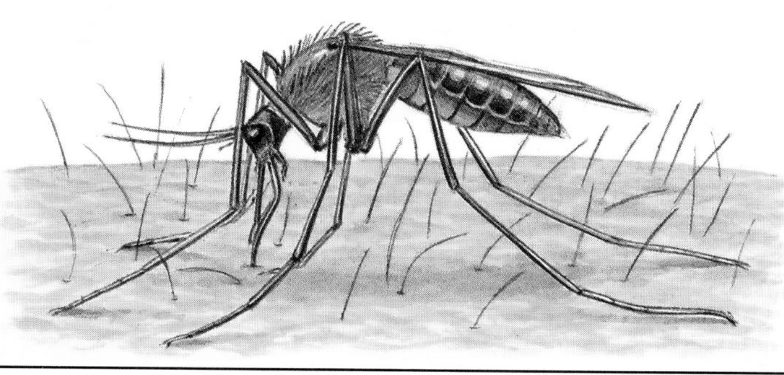

The wings of butterflies and moths are covered with tiny scales. The largest tropical butterflies have wings almost 1 ft (30 cm) across. Other butterflies are tiny, measuring less than half an inch (1 cm). Butterflies feed from plants. They "taste" their food with their feet; then they uncoil a long mouth tube to suck nectar from a flower.

Painted lady butterfly

Red underwing moth

Giant birdwing butterfly

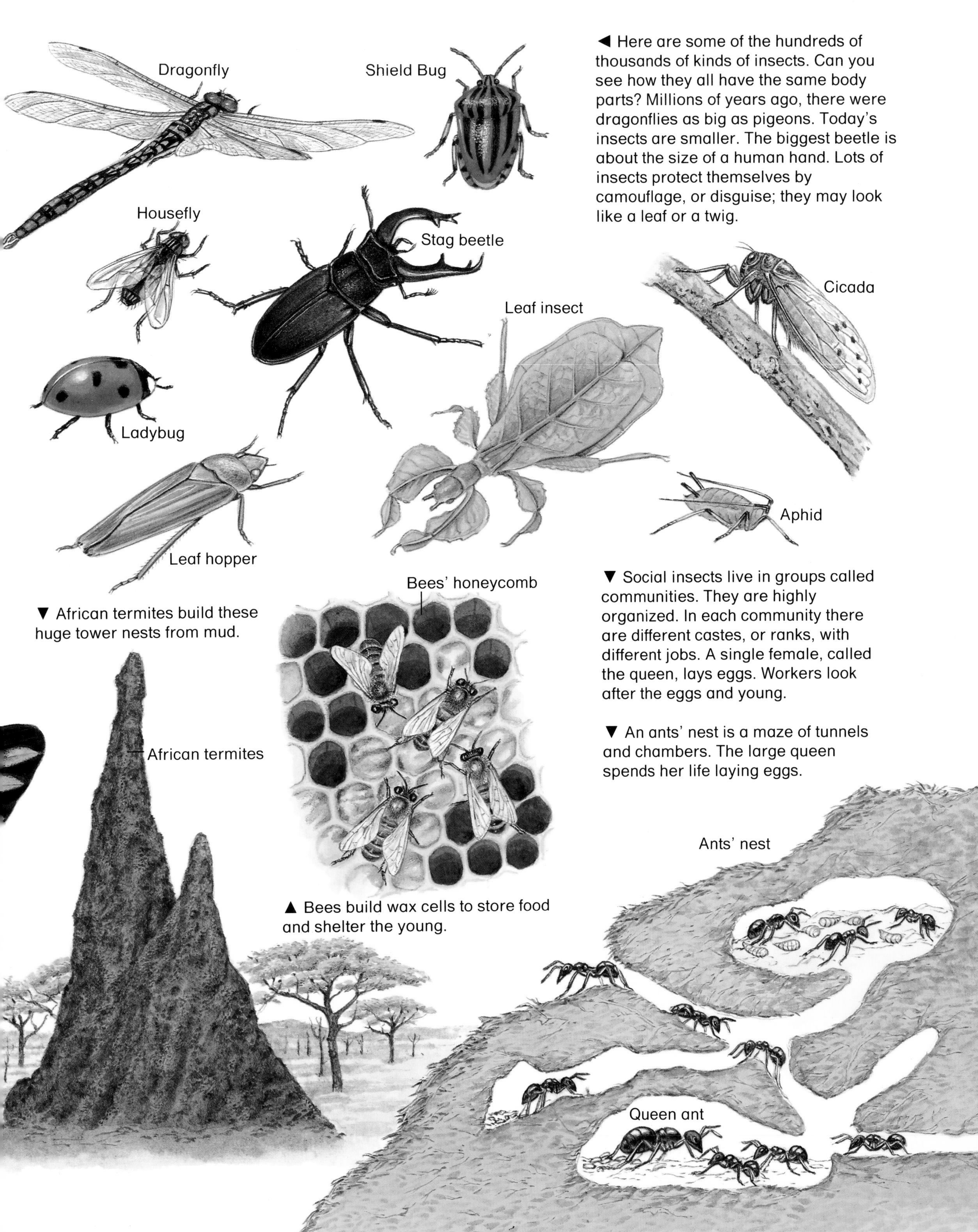

◀ Here are some of the hundreds of thousands of kinds of insects. Can you see how they all have the same body parts? Millions of years ago, there were dragonflies as big as pigeons. Today's insects are smaller. The biggest beetle is about the size of a human hand. Lots of insects protect themselves by camouflage, or disguise; they may look like a leaf or a twig.

▼ African termites build these huge tower nests from mud.

▲ Bees build wax cells to store food and shelter the young.

▼ Social insects live in groups called communities. They are highly organized. In each community there are different castes, or ranks, with different jobs. A single female, called the queen, lays eggs. Workers look after the eggs and young.

▼ An ants' nest is a maze of tunnels and chambers. The large queen spends her life laying eggs.

INVENTIONS & DISCOVERIES

Human civilization is the story of discovery and invention. Inventions succeed when people need them. The ancient peoples of Central America knew of the wheel but had no domestic animals big enough to pull carts. As a result, the wheel never developed there as a tool. Some inventions and discoveries were made by one person. Others by a team.

◀ The wheel first appeared 5,000 years ago in Mesopotamia, part of present-day Iraq. The first wheels were made from pieces of wood fastened together. On the first wagons, wheel and axle turned together.

► Ancient Egyptians, Arabs, Greeks, Indians, and Chinese were skilled in mathematics.

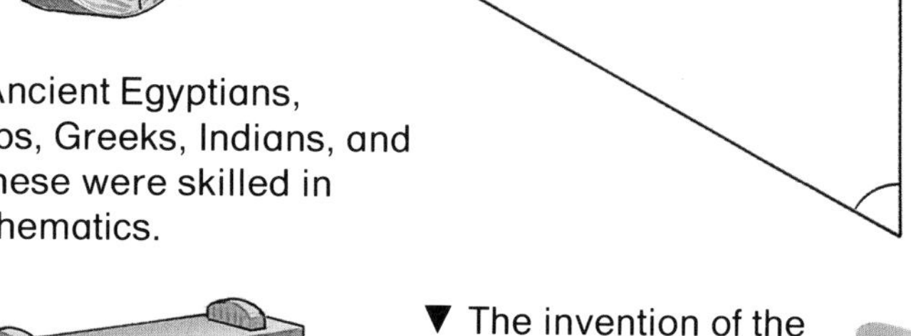

▼ The invention of the mechanical printing press, with movable type, was a revolution in communications.

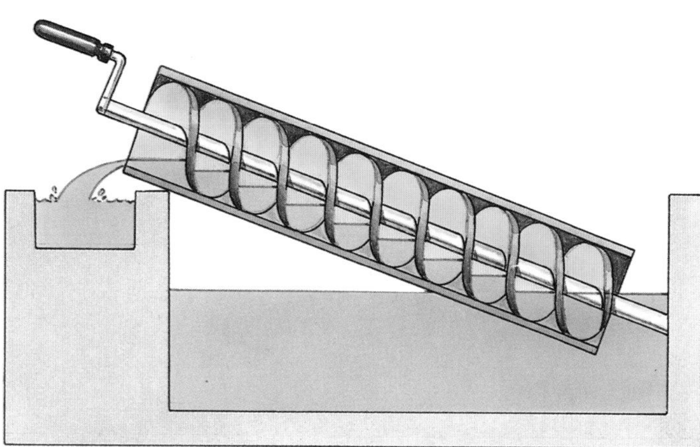

▼ Astronomers of the ancient world thought the earth was the center of the universe. In the 1500s scientists showed that the earth and other planets circled the sun.

▲ Archimedes was a famous Greek scientist. He lived from 282 to 212 B.C. He invented a screw machine to raise water from a river for watering crops.

▼ The first steam engines pumped water from mines. James Watt made great improvements to them in the 1760s.

▲ Discovering how to use such simple machines as wedges and levers was a great step forward in human progress.

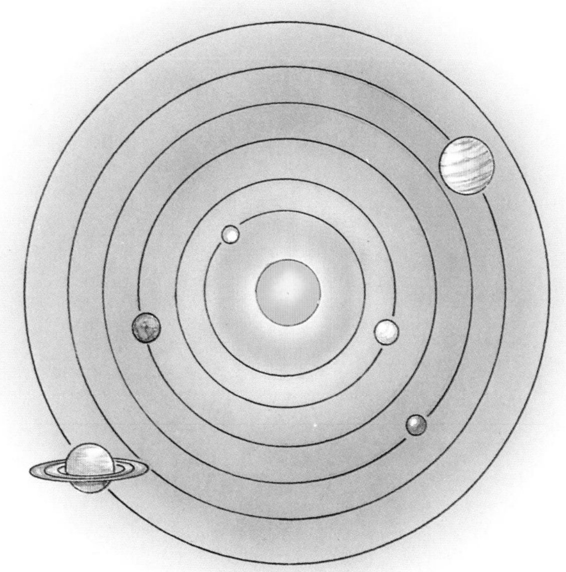

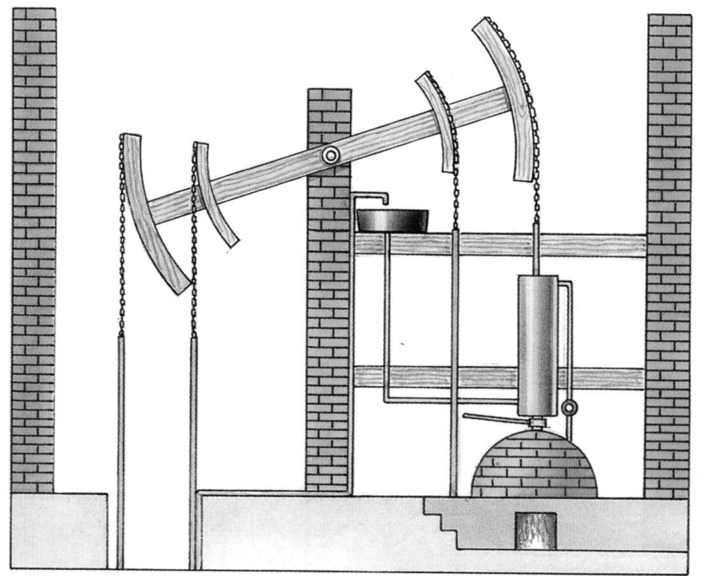

◀ The telephone was invented by Alexander Graham Bell in 1876. By 1923 a person could call from New York to London.

► Photography was invented in the 1820s. Moving pictures were first shown in the 1890s.

► The light bulb was invented separately, by Swan and Edison, in 1878–1879.

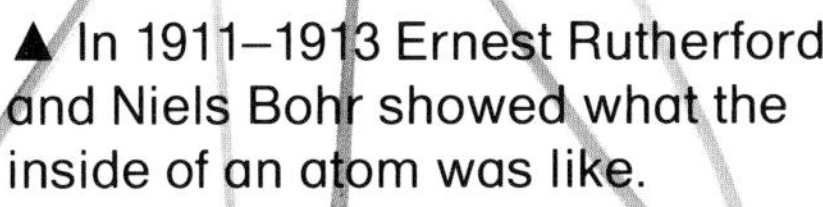

▲ In 1911–1913 Ernest Rutherford and Niels Bohr showed what the inside of an atom was like.

► Since the 1970s, microchips have brought about a revolution in electronics.

◀ Television broadcasting began in 1936. Videotape was invented in 1956. Color TV began to replace black and white TV in the 1950s.

► The first laser was made in 1960. Laser beams are very powerful and accurate. They have many different uses.

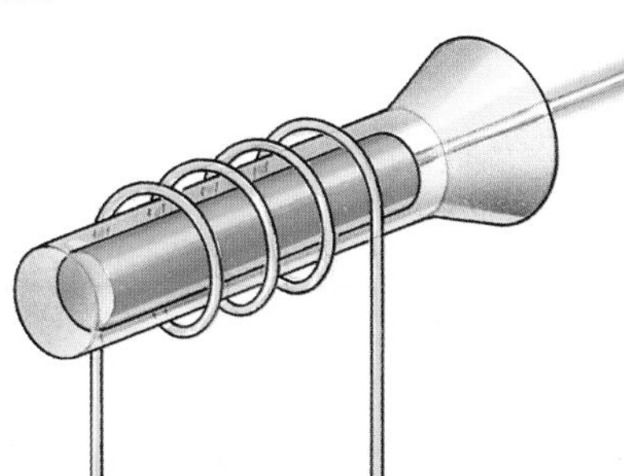

TIME CHART

Prehistory: first stone tools. People learned to use fire over 500,000 years ago.

50,000 years ago: flint tools, bone needles, bows and arrows

12,000 years ago: clay pots, tame dogs, oil lamps

10,000 years ago: first farmers, first use of copper tools

5,000 years ago: writing, wheel, plow, pyramids of Egypt, 365-day calendar

3,000 years ago: iron tools, kites, first coins, water clocks, and sundials

2,000 years ago: water wheel, cement, paper, many building and woodworking tools in use

A.D. 1000 to 1500: gunpowder rocket, cannons, magnetic compass, eye-glasses, printing by movable type, voyages to Africa, Asia, America

1500 to 1800: microscope (1590), thermometer (1593), telescope (1608), circulation of the blood (1628), laws of gravity and motion (1687), steam engine (1690s), steam carriage (1769), discovery of oxygen (1774), balloon flight (1783), inoculation (1796)

1800 to 1900: battery (1800), steamship (1807), food canning (1809), electric motor (1821), dynamo (1831), steam railroad (1830), bicycle (1839), photography (1826), airship (1852), internal-combustion engine (1860), telephone (1876), light bulb (1878–79), automobile (1885), radio waves (1887), diesel engine (1892), radio (1895)

1900 to the present: airplane (1903), theory of relativity (Einstein, 1905), model of the atom (1911), penicillin (1928), jet engine (1930), radio telescope (1937), radar (1935), photocopier (1938), nuclear reactor (1942), computer (1946), videotape (1956), artificial satellite (1957), laser (1960), first heart transplant (1967), moon landing by astronauts (1969), supersonic airliner (Concorde, 1976)

iron and steel

Iron comes from iron ore, dug from the ground. Steel is an alloy, or mixture, of iron, carbon, and sometimes another metal, such as chromium. Steel is stronger than iron and has many uses.

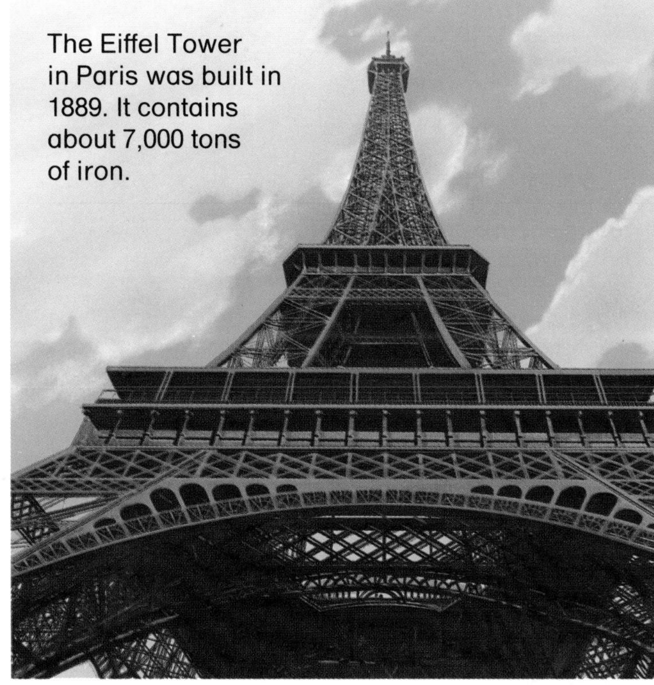

The Eiffel Tower in Paris was built in 1889. It contains about 7,000 tons of iron.

Islam

The religion of Islam was preached by the Prophet Muhammad, who was born in Mecca in Arabia about A.D. 570. After his death in 632, Islam spread rapidly. The followers of Islam are called Muslims. Their holy book is the Koran. Their place of worship is a mosque. Muslims pray five times a day. They fast during the month of Ramadan and travel as pilgrims to Mecca.

island

An island is land surrounded by water. The biggest island is Greenland. Islands form when land sinks or the sea rises. They are also made by undersea volcanoes or coral animals and plants.

jaguar see **cats**

Japan

Japan is the richest country in Asia. It is made up of four large and many small islands. Much of the country is forest, but most Japanese live in cities and work in factories. Ancient Japan was ruled by an emperor and warrior lords. The country modernized in the 1800s. Japan was defeated in World War II (1939–1945), but afterward became a very important manufacturing center. Cars, motorcycles, stereos, and computers are just some of the goods made in Japan.

Jesus Christ see **Christianity**

jet engine

In a jet engine, air is mixed with petroleum fuel and burned. The hot gases given off shoot out of the back of the engine and push it in the opposite direction. See **aircraft**, **engine**.

▼ A jet engine sucks in air at one end, burns fuel, and shoots out a jet of hot gases at the other end.

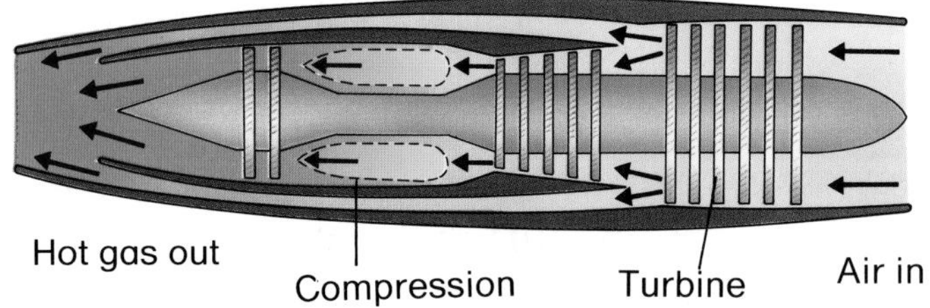

LIFE STORY

Joan of Arc

Joan of Arc was born about 1412 in a village in France. France was losing a long war with England. Joan was a simple peasant girl. Yet one day she left home and went off to save her country. She said she heard voices from heaven, telling her what to do. Joan persuaded the French king to let her lead his soldiers, and they won battle after battle. In 1430 Joan was captured. The English said she was a witch. In 1431 she was burned to death in Rouen, France. In 1920 she was declared a saint.

Judaism

Judaism is the religion of the Jews. It was the first great religion to teach belief in one God. The teachings and laws of Judaism are written in the books of the Torah and Talmud. Jews live all over the world, but regard Israel as their spiritual and historical home.

Kangaroos use their long tails to balance as they bound along.

kangaroo

Kangaroos live in Australia. They are marsupials, or mammals with pouches to carry their young. They eat plants, have long back legs, and can hop at up to 37 mi (60 km) an hour. Baby kangaroos are called joeys. See **marsupials**.

kings and queens

A country ruled by a king or queen is a monarchy. When a king or queen dies, the eldest son or daughter usually takes the throne. In the past, kings had great powers. Today, only a few countries have kings and queens. One is Great Britain, which has a "constitutional" monarchy. The queen is head of the country, but Parliament makes the laws. See **government**.

kite
Flying kites is fun. A kite soars in the sky on the end of a string. Air pushes against the kite, making it fly. The first kites were made in China about 3,000 years ago.

knight
In Europe in the early Middle Ages, knights were warriors on horseback. Later, boys learned to be knights by acting as pages or squires to other knights. Some were knighted on the battlefield. Knights practiced fighting in tournaments. See **Middle Ages**.

▼ Only the king could make a man a knight, by touching him on the shoulders with a sword.

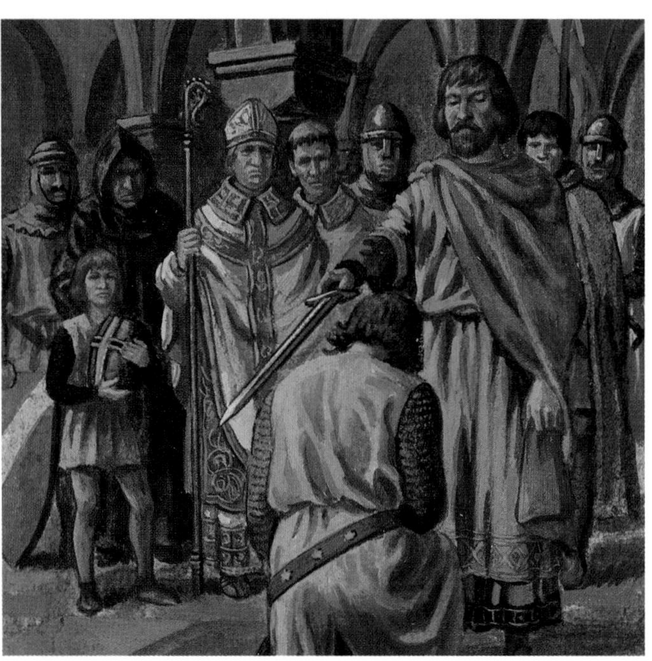

koala
The koala is an Australian mammal that looks like a teddy bear. It is not a bear at all, but a marsupial. Koalas climb in eucalyptus trees, eating leaves. The babies are first carried in the mother's pouch and, when they get older, ride on her back. See **marsupials**.

lake
A lake is a large area of inland water. Some lakes were made by glaciers scooping out hollows in the earth. Others are made when dams are built across rivers. Some big lakes are called seas.

Lake Titicaca in South America (shown here) is the highest lake on which boats sail. The largest freshwater lake is Lake Superior in North America. The deepest lake, Lake Baikal, is in the U.S.S.R.

language
Language is sounds put together to make words, which we use to talk and write. There are thousands of languages and dialects (variations of a language) in the world. More people speak Chinese than any other language. English is also spoken in many countries.

laser
A laser shoots out a narrow beam of light. The light is "pumped up" in the laser to make it much stronger than ordinary light. A laser can burn a hole through metal. Lasers can also carry television signals. Surgeons use lasers for eye operations. Soldiers use lasers to guide missiles. Lasers were invented in the 1960s. There are crystal lasers, gas lasers, and liquid lasers. See **light**.

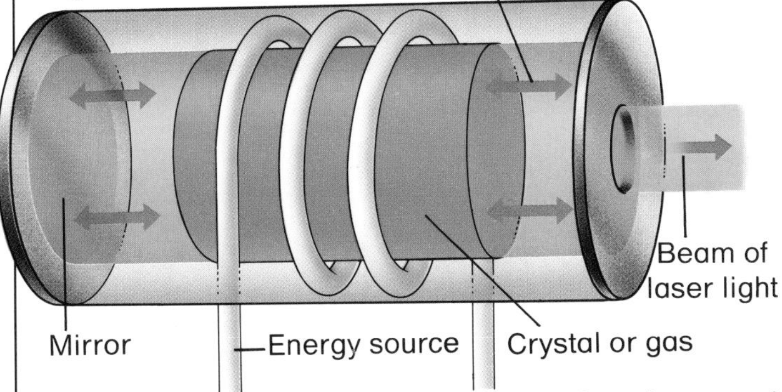

▲ Light is made stronger inside a laser by mirrors and bursts of energy, until a powerful beam shoots out.

latitude and longitude
The crisscross lines on maps are lines of latitude and longitude. Longitude lines run north and south. Latitude lines run east and west. The equator is 0° (degrees) latitude. Greenwich, in England, is 0° longitude.

laws
Laws are rules made by governments for their people to live by. The government sets out the people's rights and duties, as well as punishments for anyone who breaks the law. The police see that laws are obeyed. A person who may have broken the law is tried in court. If the court finds the person guilty, he or she may be punished, perhaps by being sent to prison. See **court, police**.

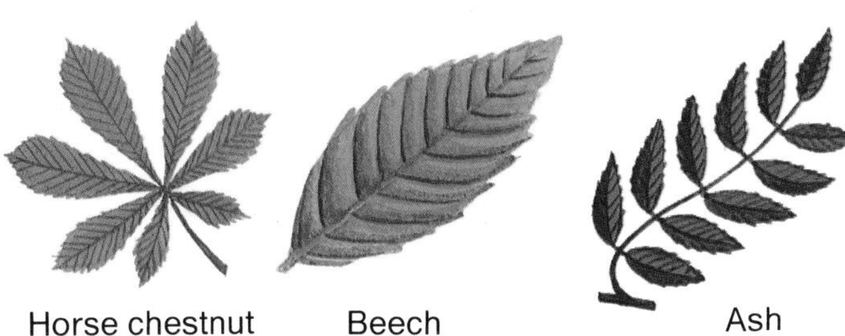

leaf
A plant's leaves make food for the rest of the plant. A leaf turns energy from sunlight into sugar, using carbon dioxide gas from the air, and water and chlorophyll, a green color in the plant. See **plants**.

Lenin
Vladimir Ilyich Ulyanov, known as Lenin (1870–1924), helped to overthrow the tsar in the Russian Revolution of 1917. He led the first Communist government of the U.S.S.R.

lens
The lens in your eye helps you to see. Plastic or glass lenses in eyeglasses curve to bend light as it passes through. Different lenses make objects look bigger or smaller. See **eye, light**.

▼ A convex lens makes things look bigger. A concave lens makes things look smaller.

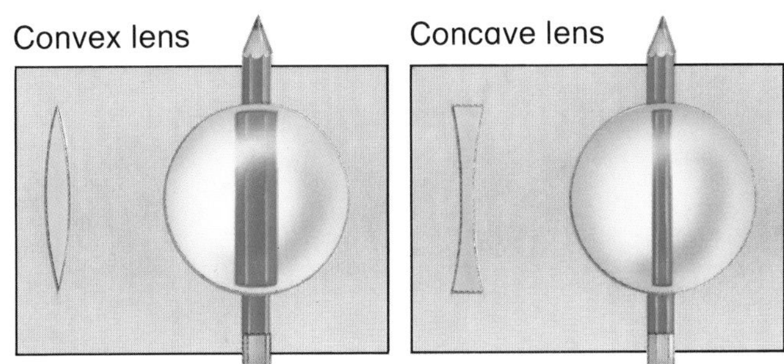

Leonardo
Leonardo da Vinci (1452–1519) was a famous painter and inventor. He lived in Italy during the Renaissance. See **Renaissance**.

leopard see **cats**

library

A library is a building where books are kept. Libraries store knowledge in books, tapes, records, and films. In a public library, you can borrow all kinds of books and look up lots of useful information. See also **museum**.

light

Light is energy from the sun and other stars. Sunlight looks white but is made up of colors. Light travels in straight lines. It is bent when it "reflects," or bounces, off a surface, such as a mirror. It also bends when it passes from air into glass or water. This is "refraction." Light travels amazingly fast: 186,282 mi (300,000 km) a second. See **color**.

▼ How to make a rainbow. Each drop of water in the hose spray bends the light passing through it. The white light is split into rainbow bands of colors.

LIFE STORY

Lincoln

Abraham Lincoln was president of the United States during the Civil War. He was born in Kentucky in 1809. "Abe" had little schooling, but he studied to become a lawyer and was elected to Congress. He spoke out against the Southern states of America, where black people were kept as slaves. In 1861 Lincoln became president. The Southern states set up their own government and declared they were no longer part of the United States. Lincoln gave the order for war. The Civil War brought great suffering. In the end the North won and slavery was ended. Lincoln was shot dead in 1865 while at a theater in Washington. Today, he is remembered as one of the greatest of all presidents. See **United States of America**.

lion see **cats**

liquids and solids
Matter can be liquid, solid, or gas. Water is a liquid. When frozen, it becomes solid ice. Heated, it becomes steam, a gas. All matter is made up of tiny parts called molecules. A liquid takes the shape of any container that it is poured into. Its molecules can move around. A solid has a fixed shape. Its molecules are packed tight in regular patterns and cannot move about. See **gas**.

▲ The frilled lizard makes itself look bigger when frightened by an enemy.

lizards
Lizards are reptiles. Some have no legs, but most run and climb on four legs. Lizards like warm climates. Most lay eggs, although some give birth to live young. They eat plants, insects, or small animals. The biggest lizard is the Komodo dragon of Asia. See **reptiles**.

Luther
Martin Luther (1483–1546) was a German priest. He protested against the practices of the Roman Catholic Church. Supporters of Luther set up "Protestant" churches, starting the Reformation.

machines
Some machines are very big. They have lots of moving parts. Others are very simple. A machine does its work when it makes something move: a lever forces open a box; a ramp makes it easier to push a load uphill; a wedge splits a log. The wheel is an important machine. See **engines, wheels and gears**.

▼ These may not look like machines, but they are all very important ones in everyday life.

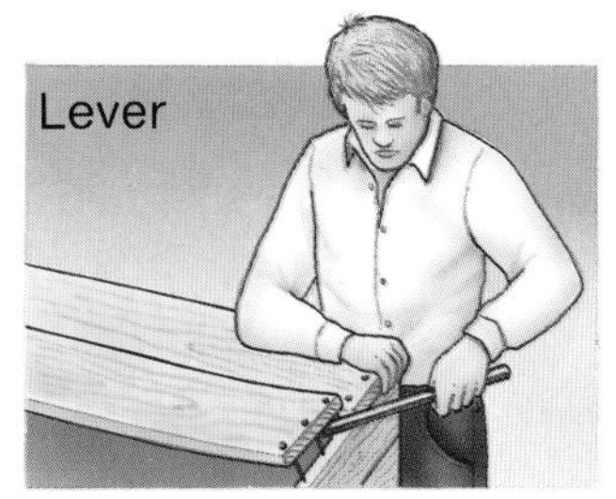

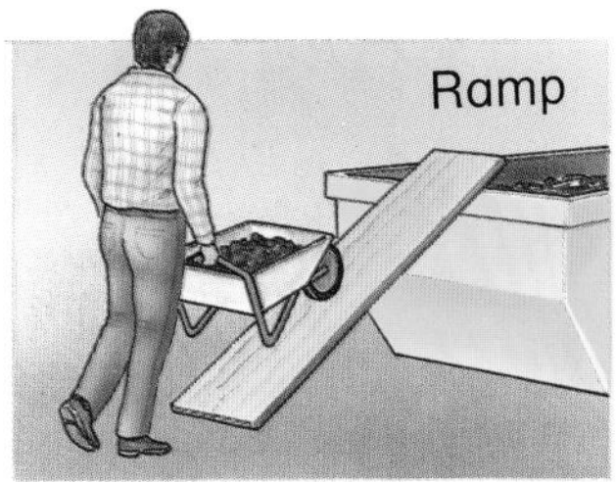

Magellan
Ferdinand Magellan (1480–1521) was a Portuguese sailor. In 1519 he led the first voyage around the world. Only one of five ships came home. Magellan was killed in the Philippines. See **explorers**.

MAMMALS

Mammals are the most advanced animals. They are warm-blooded, and have hair or fur. There are about 4,000 kinds of mammals. The smallest mammals are shrews. The biggest land mammals are elephants. Bats are flying mammals. Whales and dolphins are mammals that never leave the sea. Seals prefer water to dry land.

Humans are also mammals. We belong to the same mammal family as the gorilla and the chimpanzee. The chimpanzee is our closest living relative.

MAMMALS AND THEIR YOUNG

Most mammals give birth to live young. Some mammal babies (deer and goats, for example) can run soon after they are born, but most are helpless and have to be cared for by their mothers. Female mammals feed their babies on milk from their bodies. Two mammals, the echidna and the duck-billed platypus, lay eggs.

The Australian platypus

The blue whale is the biggest animal that ever lived.

Mammals can live in hot or cold places. They have evolved into all kinds of forms. Some of them are shown here.

magnets

Magnets attract metals, especially iron and steel. The earth has north and south magnetic poles, which are fairly close to the geographic North and South Poles. A bar magnet, such as a compass needle, turns to magnetic north. Each magnet has north and south poles. An electromagnet is made by passing electric current through a coil of wire around a metal core. See **compass**.

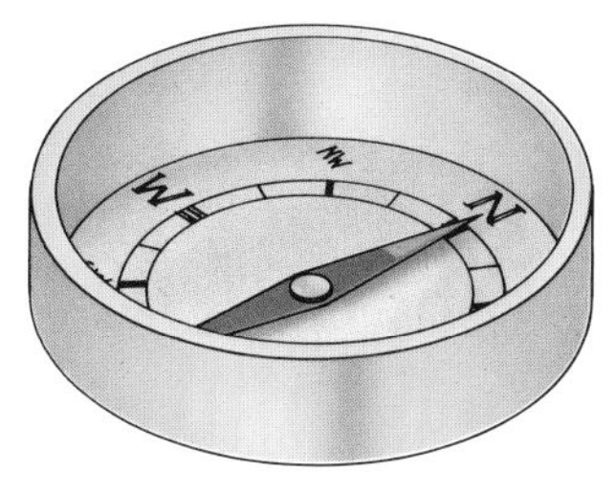

A magnetic compass needle points north. The arrows in the pictures below show the force fields around two bar magnets. North poles (N) push each other apart. North and south poles attract each other.

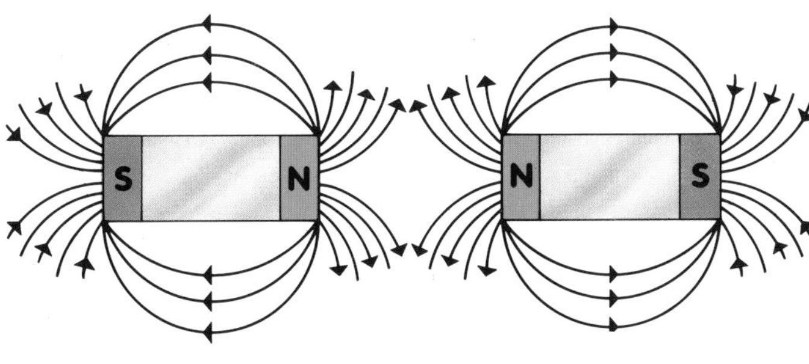

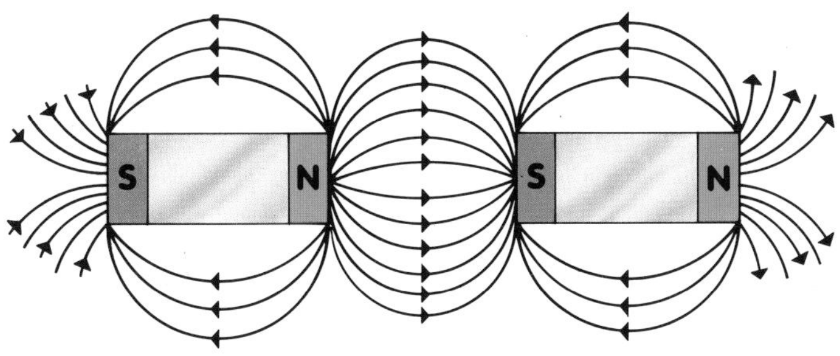

map

A map is a picture of part or all of the earth. Maps show us how to find our way. They show mountains, rivers, roads, and other features. Maps are drawn "to scale"; a small map distance means a big ground distance.

Marconi

Guglielmo Marconi (1874–1937) was an Italian inventor. He used radio waves to send signals. In 1901 he sent the first radio message across the Atlantic Ocean. See **communication**, **radio**.

LIFE STORY

Marco Polo

Marco Polo had amazing adventures. He was born in Venice, Italy, in 1254. His father and uncle were merchants. They journeyed as far as China, where few Europeans had ever been. In 1271 they set off again, taking young Marco with them. They traveled by sea, on foot, and on horses and camels, crossing mountains and deserts. In 1275 they reached China. Marco Polo traveled around China, marveling at all he saw. He remained in China for 17 years, working for the Chinese emperor, Kublai Khan. In 1292 the Polos set off for Italy. The journey took three years. Their friends had long given them up for dead. Marco Polo wrote about his travels, telling people in Europe about the wonders of Asia. See **China**.

▲ Australia is the home of many marsupials. The koala eats the leaves of eucalyptus trees. The Tasmanian devil is a fierce-looking marsupial that preys on other animals. Both these marsupials are now rare in the wild.

marsupials

Marsupials are primitive mammals. A baby marsupial is born tiny and undeveloped. It crawls into a pouch on its mother's body. There it can suck milk and be warm and safe until it is big enough to look after itself. Most marsupials live in Australia and New Guinea. The opossum is an American marsupial. Marsupials include grass-eaters such as kangaroos, tree-climbers such as koalas, and burrowers such as wombats. There are even marsupial mice, shrews, and moles. See **kangaroo**, **koala**.

Marx

Karl Marx (1818–1883) was a German writer. He believed in revolution and thought poor workers should overthrow their rich masters, who owned the farms and factories. Wealth would be shared equally in a new Communist system. Marx's writings inspired revolutionaries such as Lenin. See **Lenin**, **Soviet Union**.

mathematics

When you add up coins in your pocket, you are using mathematics. Mathematics that deals with numbers is called arithmetic. Algebra is math using letters, such as x and y, instead of numbers. Geometry is the study of lines, angles, and shapes. We use math all the time, sometimes with the help of calculators and computers. See **measurement**.

FIND OUT FOR YOURSELF

Estimating

Someone says: "Guess how many candies there are in this jar." You need to know how big the candies are and how big the jar is. How many candies would cover the bottom of the jar? How many layers of candies are there?

If you multiply the number of candies in a layer by the number of layers, you can work out roughly how many candies are in the jar.

Think of a number

Puzzle your friends. Ask them:

(1) To think of a number.
(2) Add 3 to it.
(3) Double it.
(4) Subtract 4.
(5) Halve it (divide it by 2).
(6) Take away the number they thought of.

And the answer is . . . 1. Every time!

Amazing numbers

There are 64 squares on a chessboard. Imagine that someone gives you one apple for the first square on Monday, two apples for the second square on Tuesday, four apples for the third square on Wednesday, eight apples for the fourth square on Thursday, and so on, doubling every time until you reached the 64th square. How many apples would you have?

MEASUREMENT

When we measure things, we may want to know "how many?" "how heavy?" "how long?" or "how much space does it take up?" We can measure distance, area, volume, weight, and time. We can also measure light, sound, speed, temperature, and rainfall. Scientists in particular have to measure things very accurately, with special instruments.

Abacus

Beads

Knotted cord

Notched stick

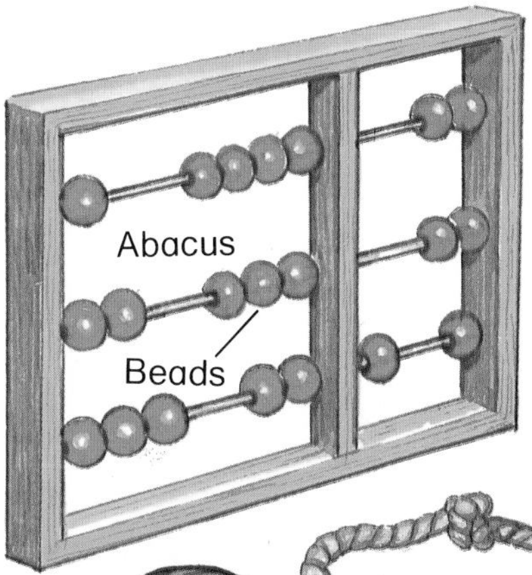

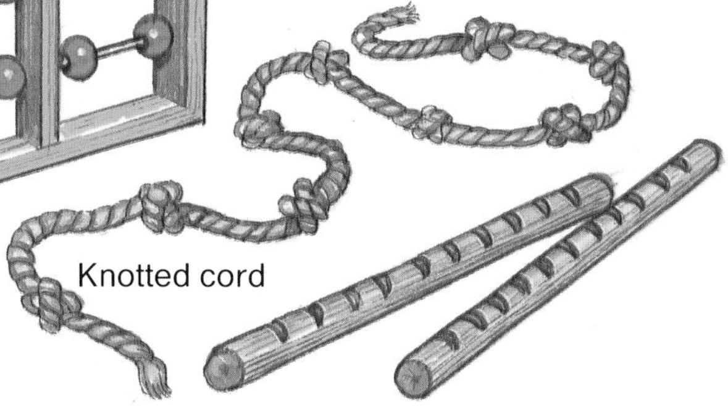

These are three ancient aids to counting: the abacus with its beads on wires, a knotted rope, and sticks with notches cut in them.

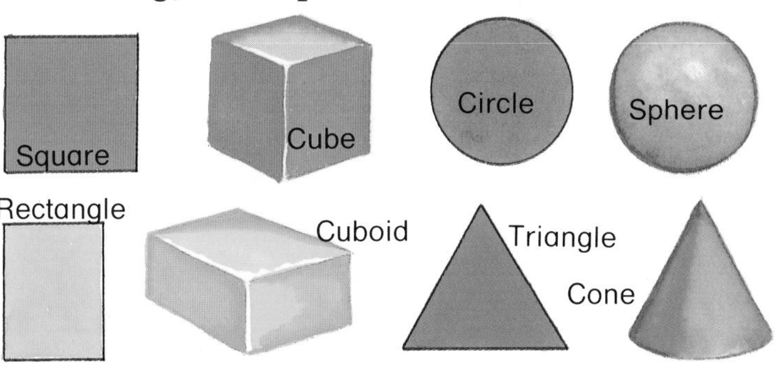

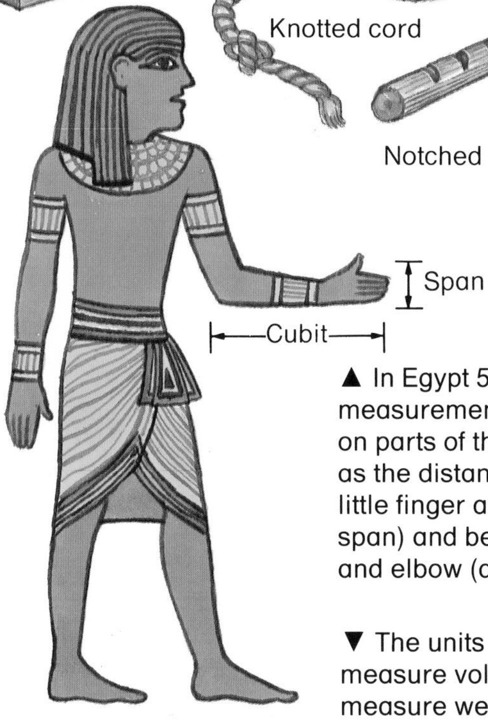

▲ We can measure the space that a flat shape, such as a square, occupies. This is called its area.

▲ Solid shapes, such as cubes and spheres, also take up space. Measuring this gives us their volume or capacity.

Span

Cubit

▲ In Egypt 5,000 years ago, measurements were based on parts of the body, such as the distance between little finger and thumb (a span) and between fingertip and elbow (a cubit).

THE METRIC AND IMPERIAL SYSTEMS

Most countries use the metric system of weights and measures. It is a decimal system (based on 10). The basic unit is the meter, which measures length. Weight is measured in grams. Volume is measured in liters. Units of the imperial system, used in the United States, include inches and feet for length, pints and gallons for volume, and pounds and tons for weight.

▼ The units on the cup measure volume. Scales measure weight, a ruler and tape measure length. A light meter shows how strong the light is; a watch measures time.

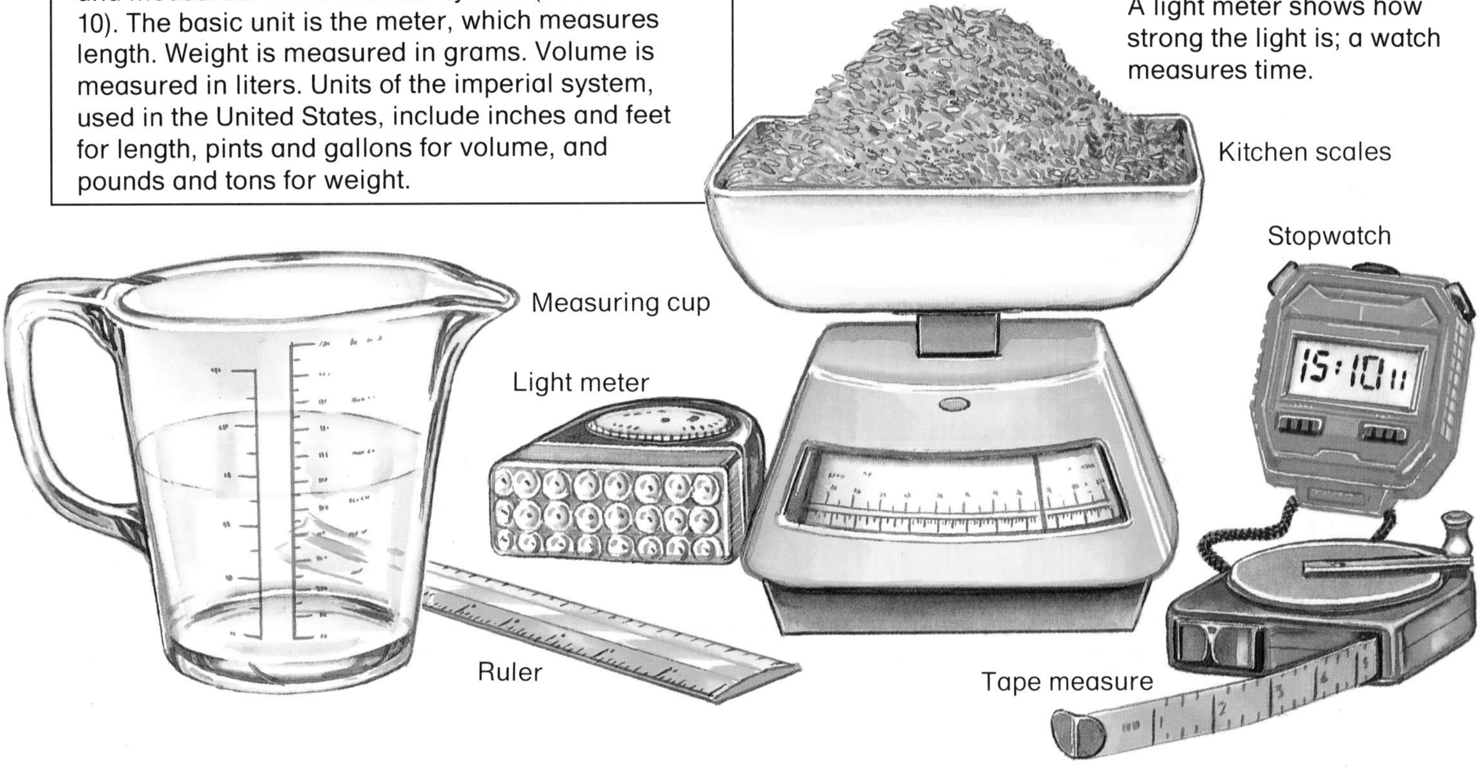

Kitchen scales

Stopwatch

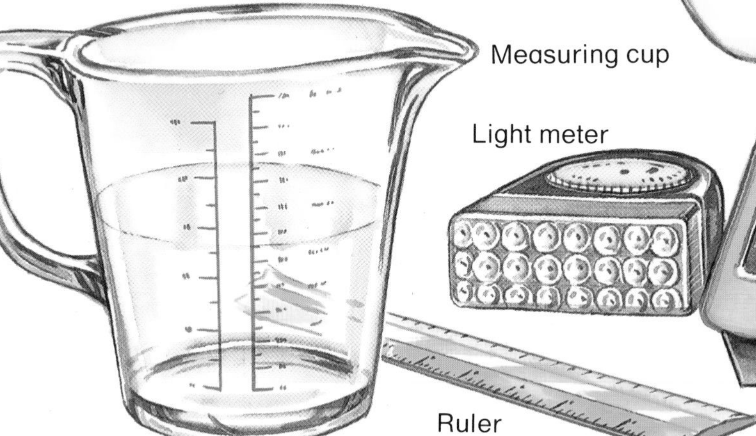

Tape measure

MEDICINE

From earliest times people have used medicines to heal wounds and cure diseases. The first drugs came from berries and herbs. People also believed magic could cure the sick. Doctors began to study anatomy (the parts of the body) in the 1500s. Modern medicine has brought such wonders as heart transplants and body scanners.

Pestle and mortar for mixing medicines

Herbs and berries

▲ Many medicines are made from plants, just as in the past. Herbs and the berries, roots and bark of certain plants contain disease-curing chemicals.

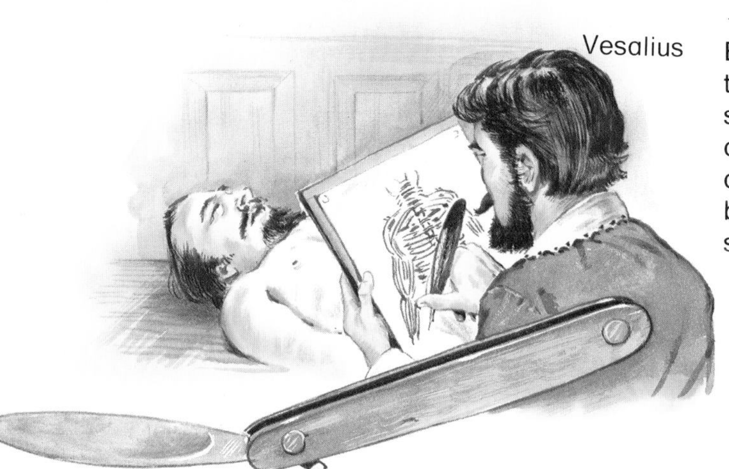

◀ Andreas Vesalius of Belgium was the first doctor to study the body scientifically. Until the 1600s doctors had to examine dead bodies in secret, because the Church banned such research.

Artificial hand

Artificial leg

▲ Artificial hands and legs were made over 2,000 years ago. In the 1500s they were made of metal or wood. They were awkward to wear and to move.

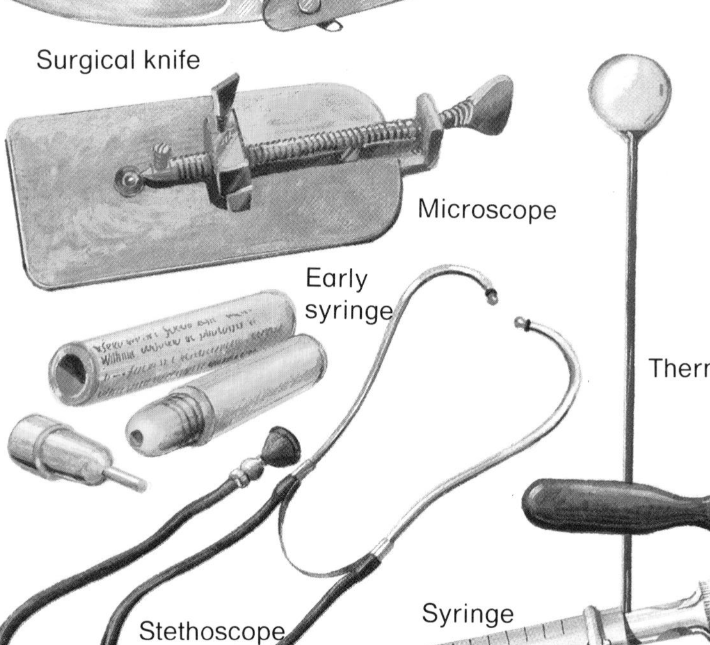

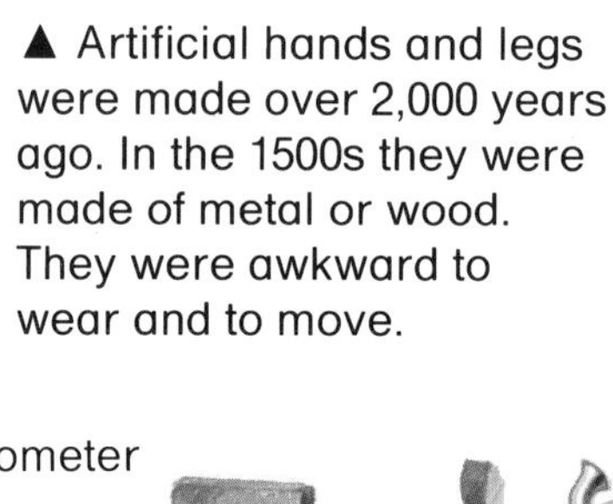

Lister's carbolic spray

▲ The first stethoscope (for listening to a patient's heart and lungs) was made in 1816. Medical thermometers were first used in the 1600s.

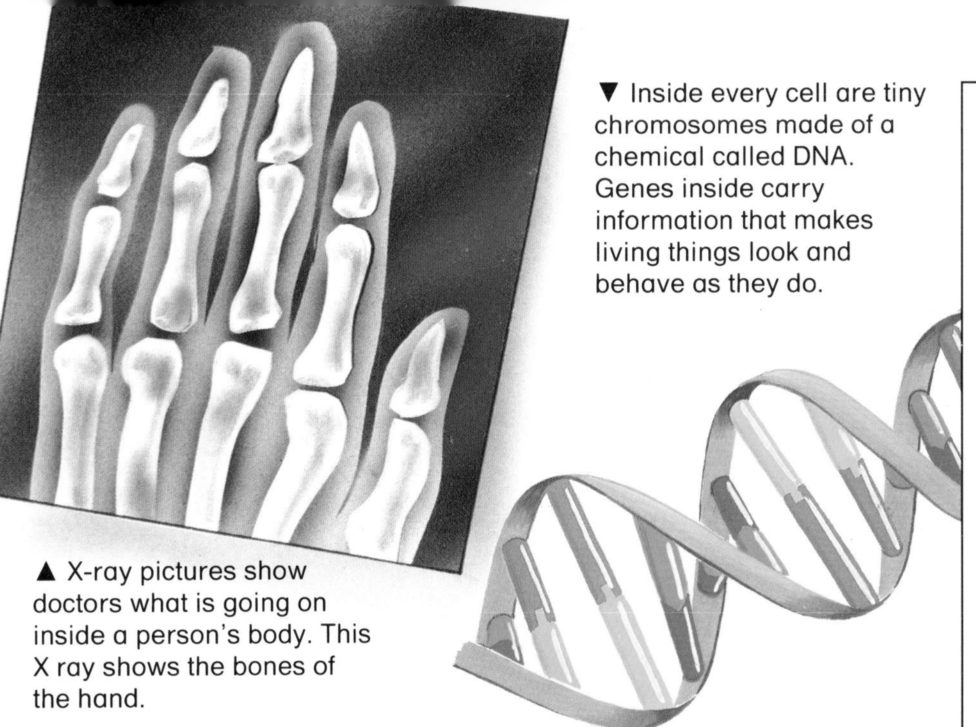

▼ Inside every cell are tiny chromosomes made of a chemical called DNA. Genes inside carry information that makes living things look and behave as they do.

▲ X-ray pictures show doctors what is going on inside a person's body. This X ray shows the bones of the hand.

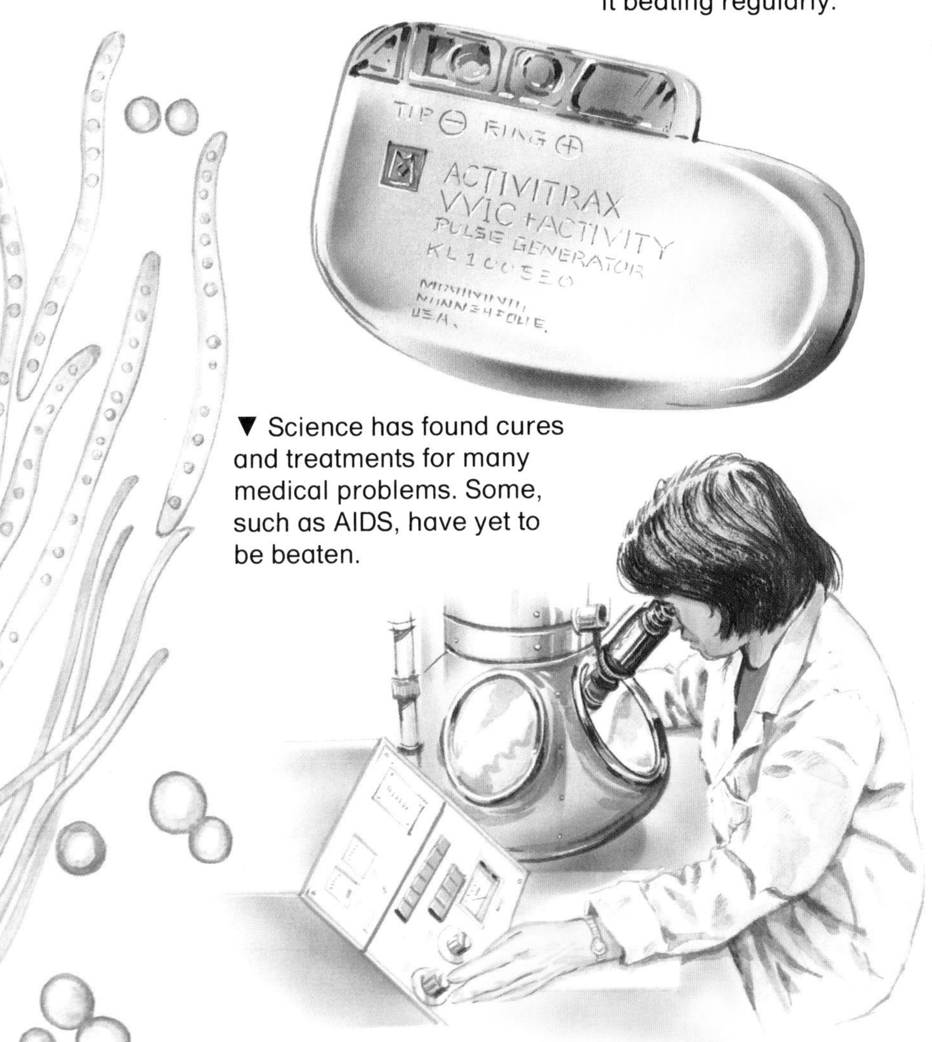

▼ Anthrax germs under a microscope. Anthrax is a dangerous disease. In 1876 Robert Koch showed that bacteria caused anthrax.

▼ A heart pacemaker helps people whose hearts do not beat properly. The pacemaker sends electrical signals to the heart to keep it beating regularly.

▼ Science has found cures and treatments for many medical problems. Some, such as AIDS, have yet to be beaten.

ADVANCES IN MEDICINE

The Greek Hippocrates (born about 460 B.C.) is known as the Father of Medicine.

The Chinese began to use acupuncture 3,000 years ago.

In 1590 Zacharias Janssen invented the microscope.

In 1628 William Harvey showed that the heart pumps blood all around the body.

Florence Nightingale founded modern nursing in the 1850s.

In 1846 William Morton used ether, the first anesthetic to kill pain, during an operation.

In the 1860s Louis Pasteur suggested that diseases were caused by germs. This was later proved by Robert Koch, using the anthrax germ.

In 1885 Pasteur used inoculation to prevent rabies.

In 1895 Wilhelm Röntgen discovered X rays.

In 1901 Karl Landsteiner showed that people have different blood types.

In 1922 Frederick Banting and Charles Best discovered the insulin treatment for diabetes.

In 1928 Alexander Fleming discovered penicillin. This was used as the first antibiotic drug in the 1940s.

In the 1950s Jonas Salk developed the first vaccine against polio.

In 1967 Christiaan Barnard transplanted a heart from one patient to another.

In the late 1970s the World Health Organization declared that smallpox, once a worldwide killer disease, was no more, thanks to vaccination.

In 1982 the first artificial heart was fitted to a person.

Mediterranean Sea

Mediterranean means "center of the world." To the ancient Romans, that's what this sea was. The Mediterranean is linked to the Atlantic Ocean by the Strait of Gibraltar, and to the Red Sea by the Suez Canal. See **Europe**.

metals

Eight of every ten elements on earth are metals. Important metals include iron, copper, and aluminum. Gold and silver are precious metals, used in jewelry.

Most metals are shiny. They let heat and electricity pass through them. Most metals are solid, unless heated until they melt. Mercury is liquid at room temperature. Some metals are very hard. Others are soft enough to be beaten into sheets or pulled into wires.

Metals mixed together make alloys. Bronze is an alloy of tin and copper. Most metals are found mixed with other substances, in materials called ores. The ore is treated to take out the pure metal. See **minerals and mining**.

Michelangelo

The artist and sculptor Michelangelo Buonarroti (1475–1564) was Italian. He painted hundreds of figures on the ceiling of the Sistine Chapel in Rome. He also made beautiful statues. See **art**.

microscope

A microscope uses lenses to make things look bigger. Scientists use microscopes to study things too small to be seen otherwise. An electron microscope can show pictures of atoms. See **atom**.

Middle Ages

The Middle Ages of Europe's history lie between ancient and modern times. They began about A.D. 500, with the fall of the Roman Empire. They ended with the new age of discovery and science in the 1400s. The Middle Ages were troubled times. There were wars, such as the Crusades, and terrible diseases, such as the Black Death. Yet the Middle Ages left us great buildings, such as castles and cathedrals. See **castle**, **Crusades**.

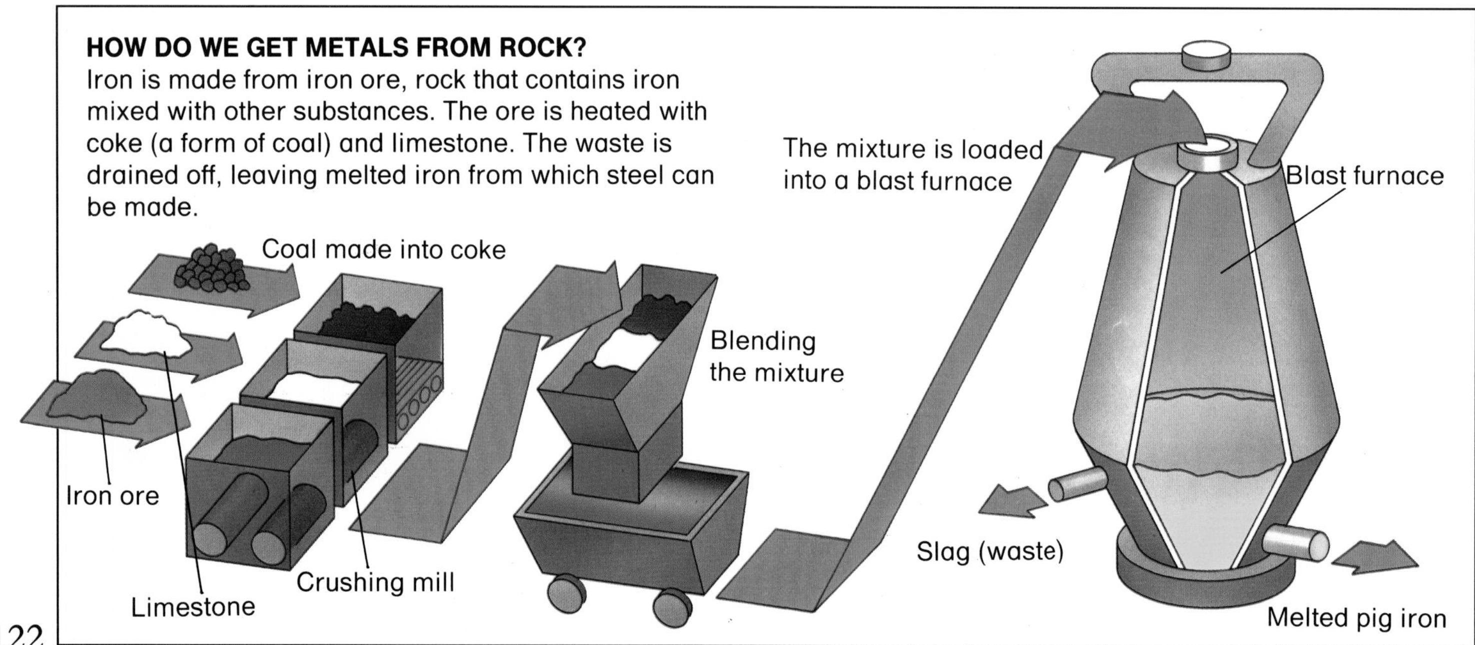

MIDDLE AGES

In Europe during the Middle Ages (A.D. 500–1500), kings were the most powerful rulers. Nobles and knights served the king by fighting for him in time of war. In return, the king gave them land. The land was used mostly for farming. Poor peasants did the farm work. The nobleman was supposed to protect them in return.

▲ Peasants, or serfs, did not own the land they farmed. They had to obey the lord of the manor, the nobleman who owned the land. Their lives were hard. They had no farm machines to help with the work.

▼ Roads were bad in the Middle Ages. Few people traveled farther than the next village. Oxen were used to pull heavy carts.

▲ A knight swears loyalty to his king. He had to obey the king's commands.

▶ Few people could read. In monasteries, monks preserved ancient learning, copying books by hand.

◀ Stonemasons and other workers toiled to build great cathedrals. The work took hundreds of years. Castles were built much faster.

▲ Islamic mosques with their towers and domes can be seen in many countries of the Middle East.

Middle East

The countries of the Middle East include Syria, Lebanon, Jordan, Israel, Iraq, Iran, Egypt, the Arabian peninsula, and part of Turkey. Much of the Middle East is desert. Oil has made some countries very rich, but others are poor. Most of the people are Muslims and many are Arabs. Since 1948 there have been wars between Israel and its Arab neighbors. There has been fighting in Lebanon. Iran and Iraq fought a war in the 1980s. In 1991 Iraq was defeated when it tried to take over Kuwait.

migration

Birds called warblers spend the summer in North America, but in fall fly to Central and South America. This kind of animal journey is called migration. Many animals migrate to find food or places to breed. African antelope cross the dry plains to find grass. The Arctic tern, a seabird, flies around the world to nest. Salmon swim from the sea back to the rivers where they hatched.

milk see **food, mammals**

minerals and mining

Rocks are made of minerals, often mixed together. The word "mineral" is also used to mean anything that is mined, or dug from the ground. People mine for things such as coal (a fuel), copper (a useful metal), and diamonds (precious stones). Sometimes miners need only to scrape away the surface of the ground, but often they must dig deep pits and tunnels in the rock. See **quarry**.

▼ Inside a coal mine. Elevators carry miners up and down deep shafts. Trains run through the main underground tunnels, pulling wagons loaded with coal.

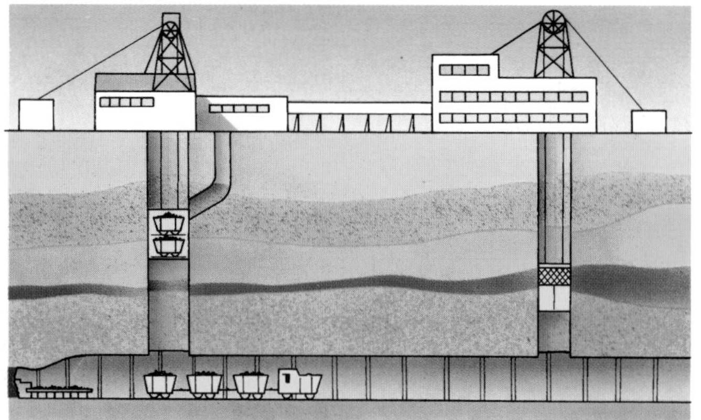

mirror

A mirror's shiny surface makes light bounce off it. We see a reflection. The "mirror image" is reversed. Look in a mirror and wave your right hand. Which hand does your image wave? Mirrors are made of glass with a silver or aluminum back. See **light**.

Mississippi

The Mississippi River is the longest river in the United States. It is 2,340 mi (3,766 km) long. The Missouri and other rivers join the Mississippi before it reaches the Gulf of Mexico.

mole

Moles are animals that spend most of their lives underground. They dig tunnels using their front claws, and find their way in the dark by touch and smell. They have very poor eyesight. Moles eat lots of worms and grubs.

mollusk

Mollusks are soft-bodied animals. Many have hard shells for protection. Some mollusks, such as the limpet, cling to rocks. Others, such as snails, move slowly. Slugs are like snails, but some slugs have no shells at all. Mollusks must keep moist to stay alive. The largest mollusks are the octopus, which has no shell, and the squid, which has a shell inside its body. See **octopus and squid, shell**.

▼ There are more mollusks on the earth than any other animals, except insects.

money

When people first began to buy and sell, they did not use money — they exchanged goods. Later, people used shells, beads, or cattle as money. The first coins were gold or silver, but cheaper metals are now used. The Chinese invented paper money, or banknotes. Checks and credit cards are another kind of money. See **bank**.

► Metal coins last a long time and are easy to carry. The coins we use today are made of cheap metals.

monkeys

Monkeys are mammals that look much like people (with tails). Monkeys and apes are called primates. Most monkeys live in hot countries. American monkeys use their tails as extra hands, to grasp tree branches. African and Asian monkeys cannot use their tails like this. Monkeys live in groups, often in trees. Some, such as the big baboons, walk on the ground. See **apes, mammals**.

MOON

The moon circles the earth in space, about 237,000 miles (382,000 km) away from it. It is kept in orbit by the earth's gravity. It is a dry lifeless world, with no air. The moon was probably formed about the same time as the earth. Nothing has changed there for over 4 billion years until the first astronauts landed on its surface in 1969.

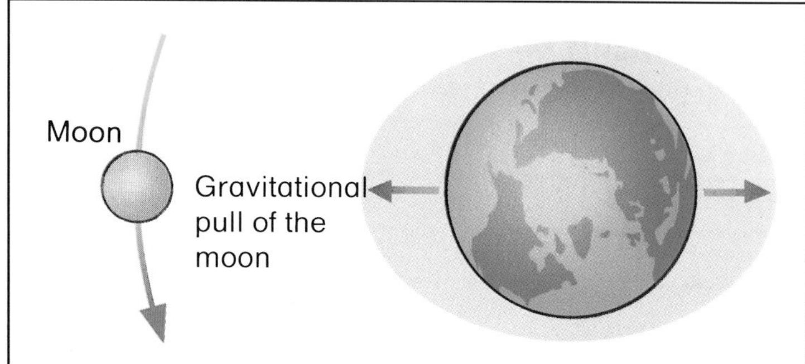

The moon has its own gravity. The pull of the moon's gravity drags at the waters of the earth's oceans, and so causes the tides. The moon's gravity makes oceans "bulge" on the side of the earth that faces the moon.

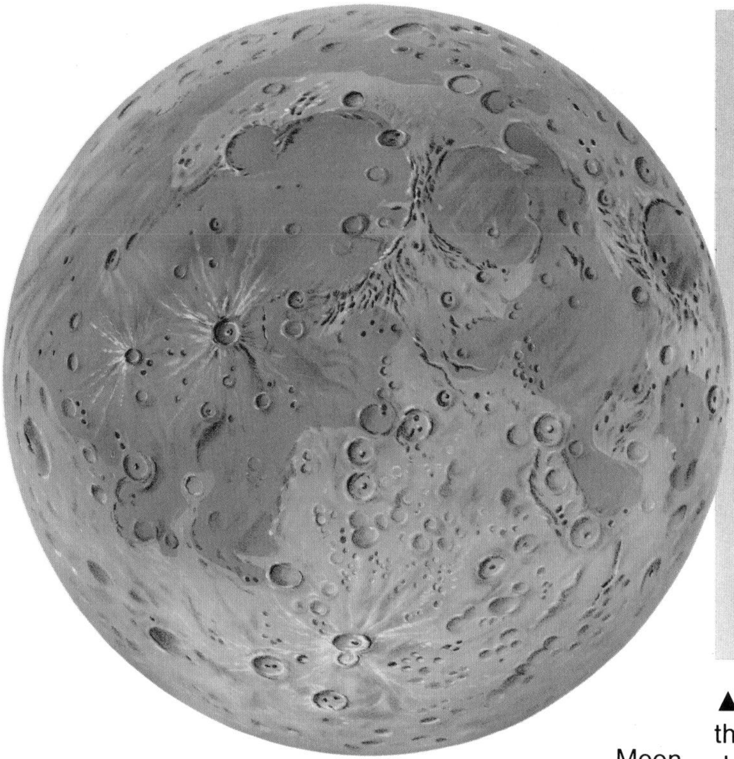

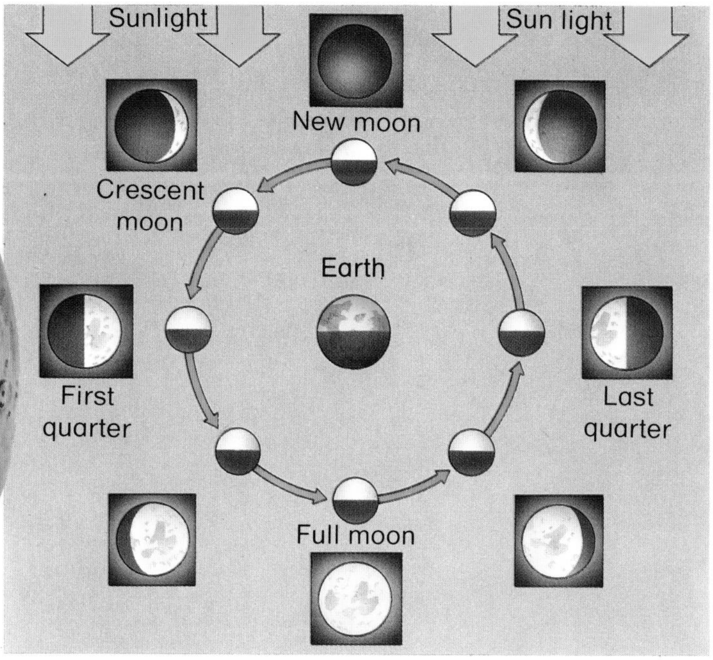

▲ The moon travels around the earth roughly every $27\frac{1}{3}$ days. We see only one side of the moon. It is lit by the sun. This shows how we see the moon during its monthly journey.

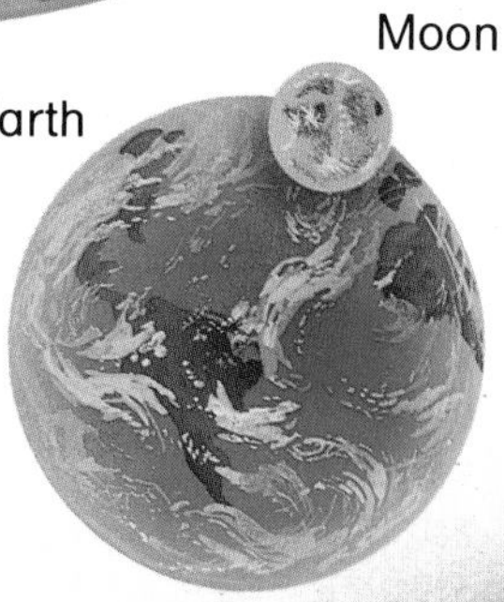

▲ The craters on the moon are made by meteorites. There are mountains, and the dark areas are plains, wrongly called "seas" by early astronomers.

► The earth is much bigger, and 81 times heavier, than the moon.

▼ Twelve *Apollo* astronauts explored small areas of the moon between 1969 and 1972. Some of them drove electric "moon buggies."

mosque see **Islam**

moth see **butterflies and moths**

motion pictures

People all over the world enjoy going to the theater to watch movies. The first moving films were made about 100 years ago by the Lumière brothers. These films were black and white, and silent. The pictures looked jerky. By the 1930s talking pictures in color had been invented. Hollywood, California, became the center of the movie industry. Films are now made all over the world. Films are made indoors in a studio, and outdoors on location. Today, we can watch films at home on television and video, as well as in a specially built movie theater.

motor see **engines**

motorcycle

A motorcycle has two wheels. It is driven by a gasoline engine like the one in a car, but smaller. The rider sits astride the bike. Some controls, such as the throttle, or speed control, are on the handlebars. Others, like the gears, are worked by the rider's feet. A chain drive connects the engine to the back wheel. A sidecar for an extra passenger can be fitted to a motorcycle. The first motorcycle was built in 1885 by a German engineer named Gottlieb Daimler. It was slow and uncomfortable. The fastest modern motorcycles can travel at 125 mph (200 km/h). See **engines**.

◀ A trail bike is a motorcycle made specially for riding over rough ground.

MOUNTAINS

The highest mountains on earth are in the Himalaya of Asia. Other ranges, or huge groups, of mountains are the Rocky Mountains (North America), the Andes (South America), and the Alps (Europe). There are even higher mountains under the sea. Some mountains are young and still growing. Others are old and being worn away.

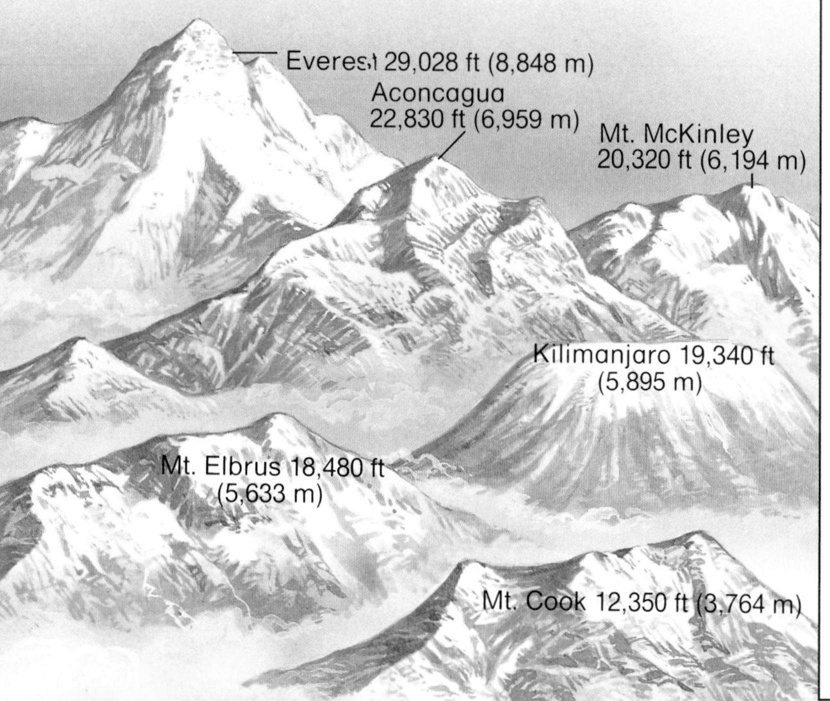

Mount Everest, above, in the Himalaya mountains of Asia, is the world's highest peak. Sir Edmund Hillary and Tenzing Norgay first reached the top on May 29, 1953. It is 29,028 ft (8,848 m) above sea level.

HOW ARE MOUNTAINS MADE?

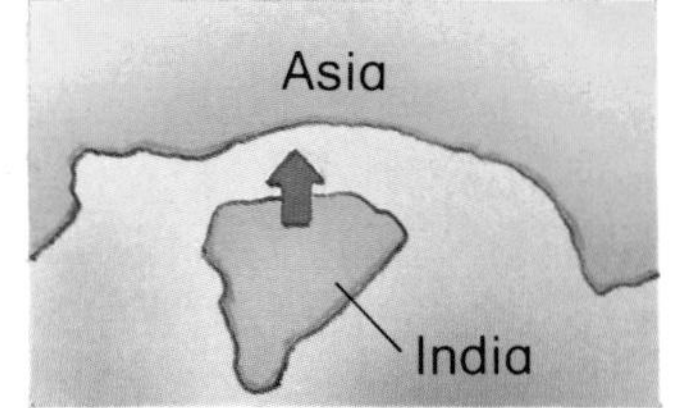

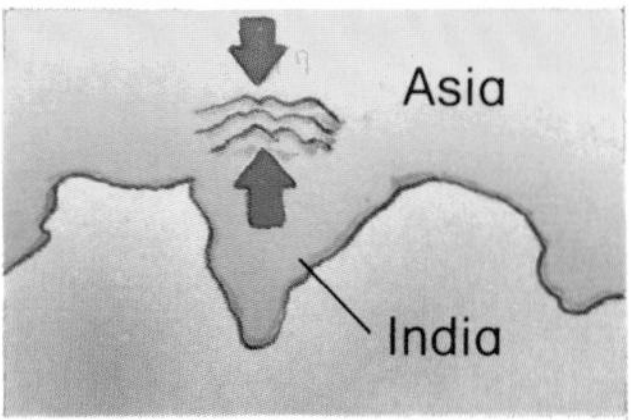

Most mountains are made when rocks are pushed upward. Some are made when volcanoes erupt. Millions of years ago, India was an island. It drifted very slowly northward and collided with Asia. The collision pushed up the rocks of the earth's crust into folds, making the mighty Himalaya mountains.

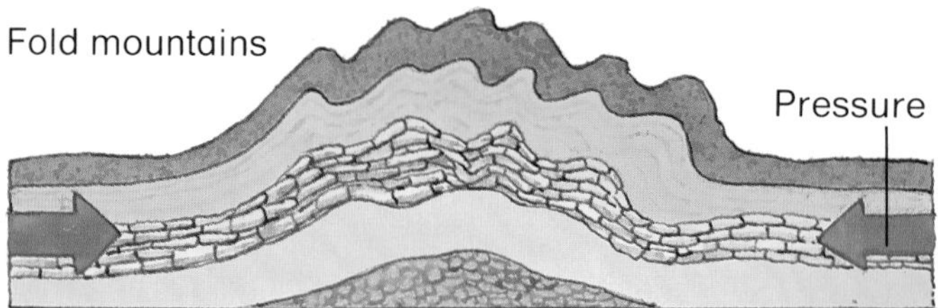

Fold mountains are made when parts of the earth's crust bump into one another. The rocks are squashed upward. Block mountains are made when blocks of rock are pushed up or down by movements within the earth's crust. The movements happen along weak spots in the crust called faults.

The map shows the earth's main mountain ranges. The world's 20 highest mountains are all in Asia, in the Himalaya-Karakoram range. All are over 26,000 ft (8,000 m) high. The highest mountain in the Americas is Aconcagua in South America at 22,830 ft (6,959 m).

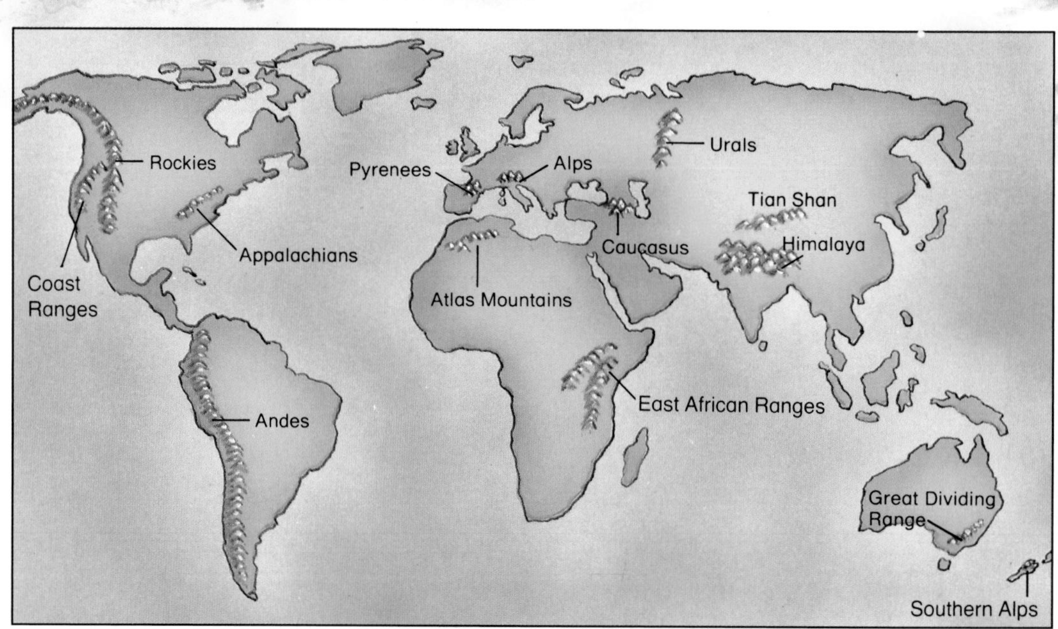

mouse and rat

The mouse and rat are rodents, or gnawing animals. Rats are larger than mice. The house mouse and brown rat spoil food and carry disease. See **rodents**.

Mozart

Wolfgang Amadeus Mozart (1756–1791) was only four years old when he began to write music. He became one of the world's greatest composers. Mozart wrote operas and music for orchestras. He died when only 35.

▼ A group of musicians in Mozart's time. Two hundred years after his death, Mozart's music is listened to and played by people all over the world.

Muhammad

Muhammad founded the religion of Islam. He was born in A.D. 570 in Mecca, in what is now Saudi Arabia. At the age of 40, Muhammad set out to tell people that there was only one true God, Allah. His enemies forced him to leave Mecca in 622. The Islamic calendar begins from this event. Muhammad died in 632, but his teachings spread rapidly. See **Islam**.

muscles see **human body**

museum

Old, precious, or interesting things are kept in a museum for people to see and study. You can see what dinosaurs were like, how machines work, and how people lived long ago.

mushrooms and toadstools

These plants are fungi. A fungus is a plant with no green chlorophyll, so it cannot make its own food. It feeds on dead matter, such as rotting wood. Mushrooms and toadstools grow best in warm, damp places. See **plants**.

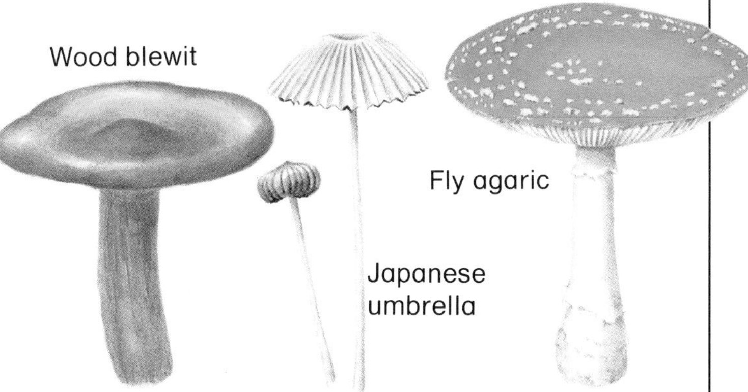

▲ Mushrooms and toadstools come in many different shapes and colors. Some are good to eat, but many are poisonous. It is safest **never** to eat wild fungi.

music

Music is made from sounds arranged in a way that is pleasant or exciting to hear. Music has a beat, called rhythm, and often a tune or melody. Music can be happy or sad, fast or slow. It can be made by musical instruments that are plucked, blown, or banged. Music can also be made by the human voice. We hear music in nature when birds sing. The notes that make up music can be long or short, loud or soft, high or low.

MUSIC

Composers (people who make up music) write it down so that others can read and play it. For each sound they use different notes, which have names from A to G. They write the notes on a "stave" of five lines. They also show how long the note should last. Many terms in music have Italian names; one example is *fortissimo* (very loud).

A quarter note equals two eighth notes, or half a half note.

A half note equals two quarter notes.

A dot after a note means it is one and a half times longer than usual.

Two eighth notes equal one quarter note.

Three eighth notes equal one and a half quarter notes.

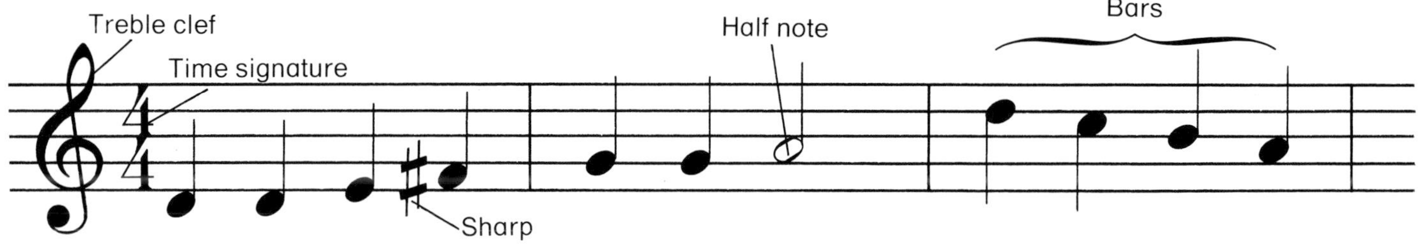

The way music is written is called notation. This shows a piece of music written down. The tune is part of the Christmas carol "Good King Wenceslas." Perhaps you can read the notes and sing them. The curly sign is the mark for the treble clef. The music is in the key of C major. The figures after the clef show that there are four quarter notes to every bar. The bar lines split the music into bars, or measures.

Music for an orchestra to play is called a score. For convenience, it is divided into parts for each instrument. All the players will have their parts on stands in front of them.

ELECTRONIC MUSIC

Most musical instruments make sounds by vibrating the air. Electronic music is made differently. The sounds are created on tape using electronics and computers. The sound from the keyboard (1) is changed into an electronic signal (2). This is passed through an amplifier and made louder (3) then played through loudspeakers (4). A synthesizer is a machine that can copy the sounds of many ordinary instruments and make its own sounds. With a synthesizer, two or three musicians can sound like an orchestra.

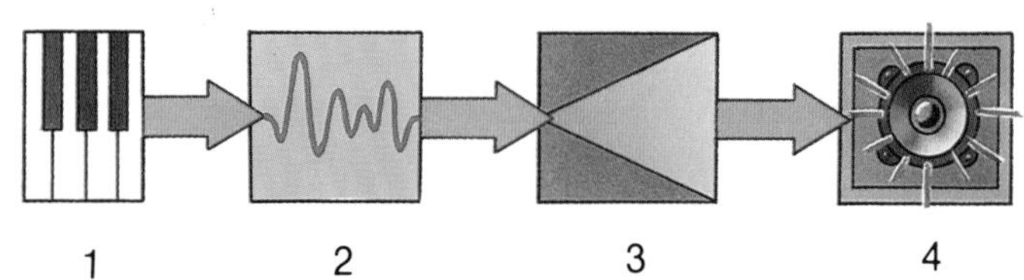

THE ORCHESTRA

The full orchestra is a large group of musicians. They are arranged like this in a half-circle in front of the conductor. The string instruments are nearest the conductor. The percussion and brass instruments are in the middle, farthest from the conductor (because they are the loudest instruments). All the musicians must be able to see the conductor, so they can follow his or her signals as they play.

Brass
Percussion
Woodwind
Brass
Second violins
Violas
Double basses
Cellos
First violins
Conductor

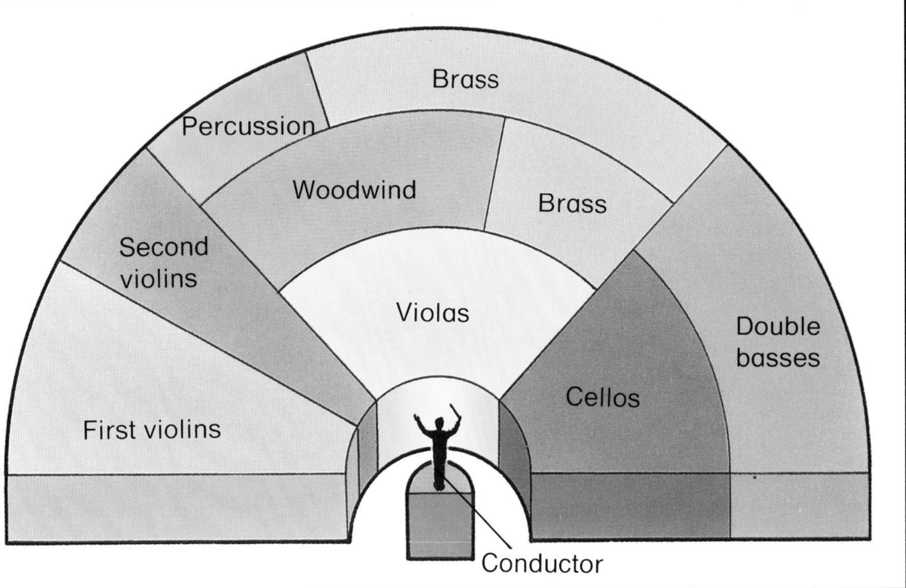

STRING INSTRUMENTS

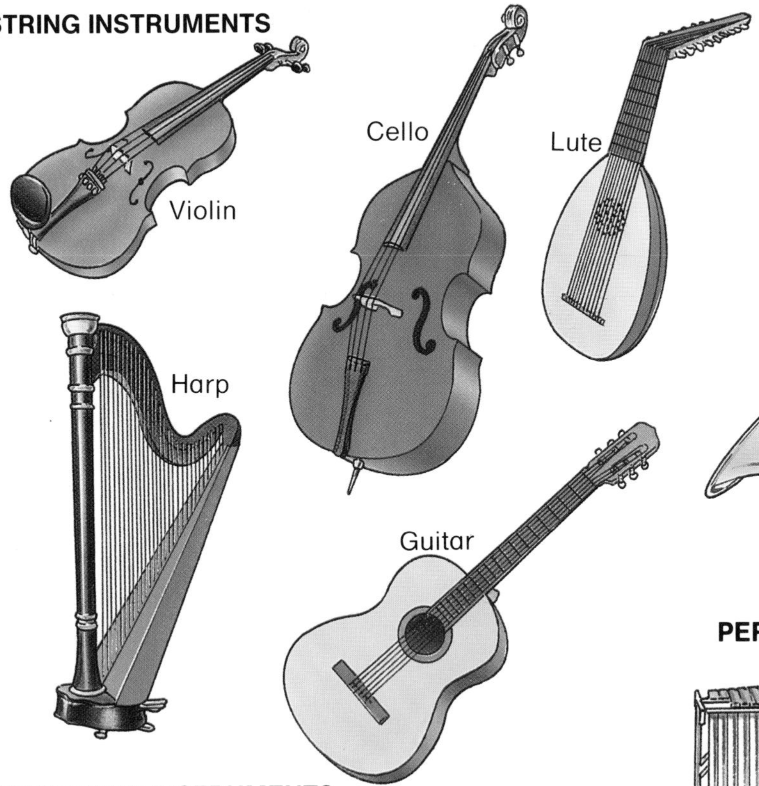

Violin
Cello
Lute
Harp
Guitar

BRASS INSTRUMENTS

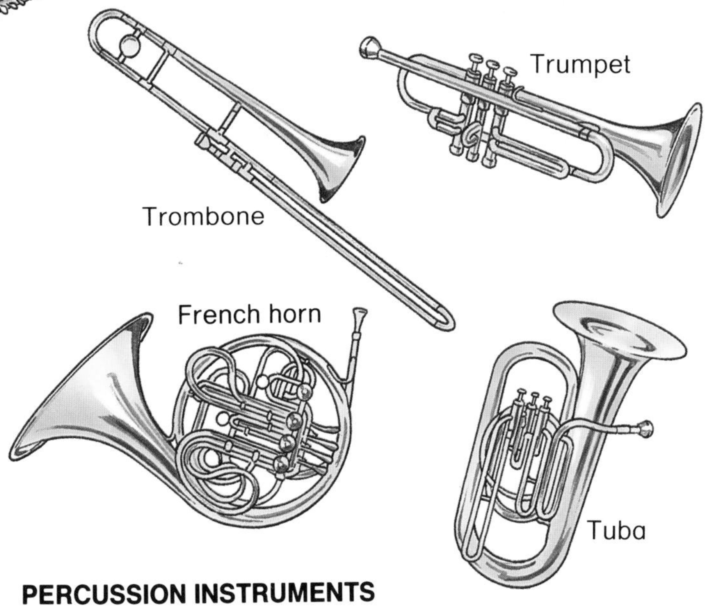

Trumpet
Trombone
French horn
Tuba

PERCUSSION INSTRUMENTS

Vibraphone
Cymbal
Kettledrum
Snare drum

WOODWIND INSTRUMENTS

Clarinet
Piccolo
Flute
Cor anglais
Bassoon

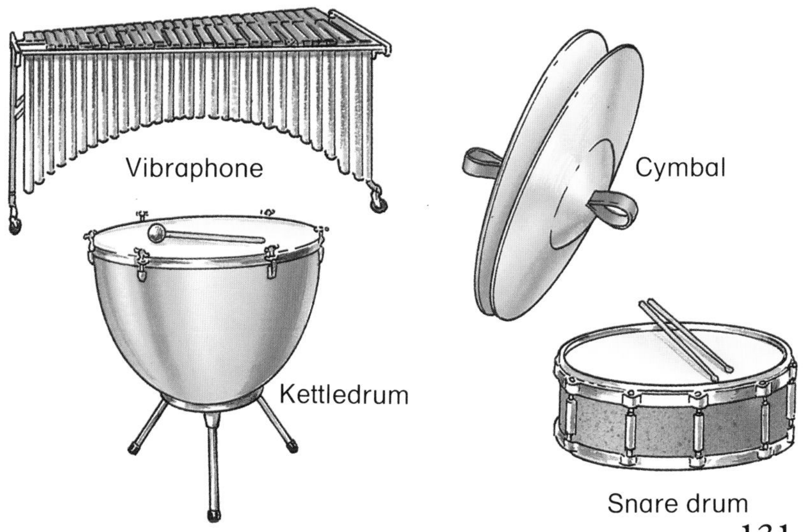

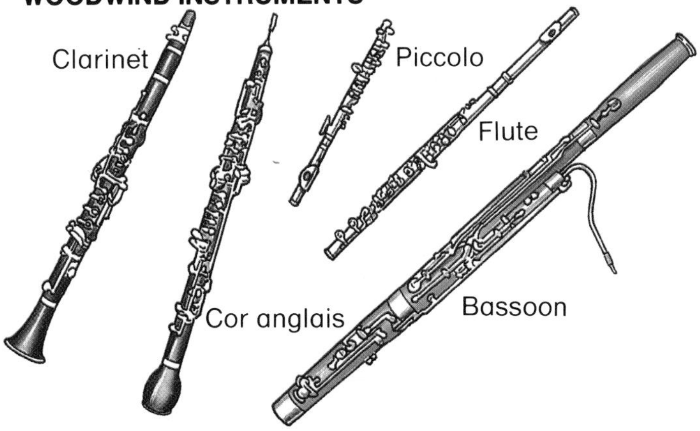

M

Muslim
A Muslim is a person who follows the religion of Islam, founded by the Prophet Muhammad. See **Islam**, **Muhammad**.

myths and legends
In ancient times people believed the world was full of gods and spirits. The sun and moon were gods. There were gods of war and thunder, of the sea, and of harvest time. People told stories, or myths, about the gods and about spirits who lived in animals, rocks, water, and plants. Many myths tell how the world was created. Others are about human heroes and their adventures in the world of the gods. The Egyptian, Greek, African, Chinese, Aztec, Indian, and Norse peoples all told myths about their gods.

A legend is a story about people who are not gods, but who often have amazing adventures. The tales of Robin Hood and King Arthur are legends. They may be based on real people, but the stories were made up later. Legends mix truth and make-believe.

▼ Demeter was the Greek goddess of farming and crops. She was pictured holding sheafs of corn. The Romans called her Ceres.

LIFE STORY

Napoleon
Napoleon Bonaparte was a great French general. He was born in Corsica in 1769 and became a soldier in the French army. He became the army's commander in 1795. He won many victories and in 1804 made himself Emperor of France. France became the strongest country in Europe, but Napoleon could not defeat the British navy. In 1812 he invaded Russia. Terrible winter weather forced him to turn back. Napoleon lost the Battle of Waterloo in 1815. He was exiled on the island of St. Helena. He died there in 1821.

N

nest

Many animals, especially birds, build nests as homes for their young. Some birds make simple nests by just scraping the ground. Others make nests with great care, using twigs, grasses, or mud. Insects such as ants make large underground nests that are really networks of burrows. The fish called a stickleback makes an underwater nest for its eggs. See **birds, insects**.

DID YOU KNOW?

The huge mud nest of the African termite, an insect, may be 20 ft (6 m) high. Inside is a maze of tunnels and rooms. The king and queen termites live in the center of the nest. Aardvarks and anteaters dig into the nests with sharp claws and lap up termites with their sticky tongues.

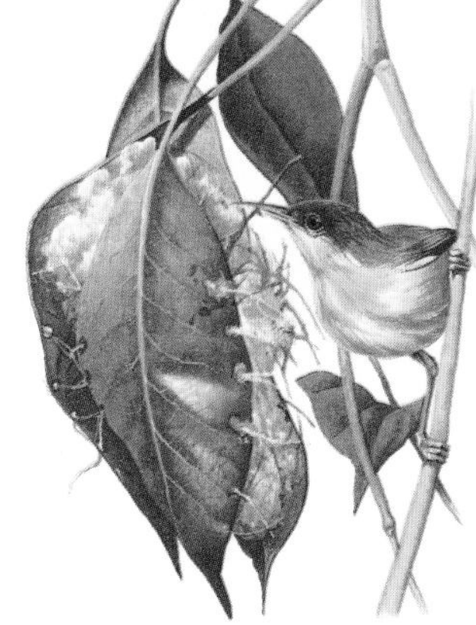

► The tailorbird of Australia uses its beak as a needle to sew leaves together for its nest. It fills the nest with grasses.

▼ European storks build big, untidy nests of sticks. Often they choose a chimney to nest on.

newspapers and magazines

In newspapers we read what is going on in the world. Some newspapers are printed every day. Most magazines are printed every week or month. Magazines may be about one subject, such as cars or sports. Editors, writers, artists, photographers, and printers all work for newspapers and magazines.

The first newspapers as we know them were published in the 1600s and 1700s. *The New York Times*, a famous newspaper, has been published since 1851. Pictures were rare in newspapers before the 1900s. See **printing**.

newt see **amphibians**

Newton

Isaac Newton (1642–1727) was a British scientist and mathematician. He was the first person to describe the laws of gravity — the force that pulls an object to earth and keeps the moon in orbit. Newton also experimented with light (showing that white light is made up of colors), and built the first reflecting telescope. See **gravity, light**.

▼ Newton used a glass prism to bend light and split it up into the band of colors called the spectrum.

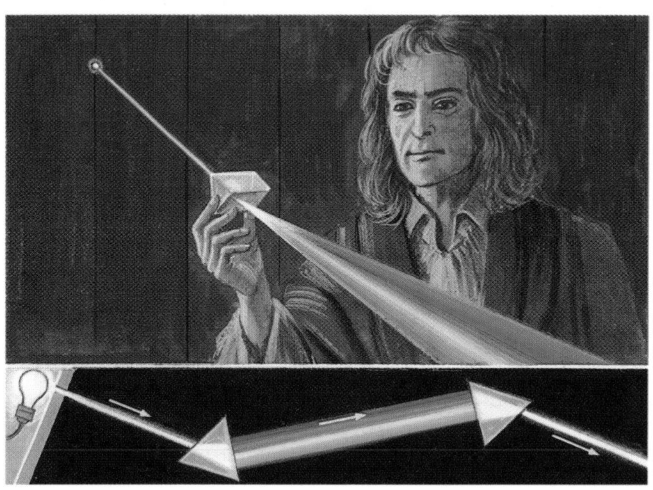

LIFE STORY

Florence Nightingale

Florence Nightingale, the founder of modern nursing, was born in 1820. She shocked her parents by becoming a nurse; nursing was not considered ladylike. Florence trained in Germany and worked in London. In 1854 the British government asked her to go and nurse soldiers wounded in the Crimean War. In the army hospital at Scutari, in Turkey, she found sick men lying on the filthy floor. There were rats everywhere, no good food, and no soap and water for washing. Florence Nightingale worked night and day to set things right. The soldiers loved her. The generals and doctors at first did not help her, but then came to admire her courage and skill. On her return home she set up a school for nursing and her ideas were copied in hospitals everywhere. She died in 1910.

Nile

The Nile is the world's longest river. It flows for 4,143 mi (6,671 km) from near the Equator in Africa to the Mediterranean Sea. It passes through Sudan and Egypt, where farmers rely on its water. Until the Aswan High Dam was built, in 1960–1970, the Nile flooded each year, spreading rich soil on farmland.

▼ Without the Nile River, Egypt's ancient civilization would not have been possible. Modern Egypt still depends on the mighty river.

North America

North America is the third-largest continent. It stretches from Alaska to the tropical forests of Central America. Two huge countries, Canada and the United States, cover most of it. High mountains include the Rocky Mountains. The Great Lakes are the world's largest freshwater lakes. There are huge cities and also areas with few people.

North America stretches from the cold Arctic to hot southern deserts and subtropical swamps. Central America is a narrow strip of land joining North and South America.

▼ A busy highway intersection. Most North Americans travel by car. There are more cars in North America than anywhere else.

NORTH AMERICA

Most people in North and Central America speak English, Spanish, or French. Many are descendants of people who came from Europe, Africa, or Asia. Others are American Indians and Eskimos. Famous natural wonders of North America include Niagara Falls and the Grand Canyon. A lot of wheat is grown on the Great Plains.

FACTS AND RECORDS

Area: 9,362,500 sq mi (24,249,000 sq km)
Number of countries: 23
Population: 427,000,000
Largest country: Canada 3,851,790 sq mi (9,976,130 sq km)
Country with most people: U.S. (249,928,000)
Largest city: Mexico City (Mexico) 20,207,000
Highest mountain: Mt. McKinley (Alaska)
Longest rivers: Mississippi–Missouri, Mackenzie

nose and smell

Your nose is the part of your body that receives smell signals. Smell is an important sense, like sight and hearing. Scents given off by flowers, food, or anything else are picked up by special cells in the nose. Other cells send messages to the brain, which recognizes what the smell is. See **human body**.

nuclear energy

Nuclear energy is set free when radioactive atoms of a substance called uranium are split. These split atoms send out great amounts of energy as heat and light. When the tiny nucleus of an atom is hit by a neutron, the nucleus

▲ In a nuclear bomb explosion, a huge amount of uncontrolled energy is released in a split second.

breaks apart and frees more neutrons to hit other atoms. This is called a chain reaction. Heat from the reaction is used to make electricity. If the reaction is not controlled there is a terrible explosion. See **atom**, **energy**.

numbers

People first learned to count by making marks. For example, ten marks meant 10. Later, people used signs to stand for numbers. These number signs are numerals, such as 1, 2, 3, and so on. Not all peoples use the same kinds of signs. The Romans wrote 28 as XXVIII. The numerals we use were invented in India and Arabia. We use numbers to do calculations. Our system for writing numbers is called the decimal system. See **mathematics**, **zero**.

nut

Nuts are the fruits of certain trees. Inside the nut is a seed, protected by the nut's tough shell. Many nuts are good to eat. Animals break open the shell to eat the seed inside. Not all nuts are eaten. Some fall to the ground, where the seed can sprout. In time, a new tree will grow.

◀ The hazelnut (left) and Brazil nut (right) are good to eat.

▶ The peanut is more like an underground pea pod than a real nut.

◀ The sweet chestnut is delicious when roasted.

▼ Walnuts have tough shells.

▶ The horse chestnut has a spiky jacket to protect the nut inside.

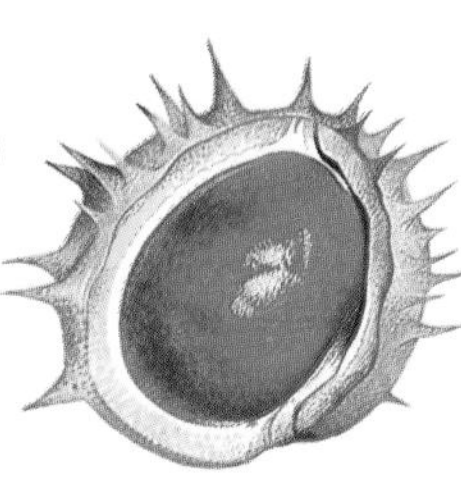

oasis

An oasis is a patch of green in a hot, dry desert. Palm trees and other plants grow there because there is water. The water comes from wells or underground streams. Travelers stop at oases to drink and rest. Around some big oases people build farms and houses. See **desert**.

▼ An oasis is like an island with water, green palm trees, and other plants amid the desert sands.

obelisk

The ancient Egyptians set up tall pillars of stone called obelisks, to mark rulers' tombs. They cut obelisks from huge blocks of granite rock. On the four sides they carved picture signs, or hieroglyphs. The top of the obelisk was pointed like a pyramid. Two obelisks, called Cleopatra's Needles, now stand in New York and London.

◀ This obelisk, called Cleopatra's Needle, stands on the Embankment in London. It was brought from Egypt in the 1900s. It is about 3,500 years old.

oceans

The surface of the earth is seven-tenths water. The large areas of water separating the seven continents are oceans. Smaller areas are seas. The water in the ocean is salty, because minerals are washed into it from rivers.

There are four oceans. The biggest and deepest is the Pacific Ocean. The other oceans are the Atlantic, Indian, and Arctic. The oceans are never still. Tides rise and fall about every 12 hours. Winds push the water into waves. Currents of cold and warm water flow below the surface. See **fish, tides and currents, waves, whale**.

OCEANS AND SEAS

The oceans were formed millions of years ago. More than nine-tenths of all the water on earth is seawater. Water from the oceans is drawn up into the atmosphere, to fall as rain. The undersea world is mostly dark and cold, for no sunlight reaches deeper than about 5,000 ft (1,500 m). Yet animals can live even at the greatest depths.

FACTS AND RECORDS

Biggest ocean: the Pacific (64 million sq mi (166 million sq km)).
Second biggest: the Atlantic is only half the size of the Pacific, with an area of 32 million sq mi (82 million sq km).
Deepest point: the Mariana Trench in the Pacific Ocean is 36,000 ft (11,000 m) deep.
Highest wave: in 1933 a wave 112 ft (34 m) high was recorded in a storm.

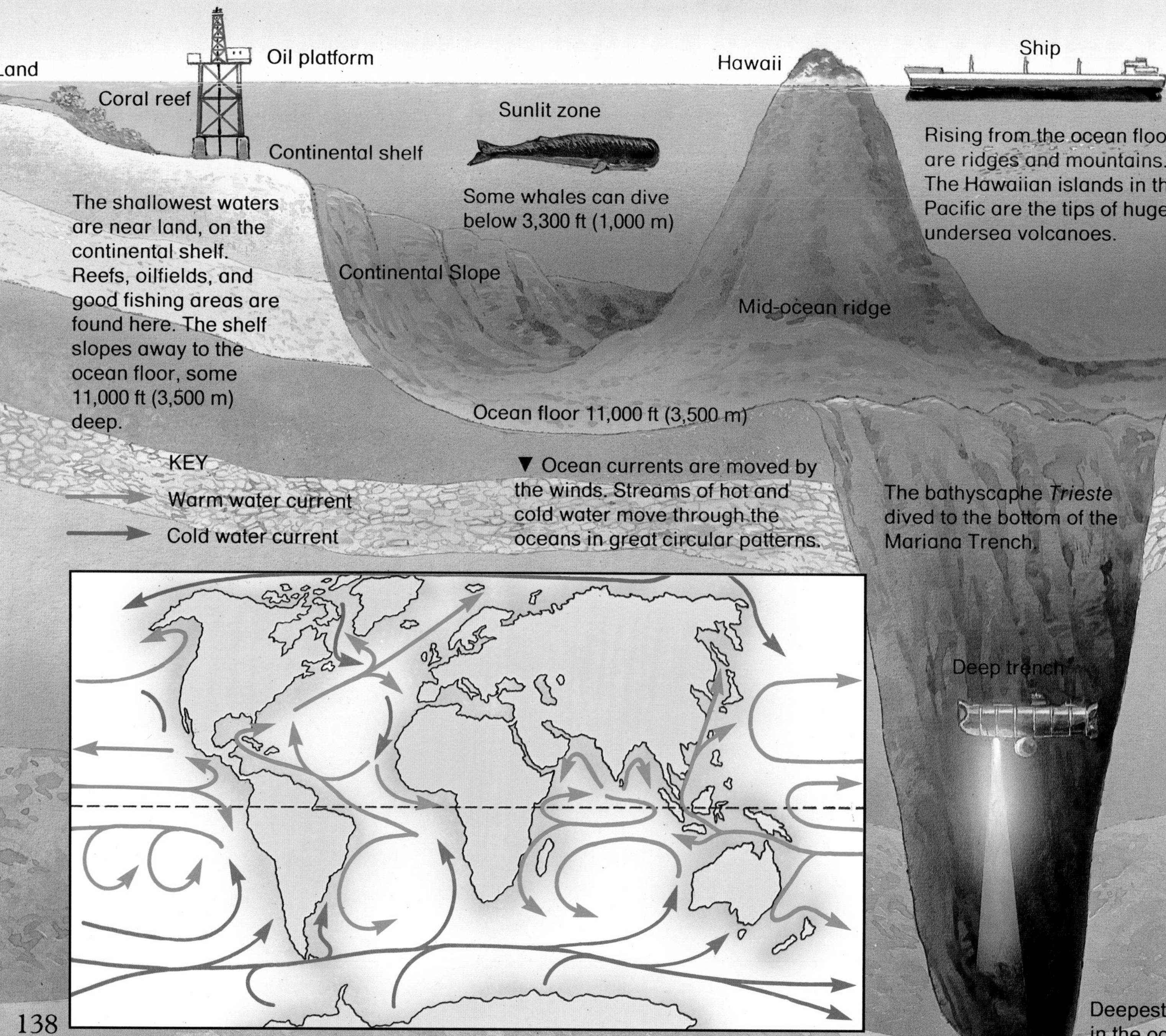

Rising from the ocean floor are ridges and mountains. The Hawaiian islands in the Pacific are the tips of huge undersea volcanoes.

The shallowest waters are near land, on the continental shelf. Reefs, oilfields, and good fishing areas are found here. The shelf slopes away to the ocean floor, some 11,000 ft (3,500 m) deep.

▼ Ocean currents are moved by the winds. Streams of hot and cold water move through the oceans in great circular patterns.

The bathyscaphe *Trieste* dived to the bottom of the Mariana Trench.

octopus and squid

The octopus and squid are mollusks that live in the ocean. The octopus is quite intelligent. To catch prey, such as crabs, these animals use suckers on their long arms, or tentacles. Octopuses have eight arms. Squid have ten arms. When frightened, an octopus can change color and shoot out a cloud of ink. It escapes quickly by squirting water from a tube in its body.

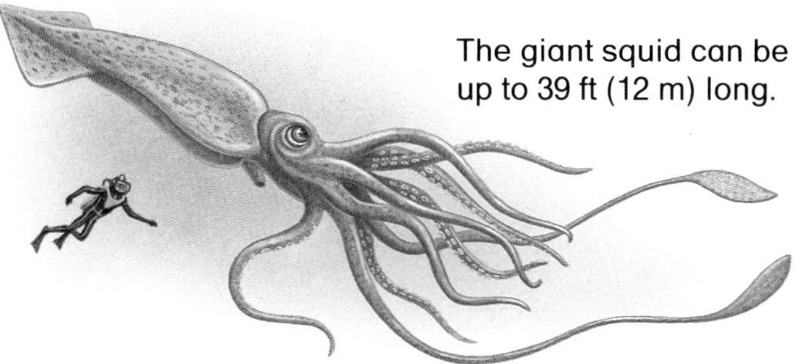

The giant squid can be up to 39 ft (12 m) long.

oil

The oil we use for cooking, such as olive oil, comes from plants. The oil we use in machines and burn as fuel comes from under the ground. It was formed millions of years ago from the remains of dead plants and animals. To reach the layers of oil, engineers drill deep into the rock. When they find oil, it gushes out or is pumped to the surface. The oil is purified, or refined, and used to make gasoline, or plastics, and detergent. See **minerals and mining**, **plastics**.

► To reach the oil, a hole is drilled through the rock layers. The drill bit (below) has wheels with sharp teeth.

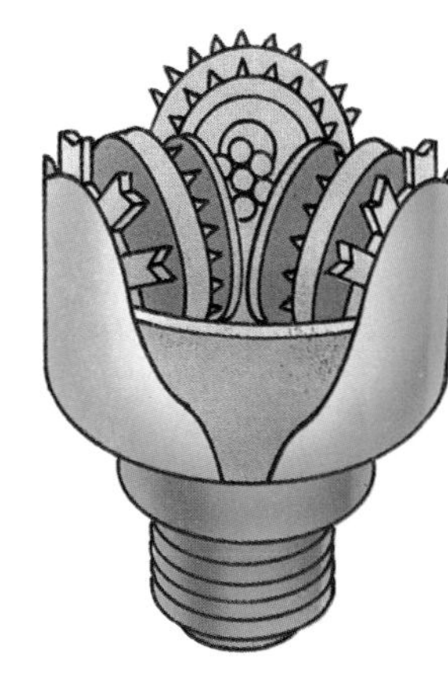

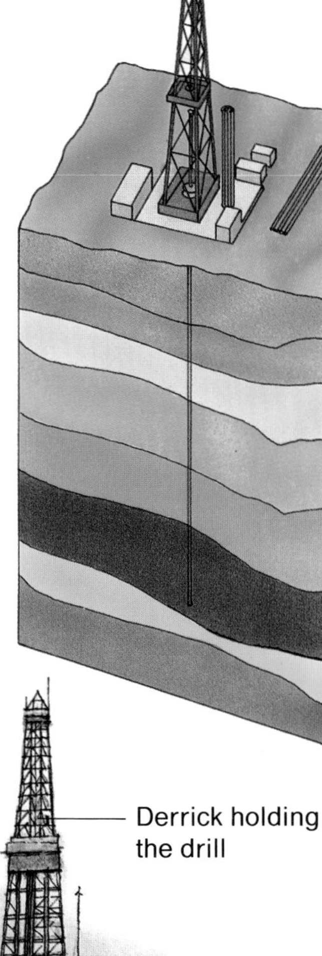

▼ Drilling for undersea oil. Some oil rigs float. Others are huge platforms that stand on the seabed.

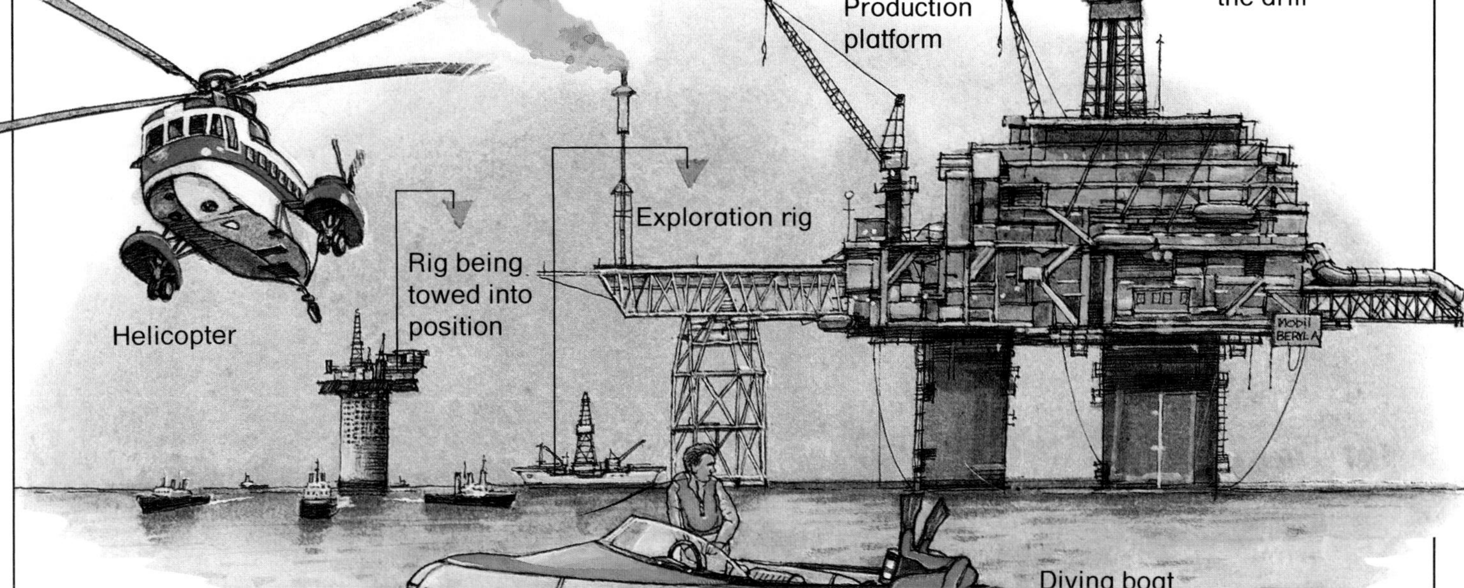

O

Olympics
The first Olympic games were held in Greece in 776 B.C. Poets as well as athletes took part. The modern Olympics have been held every four years (except during the two World Wars) since 1896. See **sports**.

opera
An opera is a play with music. The actors sing most of their words. The first operas were performed in Italy in the 1600s. Some famous composers of opera are Mozart, Verdi, and Wagner.

orchestra
An orchestra is a collection of musicians playing different instruments. It has four main groups: strings, woodwinds, brass, and percussion. A band is a small orchestra. See **music**.

ostrich
The biggest bird, the ostrich, lives in Africa. It has wings but cannot fly. It can run as fast as a galloping horse. The emu and the rhea are ostrich-like birds. See **birds**.

otter
The otter is a mammal that is at home in water. It is a relative of the weasel. River otters live in fresh water and catch fish. Sea otters live in the ocean and feed mostly on shellfish.

▲ The otter has webbed feet. Its tail acts as a rudder.

▲ The snowy owl keeps her chicks safe and warm underneath her feathers.

owl
Owls are birds of prey that hunt by night. They have large front-facing eyes to spot mice, birds, and frogs in the darkness. They can also hear the slightest rustling sound. Owls fly silently on broad wings. The biggest owl is the great gray owl of North America.

oxygen
Oxygen is a gas that makes up roughly one-fifth of the air. There is also oxygen in water and in rocks. Animals must have oxygen to live. We take in oxygen when we breathe. Fish take in oxygen from the water. Plants give off oxygen into the air. See **air, breathing, plants**.

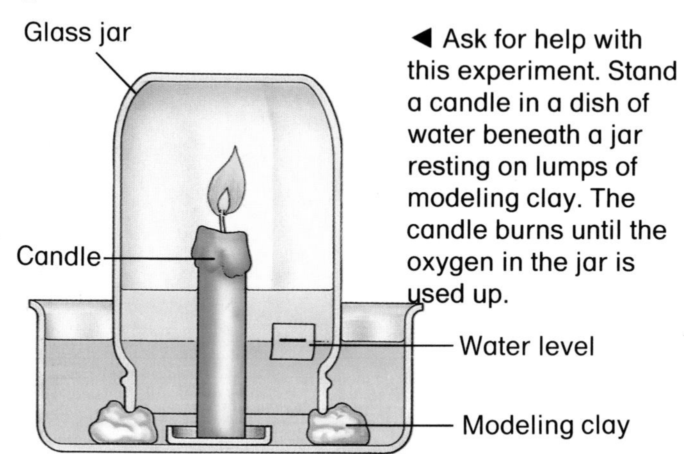

◀ Ask for help with this experiment. Stand a candle in a dish of water beneath a jar resting on lumps of modeling clay. The candle burns until the oxygen in the jar is used up.

P

FIND OUT FOR YOURSELF

Paints and inks are made from pigments. They don't mix the same way the colors of light do. Try mixing colored paints to see what happens. What color do you get when you mix yellow and blue paints? Or blue and red? What happens when you mix yellow, blue, and red paints together? Yellow, red, and blue are called the primary colors of paint.

Pacific Ocean see **oceans and seas**

painting and drawing

You can make pictures in lots of ways. You can use paints or draw with pens, pencils, or crayons.

The first artists were Stone Age painters who drew pictures of animals on cave walls. There are many different kinds of painting. A portrait is a picture of a person. A landscape is a picture of a scene in town or country. A still life is a picture of objects. Some artists try to show things as they look. Others use shapes and colors in "abstract" pictures. See **art**.

▼ You can make pictures in lots of ways, using paints or drawing with crayons. Shown below are some materials you can use.

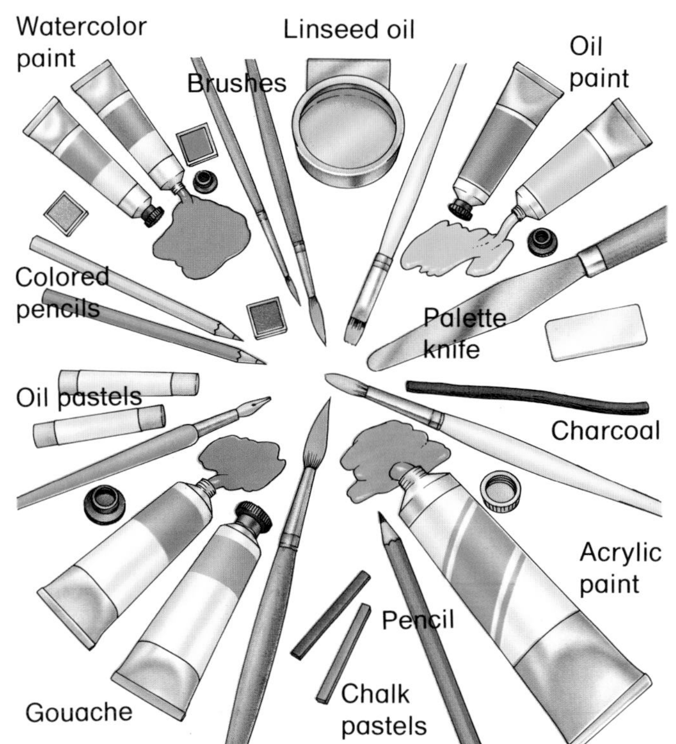

panda

There are two animals called pandas. The giant panda lives in China. It looks like a black and white bear, but it is not a bear. It eats mainly bamboo shoots. The smaller lesser panda of Asia has a bushy tail.

▼ The giant panda lives in China. It eats the leaves of the bamboo.

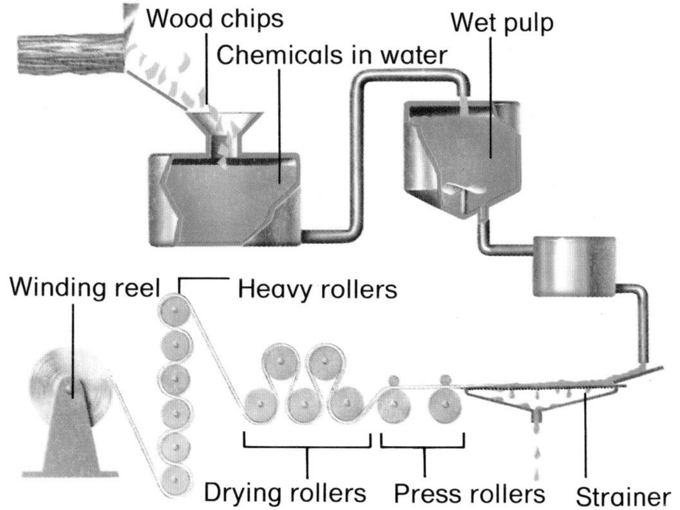

▲ To make paper, wood chips are mashed to pulp in water and chemicals. The pulp is rolled out and dried.

paper

Before paper was invented, people wrote on clay tablets or animal skins. The Egyptians wrote on a kind of paper made from papyrus reed. This plant's name gives us our word "paper." Most of the paper we use is made from wood mashed up with water, rolled, and dried.

parrot

Parrots are brightly colored birds of warm forests. They eat nuts and fruit, using their strong beaks and claws as "tools." Parakeets, cockatoos, and macaws are examples of parrots. Some pet parrots and parakeets "talk" by copying the sounds of words.

◀ A Cuban parrot. Parrots can fly, but also climb in trees. They hold on to branches with their beaks. They can also hold food in their strong claws.

LIFE STORY

Pasteur

Louis Pasteur (1822–1895) was a French scientist, who showed that diseases were caused by bacteria. By the time he was 26 he was a famous chemist. He became interested in what causes disease and why food goes bad. He found that wine turns bitter when germs get into it. Heat kills the germs. Pasteur tried the same method to keep milk from going bad. Today, we call this process "pasteurization," after him.

Pasteur also proved that animals and people could become immune to (protected against) certain diseases after vaccination with a weak form of the disease. He made a vaccine to protect sheep against the disease anthrax. In 1885 he used a vaccine to save the life of a boy bitten by a dog infected with the dangerous disease rabies. See **bacteria**, **medicine**.

penguin
The penguin is a swimming bird that cannot fly. It uses its wings like flippers. On land, penguins waddle around upright, or slide on their stomachs. They live south of the equator. See **birds**.

▼ Emperor penguins live in the icy Antarctic. The chick's thick layer of feathers keeps it warm.

pens and pencils
The first pens were hollow reeds; then birds' feathers, called quills, were used. Fountain pens were invented in the 1880s, ballpoints in the 1940s. Pencils have been used since the 1500s.

photography
Photography is the making of pictures with light. It was invented in the early 1800s. Joseph Niepce of France took the first photograph in 1826. When you push a camera's shutter button, the shutter opens to let light into the camera through the lens. Inside the camera is a plastic film coated with light-sensitive chemicals. The light makes an image on the film. The image on the film is "negative," so dark areas look light and light areas look dark. This image

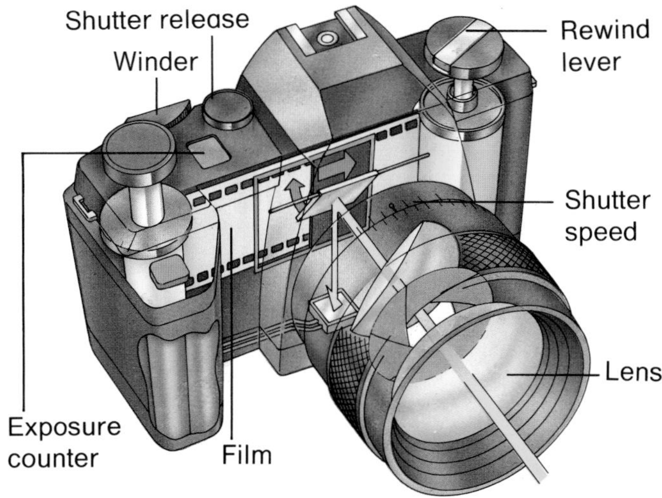

▲ Light enters the camera through the lens and exposes the film inside.

becomes "positive" when the picture is developed, by being treated with other chemicals. The picture can even be developed inside the camera. See **camera, light, television and video**.

physics see **science**

pig
The farm pig is a relative of the wild boar. Male pigs are called boars. Females are sows. From pigs we get bacon, ham, and pork. Wild pigs live in Africa, Asia, and South America.

planet see **solar system**

plants
There are more than 375,000 kinds of plants. Scientists believe many more have yet to be found. The biggest (most massive) living thing, the giant sequoia, is a plant. Other plants are so small you need a microscope to see them. The oldest living plants are lichens and bristlecone pine trees. Unlike animals, plants cannot move far by themselves, but they can make their own food.

PLANTS

Without plants, animals could not live on the earth. Plants are the only living things that can make their own food, and in turn they provide food for animals. By a process called photosynthesis, plants use the energy from sunlight to build new living matter.

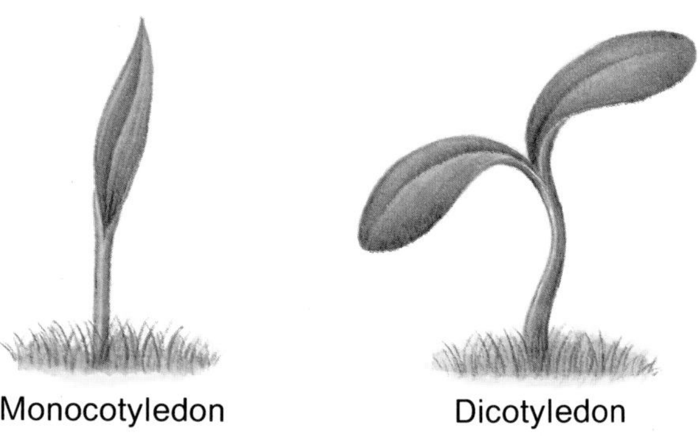

More than half of the world's plants are flowering plants. One group, called monocotyledons, has seeds that sprout a single leaf. The other group, called dicotyledons, has seeds that send out two leaves.

HOW PLANTS FEED AND GROW

Plants make their own food by a process called photosynthesis. This happens mainly in a plant's leaves. The leaves take in carbon dioxide gas from the air. They give off oxygen and water. When sunlight strikes the green chemical chlorophyll in the leaves, food is made. It is carried to all parts of the plant through the stem.

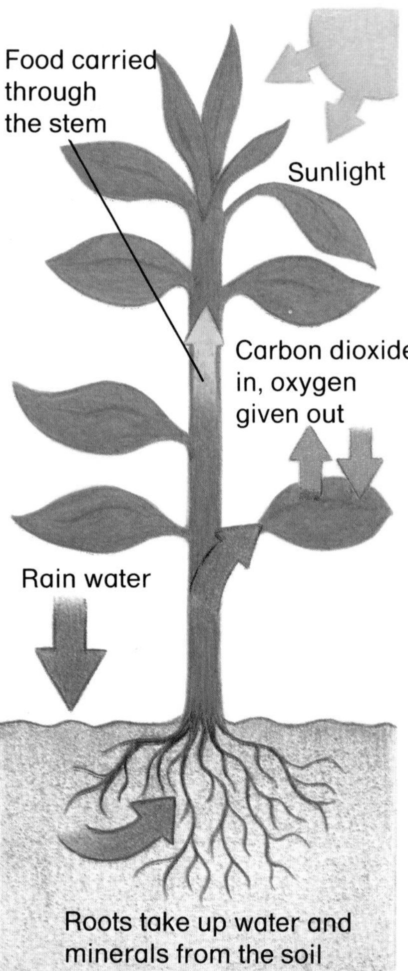

THE PLANT KINGDOM

The study of plants is called botany. Botanists have classed plants into groups, mainly by the way they are built and by the way they reproduce. The groups range from tiny algae, which do not have roots, stems, or leaves, to the so-called higher plants, known as angiosperms, which include most garden flowers, shrubs, and flowering trees.

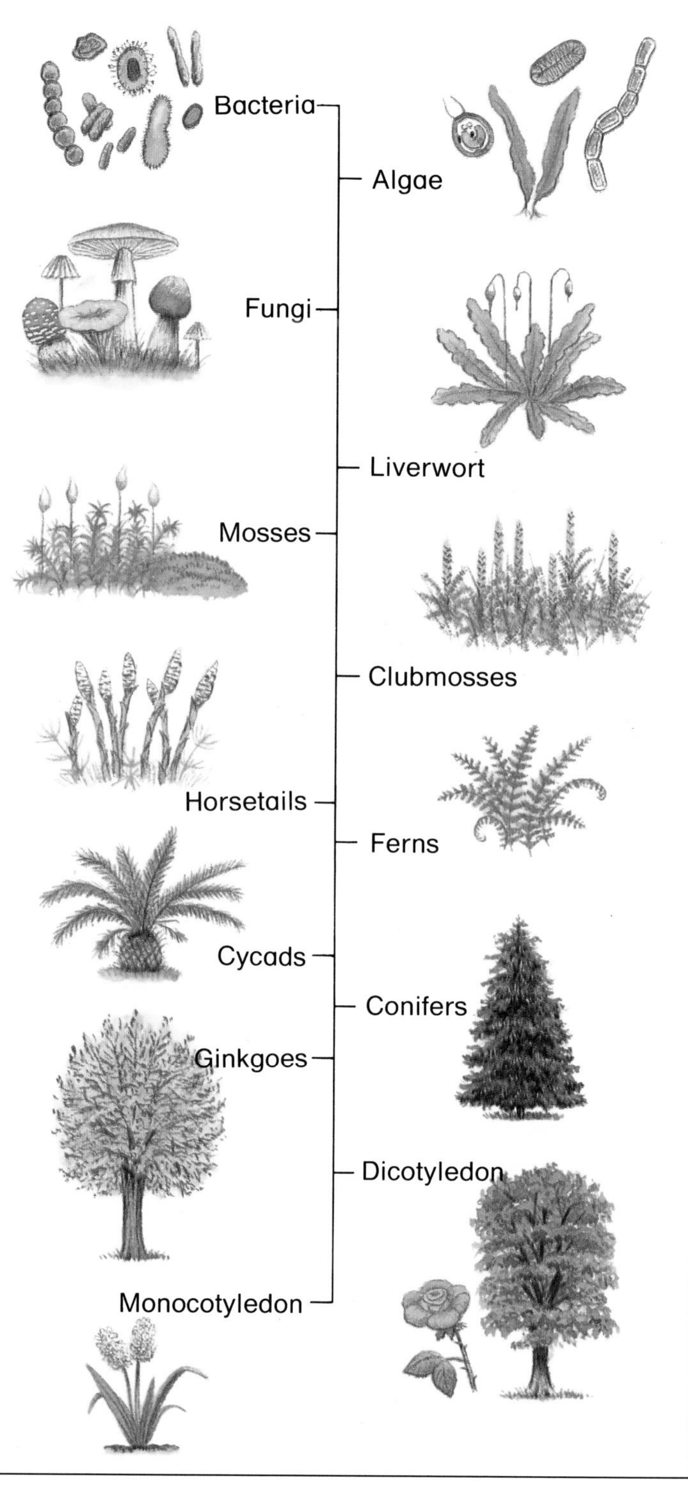

SOME STRANGE PLANTS

▲ The largest flower belongs to the rafflesia. This plant grows in Southeast Asia. Its flower measures a yard across.

▲ Fungi cannot make their own food. They feed on other plants, living or dead.

▲ Some plants trap insects for extra food. The Venus's flytrap, above, catches flies in its "jaws." The pitcher plant (right) looks like a pitcher. Insects fall to the bottom, where they are digested.

▼ The oldest trees are bristlecone pines, which grow in the southwest of the United States. Some are over 4,500 years old. Some Antarctic lichens are probably twice as old. Trees grow in a variety of shapes. The tallest tree alive is a giant redwood in California. It is 360 ft (110 m) tall.

P

plastics

Plastics are useful because they can be shaped easily. The word "plastic" means "can be shaped." Plastics can be solid or liquid and can look like glass or metal. They can be made into thin threads and woven into textiles. They can be clear or any color. All plastics belong to a family of chemicals called polymers. Plastics are made from chemicals found in oil. Some plastics are very hard. Others are soft. Some plastics melt when heated and harden again when cooled. Others do not melt at all.

▲ Bakelite was an early plastic. It was invented in 1908 and used for many household objects.

plays see **drama**

poetry

Stories told as poetry are easy to remember. The oldest stories we know were first sung as poems. The words of a poem are arranged to a musical beat or rhythm. Some poetry rhymes; this means that words at the end of lines sound similar, like "light" and "sight."

police

In all countries people live by rules or laws. The police make sure that everyone obeys these laws. Police prevent crimes, such as stealing. They control traffic on the roads and watch out for dangerous drivers. They also keep order when there are big crowds of people. Most police wear uniforms. Detectives are police who investigate crimes and try to catch criminals. They often wear ordinary clothes. In some countries, secret police arrest anyone who opposes the government.

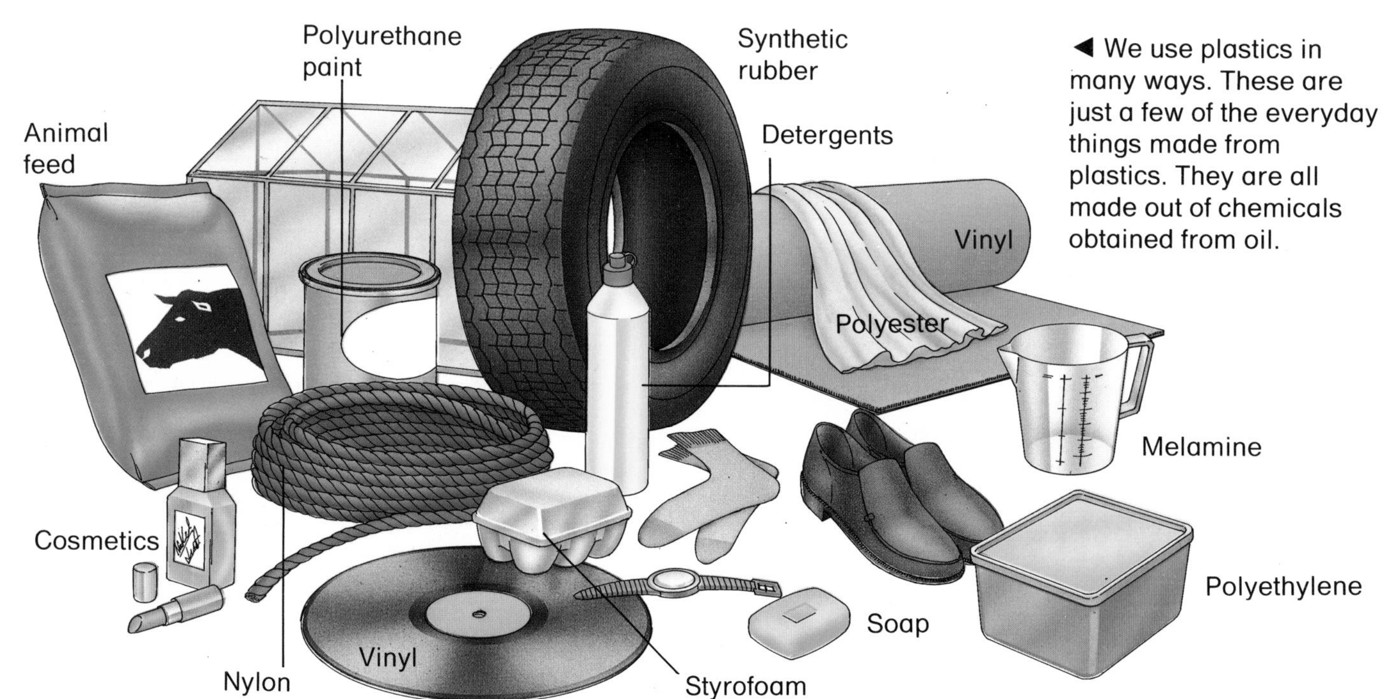

◄ We use plastics in many ways. These are just a few of the everyday things made from plastics. They are all made out of chemicals obtained from oil.

pollution
Every day people throw away lots of garbage. Much of this stays wherever it is dumped. Garbage that does not rot and cannot be used again causes pollution. Factories pour away harmful chemicals that can make soil and rivers unsafe for people, animals, and plants. Car engines puff out poisonous gases. To care for the earth, we must stop polluting it. See **conservation**.

porcupine
Few animals have better protection than the porcupine. It is covered in long spines, or quills. Porcupines are rodents. Some live in Asia and Africa. The American porcupine climbs trees.

pottery
Pottery is made from clay. The clay is shaped while wet. It is put into an oven called a kiln, and heated to dry and harden it. Earthenware pottery is made at low heat. Fine porcelain, or china, is made at high heat. People first made pottery about 10,000 years ago. Some pottery is made by hand, using a spinning wheel to shape the wet clay. Most of the plates, cups, and dishes we buy are made in pottery factories.

DID YOU KNOW?

◀ The first farmers made the first pots. They needed waterproof containers to store grain in. This pot was made in Turkey nearly 8,000 years ago.

▶ This pot was found in Turkey, near the ruins of the ancient city of Çatal Hüyük.

▼ The Chinese learned to make fine decorated porcelain over 1,000 years ago.

prehistoric animals
The first animals lived in the oceans over 600 million years ago. They were primitive single-celled animals. Over millions of years, crablike animals, shellfish, and fishes appeared. About 350 million years ago insects began to live on dry land. Some fishes crawled out of the water. These were the first amphibians. Then came the age of reptiles. Dinosaurs ruled the world until they mysteriously died out about 65 million years ago. Mammals took their places. We know about prehistoric animals from their fossils. See **evolution**, **fossil**.

PREHISTORIC ANIMALS

Reptiles called dinosaurs roamed the earth about 200 million years ago. Dinosaurs died out about 65 million years ago. Some dinosaurs, like the huge Apatosaurus, were plant-eaters. Others were fierce flesh-eaters.

Corythosaurus was a duck-billed dinosaur.

Hypsilophodon used its tail to balance as it ran.

Tyrannosaurus was a powerful hunter.

Triceratops had bony armor for defense.

THE FIRST AMPHIBIANS

About 400 million years ago, some fish crawled out of the water onto land. These were the first amphibians. Very gradually, the paddles they had used for swimming developed into legs for walking.

THE FIRST MAMMALS

The first mammals were rat-like animals. When the dinosaurs died out, the mammals took over. The animals shown here are extinct too.

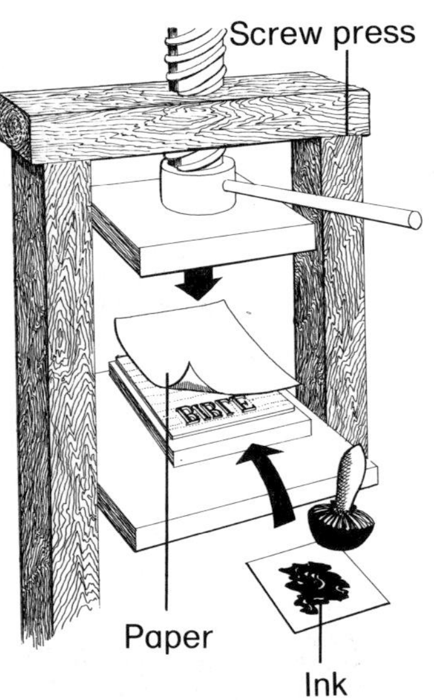

◀ An early printing press, like that invented by Gutenberg. Sheets of paper were placed over pages of inked letters, or type. A screw press, worked by hand, squeezed the paper against the inked page.

printing

Nowadays, printing uses machines, computers, and lasers. Early printing was done by hand, using inked blocks. Johannes Gutenberg invented printing with type (movable metal letters) about 1440. See **communication**.

puppet

A puppet is a doll that moves. A glove puppet is worked by hand. Marionettes are puppets with strings.

pyramid

People in ancient Egypt and Central America built pyramids. These huge buildings were used as tombs or temples. See **Egypt**.

▼ A pyramid built by the Aztecs of Central America.

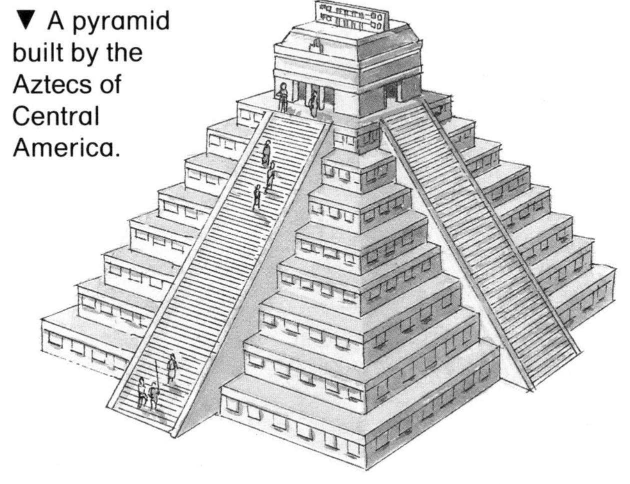

Setting the explosives

Blasting the rock

Scooping up the pieces

quarry

A quarry is a hole in the ground from which rock is dug out. Workers drill holes and set explosives to blast away the rock. Huge diggers scoop it up.

quartz

Quartz is a hard mineral. It may be clear or colored. Many rocks, such as sandstone, are made of quartz. So is sand itself.

▼ Quartz crystals are glassy but don't break easily. Each crystal has six faces and pyramid-shaped ends.

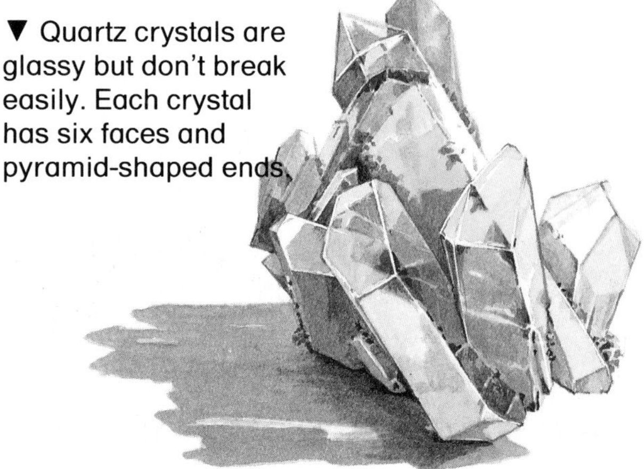

rabbits and hares
Rabbits eat grass, move by hopping, and live underground in burrows. A group of burrows is called a warren. Hares are bigger and have longer legs and ears. See **animals**.

raccoon
The raccoon is a North American mammal. It lives in woods and climbs trees, but also comes into towns. Raccoons eat almost anything, such as birds' eggs and small animals.

► The raccoon is a common North American animal. It climbs well and often makes its home inside a hollow tree.

radar
When a beam of radio waves hits an object, such as a plane in the sky, it bounces back like an echo. The echo shows as a light "blip" on a screen, showing where the plane is. Radar was invented in the 1930s. Ships and planes use radar for navigation. See **airport**.

radio
Voices and music that you hear on the radio travel through the air as radio waves. The sounds in a studio are changed into electrical signals by a microphone. The signals are carried by radio waves. Inside the radio set, the signals are turned back into sounds by a loudspeaker. See **electronics**, **Marconi**.

railroads
Railroad trains are good for moving heavy loads quickly. Some cities have tunnels with underground trains, called subways. Monorail trains travel on a single rail. The railroad age began in 1825 when the first steam passenger railroad opened in England. Railroads were built all over the world. America was crossed by rail tracks in 1869.

The first trains were pulled by steam locomotives. Today, electric and diesel trains are used. Electric trains take current from overhead wires or from the track. Diesel-electric trains have motors to make their own electricity.

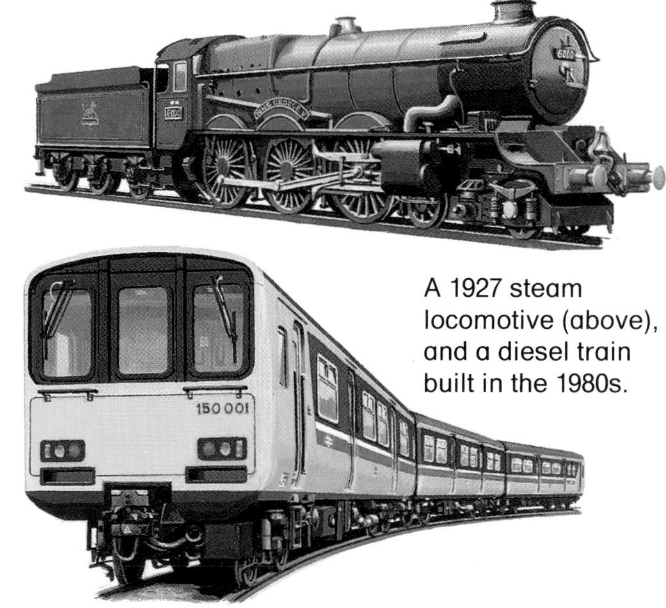

A 1927 steam locomotive (above), and a diesel train built in the 1980s.

R

rain see **cloud, water, weather**

recording
To make a record, sound must be turned into electronic signals by a microphone. These signals can be stored on a record, a tape, or a compact disk. To play back the recording, the electrical signals are turned back into sounds we can hear. This is done with an amplifier, which makes the sounds strong enough to vibrate a loudspeaker. See **sound, television and video.**

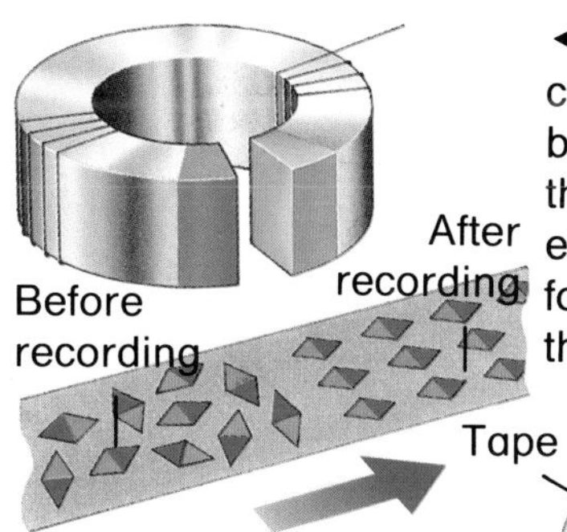

◀ Recording tape is coated with particles that become magnetized as the tape passes an electromagnet. They form a pattern like that of the sound waves.

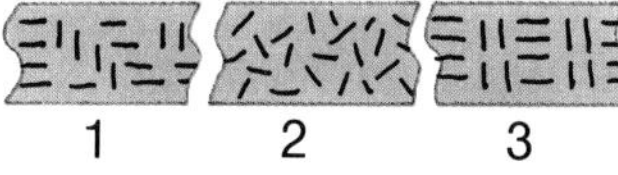

▶ An old recording (1) is wiped clean by the erase head (2). The playback head picks up the sounds of a new recording (3).

Red Cross
This international aid organization started in 1863. It helps sick and hungry people, especially victims of famine or war. Muslim countries have an organization called the Red Crescent.

refrigeration
Inside a refrigerator are pipes filled with a gas. The gas is heated. When it cools it becomes a liquid. As the liquid passes through the pipes it absorbs heat and becomes a gas again. Each time this cycle occurs the refrigerator gets colder and keeps food inside it fresh.

religion
A religion is a belief and a way of life. People who follow a religion believe in a god or gods with powers greater than those of humans. Religion sets out rules for life. It may involve saying prayers and going to worship in a building such as a church, mosque, or temple. The world's most famous religions began in Asia. See **Christianity, Hinduism, Islam, Judaism.**

▼ Shown below are symbols of six world religions. Top: (1) the Hindu goddess Kali, (2) the Jewish candelabrum, or menorah, (3) a Shinto temple. Bottom: (4) the Christian cross, (5) the Islamic crescent moon, (6) a statue of Buddha.

Renaissance
From the 1300s Europeans began to rediscover the learning of ancient Greece and Rome. Much of this knowledge was ignored during the Middle Ages. The Renaissance, or "rebirth," was an exciting age. Artists such as Leonardo da Vinci and Michelangelo made great paintings and sculptures. Scientists such as Copernicus and Galileo had new ideas about the universe. Explorers such as Columbus visited lands Europeans had never seen. The invention of printing spread this new knowledge.

REPTILES

Alligators, snakes, turtles, and lizards are all reptiles. They are "cold-blooded" animals, which means their blood is the same temperature as the surrounding air. Most live on land in warm countries. Some, such as turtles and sea snakes, live in the ocean. When the air is cold, reptiles become slow-moving. Many reptiles sleep through the winter.

DID YOU KNOW?

Some lizards have no legs. The slowworm has the long slender body of a snake, but it is actually a legless lizard.

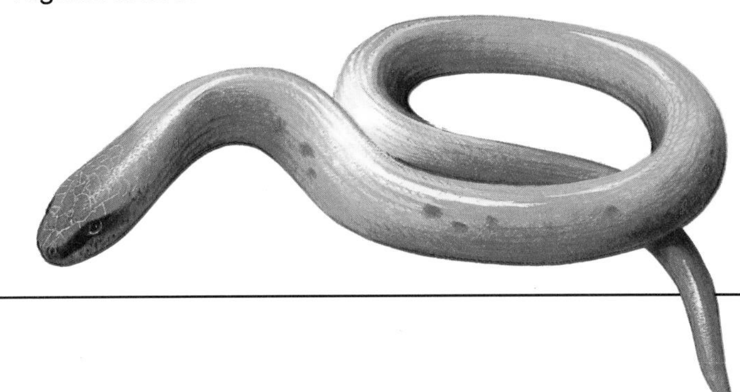

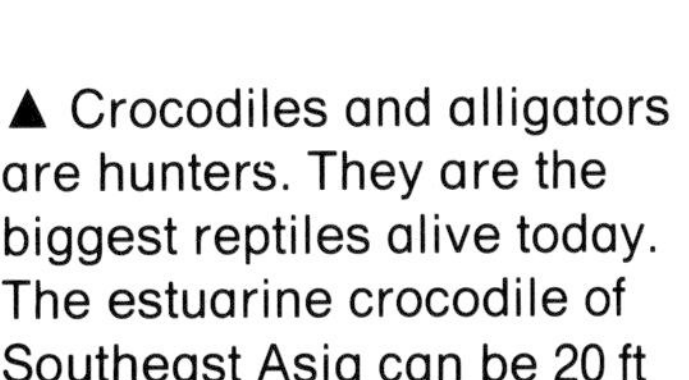

▲ Crocodiles and alligators are hunters. They are the biggest reptiles alive today. The estuarine crocodile of Southeast Asia can be 20 ft (6 m) from nose to tail.

▼ Reptiles have scaly skins. Many live in deserts and most lay eggs. Some, like the gaboon viper, have poisonous bites.

▲ A baby turtle, above, hatches from its soft-shelled egg. It will spend its life in the sea. Tortoises, below, live on dry land.

The komodo dragon is the biggest lizard.

The chameleon shoots out its tongue to catch insects.

The gila monster is poisonous.

Frilled lizard

Tortoises have shells.

Gaboon viper

R

revolution

A revolution is a "turn around." When a country has a revolution, its government is changed, sometimes by violence. New laws replace old ones. Famous revolutions took place in America in 1776, in France in 1789, and in Russia in 1917. See **Industrial Revolution**.

rhinoceros

The rhinoceros is the second-biggest land animal, after the elephant. Rhinos live in Africa and Asia. Only a few are left. Hunters kill rhinos for their horns, used in medicine in the Far East.

An African white rhino

rice

People all over the world eat rice. It is a cereal and grows best in warm, wet lands. Young rice plants are grown in flooded fields. The water is drained away when the rice is harvested. See **food**.

▼ In Asia, rice is the most important grain crop. The fields, called paddies, are flooded because the rice seedlings must have plenty of water.

▲ Rotterdam in the Netherlands is Europe's busiest port. It stands on the Maas River, which is a mouth of the Rhine River.

rivers

Many rivers start from underground springs on hillsides. The water rushes downhill, carrying stones that cut a deep, wide riverbed. In lowlands the river flows slowly. A river that joins a bigger river is called a tributary. Rivers flow to the ocean, and their fresh water mixes with salt water in the estuary, or river mouth.

roads

The best roads of ancient times were built by the Romans. They were straight and paved with flat stones. Most other roads were dirt tracks made by travelers' feet and cart wheels. Modern roads have layers of stone, cement, and tar. The first highways were built in Italy in the 1920s.

robot

Robots are machines that can work on their own. Some robots have mechanical arms and hands, worked by motors. Computers control robots in factories. The robots do the same tasks over and over again without ever getting tired or making mistakes. Some robots move around on wheels or legs. They can even find their way through a maze.

TV and film robots, like the Dalek from the TV series *Dr. Who* (right) are not real robots. Most are models worked by people. A real robot (below) is worked by electric motors and controlled by a computer "brain." Its arm has joints that can move like a human arm.

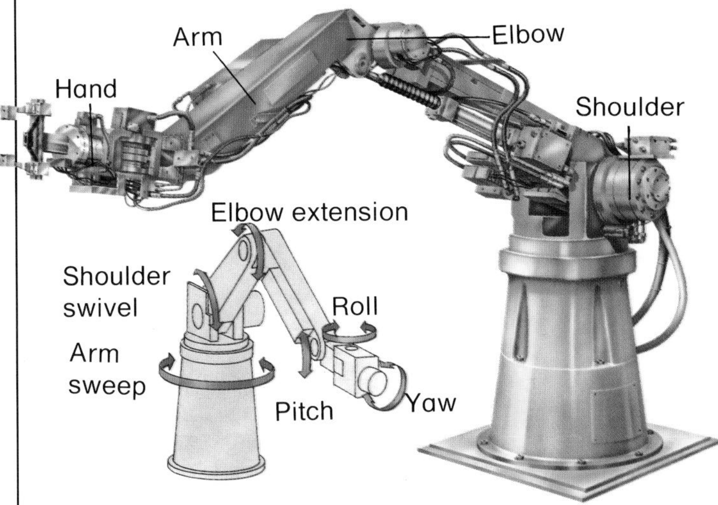

rocket

The rocket engine works well in space. Unlike a jet engine, a rocket needs no air. Its fuel contains oxygen to make the fuel burn. Gunpowder rockets were invented in about A.D. 1000 in China. The first big rocket was the German V2 of World War II. It was the first guided missile. Rockets are used as weapons, to carry bombs, and to launch satellites and other spacecraft. See **space flight**.

Rocky Mountains

The Rocky Mountains stretch over 3,000 mi (4,800 km) in the western part of North America. The tallest peaks are over 14,000 ft (4,270 m) high. See **North America**.

rodents

Rodents are animals with chisel-like front teeth. They gnaw tough plants and nuts. Squirrels, beavers, rats, hamsters, and porcupines are rodents. The biggest rodent is the capybara of South America.

Romans see **page 156**

rubber

Rubber comes from the sap of the rubber tree. It is very tough and stretchy. Rubber can also be made from chemicals.

Making rubber: (1) tapping the rubber tree; (2) adding acid to make the rubber particles stick together; (3) rolling; (4) drying the sheets; (5) rubber ready for dying and shaping.

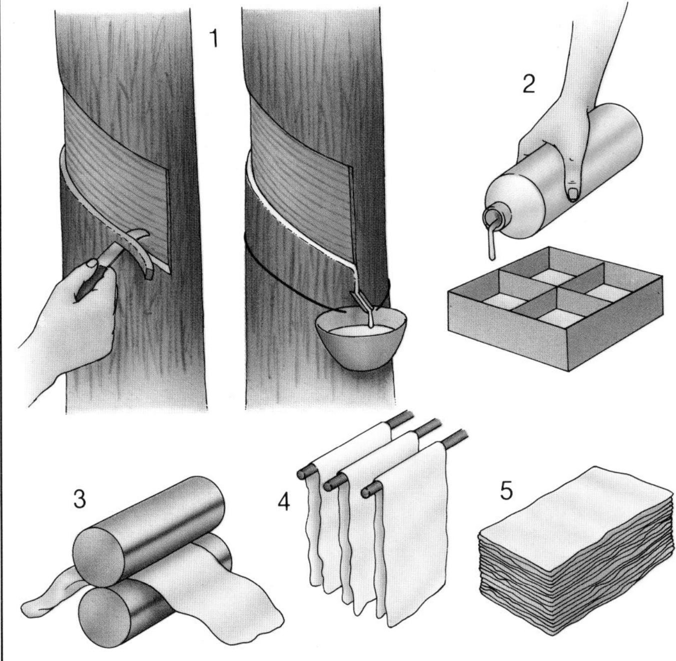

Russia see **Soviet Union**

ROMANS

Legend tells how, about 2,700 years ago, Rome was founded by Romulus and Remus. Rome grew from a cluster of villages beside the Tiber River in Italy to be the center of a mighty empire. The Romans first set up a republic, with elected officials, but were later ruled by emperors. In A.D. 395 the empire was divided. By A.D. 476 it had collapsed.

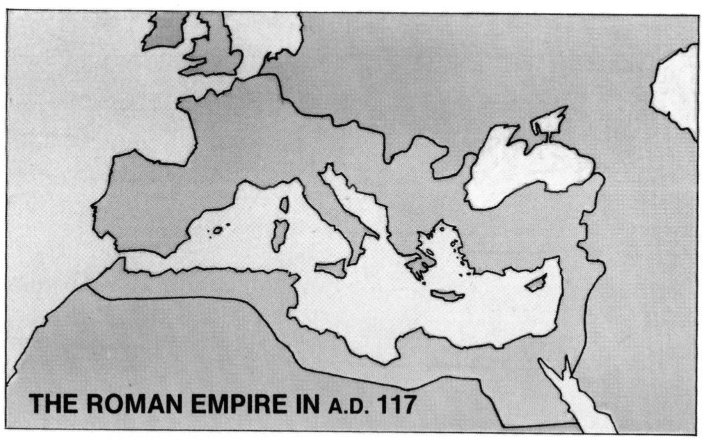

▲ A busy street in a Roman town. The shops have open fronts. The wine shop has a sign showing a wine jar outside.

◄ At its peak, the Roman Empire covered most of Europe and lands around the Mediterranean Sea.

► The Roman army was organized into legions. This soldier is carrying his equipment and weapons.

▼ Builders at work. The Romans were fine builders of homes, roads, and bridges.

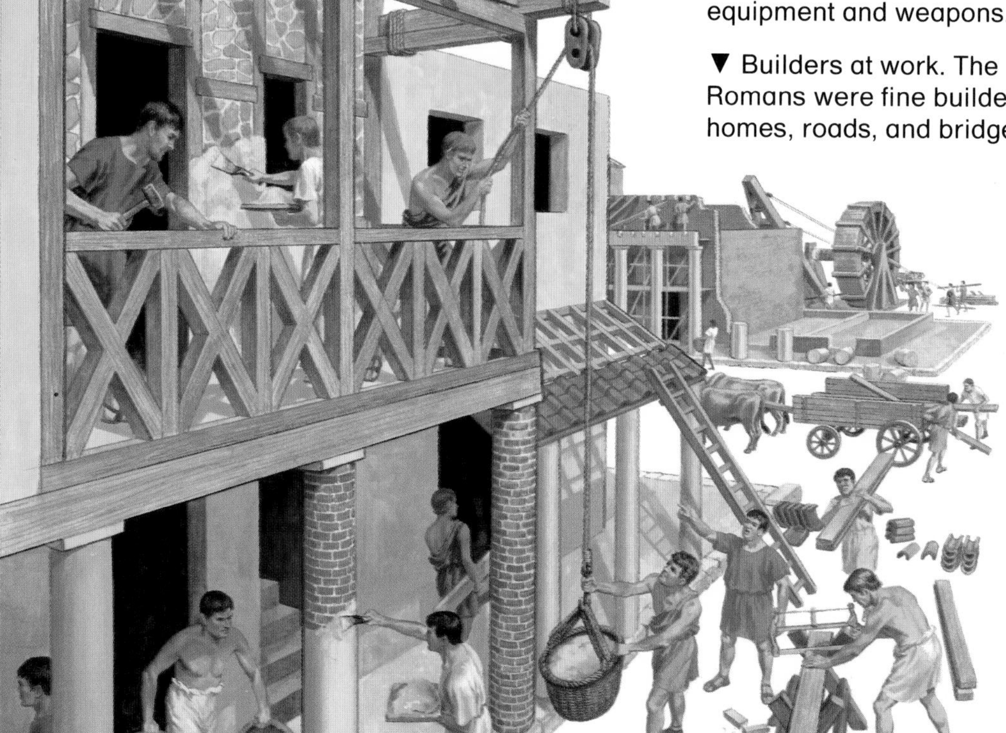

▲ The first Roman emperor was Augustus (27 B.C.). Roman coins bore a picture of the emperor. The words around the edge are in Latin, the Romans' language.

Sahara
The Sahara is the world's biggest desert. See **Africa**, **desert**.

salmon
Salmon are large fish. They lay their eggs in rivers. The young swim to the sea, but to breed they return to the rivers where they were born. Most salmon die after laying their eggs. See **migration**.

satellite
Artificial satellites circle the earth in space. They are held in their paths, called orbits, by the earth's gravity. Rockets launch satellites. In space, a satellite uses the sun's energy to make its electricity. Weather satellites send back pictures of clouds and storms. Communications satellites send TV and telephone signals around the world. Other satellites are used to make maps or study the earth. The first artificial satellite was the Soviet Sputnik 1 of 1957. The moon is a natural satellite. It orbits the earth. Other planets also have satellites, or moons. See **space flight**.

science
The word "science" means "knowledge." Early science was often mixed up with false beliefs or superstitions. Modern science began in the 1500s. Scientists such as Copernicus and Galileo showed that old ideas about the universe were wrong.

Modern scientists observe, or look at, things. They make a theory, or idea, and test it with experiments. There are many branches of science. Biology is the study of living things. Chemistry and physics deal with materials and energy. Geology is the study of the earth. Medicine is the science of health and healing. See **medicine**, **solar system**.

scorpion
Scorpions are related to spiders. They live in hot countries. They have eight legs and two big claws. The scorpion uses a stinger in its tail to poison its prey.

sculpture see **art**

▼ The Solar Max satellite took X-ray pictures of the sun.

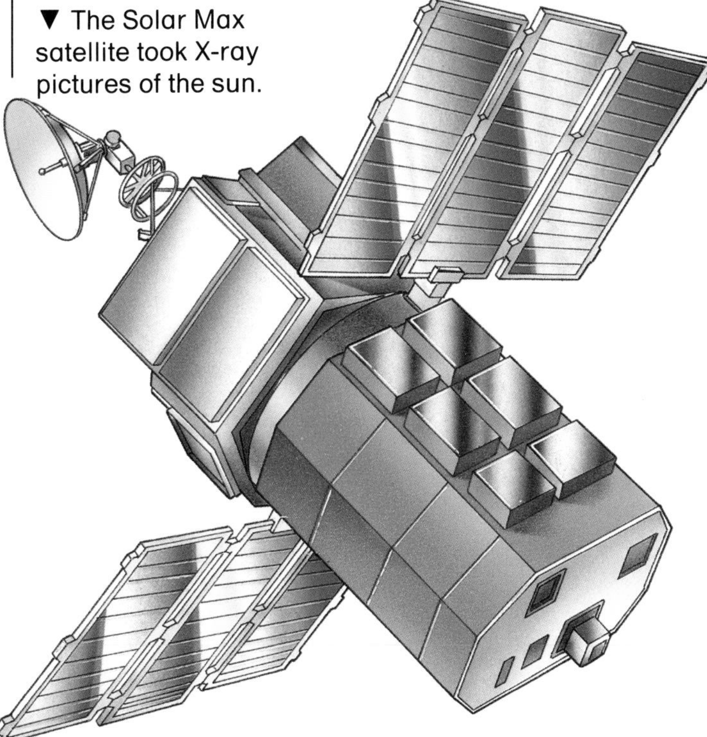

S

sea see **oceans and seas**

seals and sea lions
Seals and sea lions are sea mammals. On land they move clumsily because their legs have become flippers for swimming. They catch fish to eat. A layer of blubber keeps them warm.

▲ Seal pups are born on land. The mother seal swims out to sea to find food for them.

seasons
In some parts of the world there are four seasons: spring, summer, autumn (fall), and winter. Hot countries may have only two seasons: dry and rainy. Each season has its own weather. See **earth**, **weather**.

seaweed
Seaweeds are plants of the ocean and shore. There are about 7,000 kinds. Most are algae, simple plants. There are brown, green, and red seaweeds. Some float, others cling to the seabed.

seed see **flowers**, **plants**

senses
Our senses tell us what is going on around us. We hear, see, feel, taste, and touch. See **brain**, **ear and hearing**, **eye**, **human body**, **nose**, **smell**, **taste**.

LIFE STORY

Shakespeare
William Shakespeare was probably the greatest writer who ever lived. People everywhere still read and perform his plays and poems. He was born in 1564 in Stratford-upon-Avon, England.

In 1582 Shakespeare married. Later he went to London and became an actor. In 1594 he became the playwright for an important company of actors. Shakespeare wrote 37 plays in all. They include tragedies (*Hamlet, Macbeth, King Lear*), histories (*Julius Caesar, Henry V, Richard III*), and comedies (*As You Like It, A Midsummer Night's Dream*). He retired to Stratford, where he died in 1616.

shark

Sharks are fish that people fear and admire for their strength and ferocity as hunters. They are sometimes called the "tigers of the sea." Some sharks, such as the dogfish, are small. The huge whale shark, the biggest of all fishes, is harmless; it eats only tiny plankton. The most feared shark is the great white shark, which sometimes attacks swimmers. It can swallow a seal whole. Sharks do not have bones. Their skeletons are made of gristly cartilage. A shark must keep swimming, or it will sink. It cannot float, like other fish.

▼ The huge whale shark feeds on plankton. All the other sharks here are hunters. The carpet shark ambushes its prey on the seabed.

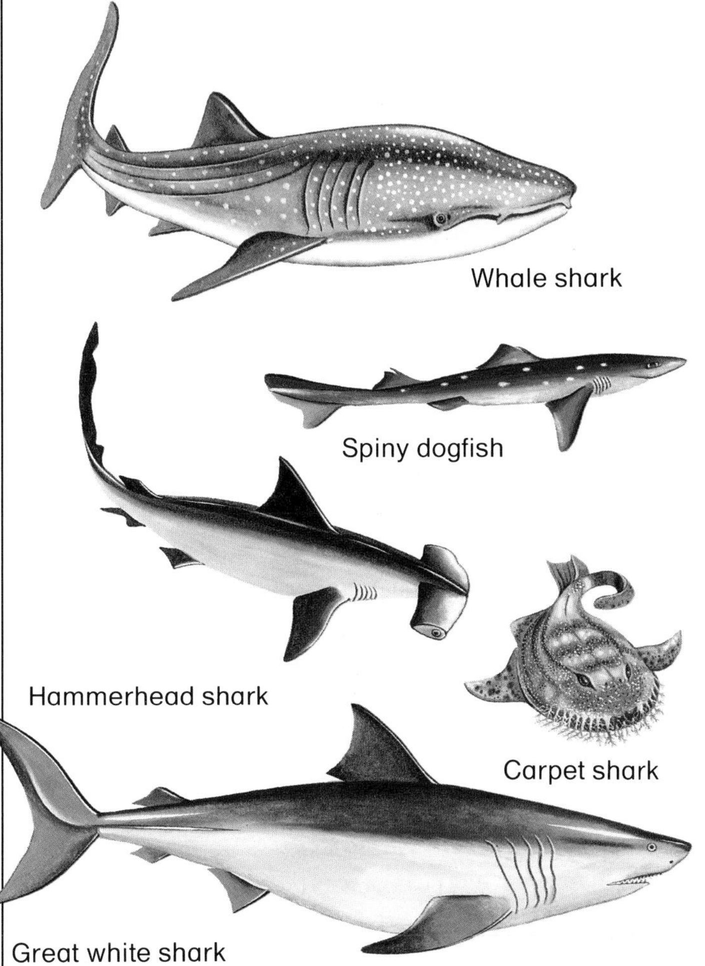

sheep

People raise sheep for their wool and meat. In Australia and New Zealand there are ten times as many sheep as people. Sheep live in flocks. Females are called ewes, males are rams, and the young are lambs. Wild sheep have long curling horns. See **farming**.

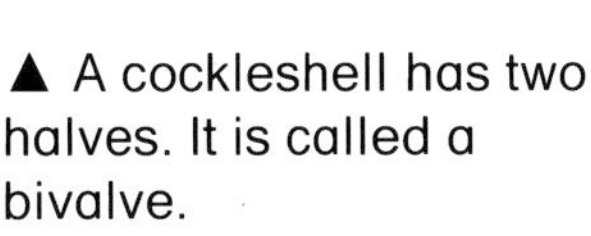

▲ A cockleshell has two halves. It is called a bivalve.

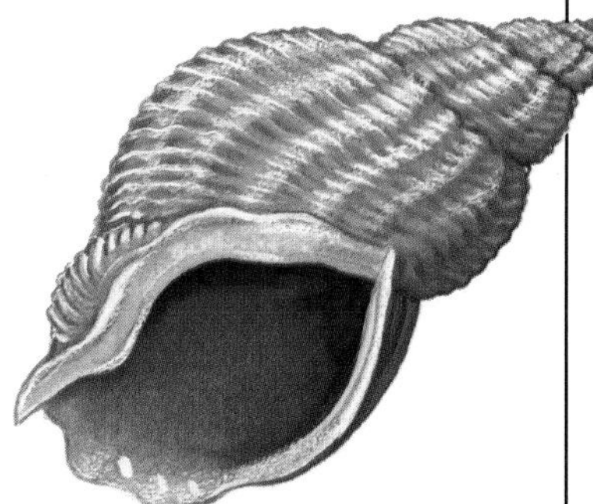

▼ Water and land snails have one-piece shells. They are univalves.

shell

A shell is a hard covering that protects a soft animal, such as a mollusk. A snail's shell grows as the snail gets bigger. It is made of a chalky substance produced in the snail's body. Snail shells are in one piece. The shells of cockles and clams are in two pieces. Animals with two-piece shells are called bivalves. A muscle opens and shuts these shells.

ships

Ships carry people across the oceans. They also carry heavy cargoes such as oil, liquid gas, and grain. Modern ships have steam turbine or diesel engines. The engines turn screw propellers, which push the ship through the water. A navy is a force of armed warships. Fast naval ships have gas turbine engines. The biggest ships are aircraft carriers and oil tankers. Submarines are ships that can travel underwater.

SHIPS

Until about 150 years ago all ships had oars or sails. Early ships had a single mast and one sail. Later, ships had three or more masts, fitted with sets of sails. When the steam engine was invented, ships no longer relied on the wind. The modern tanker and aircraft carrier are giants compared with ships of the past.

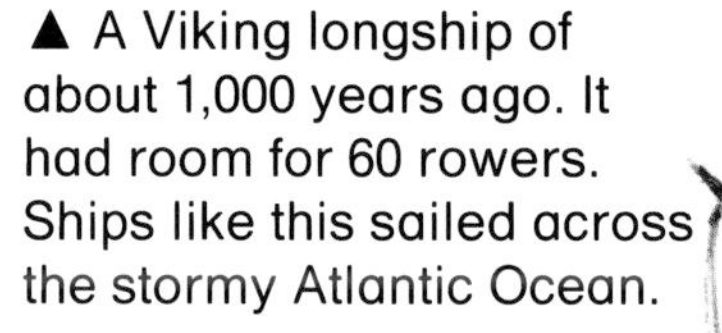

▲ A Viking longship of about 1,000 years ago. It had room for 60 rowers. Ships like this sailed across the stormy Atlantic Ocean.

► A galleon of the 1500s. Spanish galleons sailed in the great Armada of 1588.

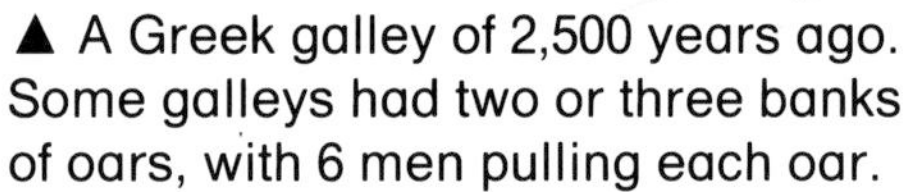

▲ A Greek galley of 2,500 years ago. Some galleys had two or three banks of oars, with 6 men pulling each oar.

▼ The last great sailing ships were the clippers of the 1800s. They could cross the Atlantic in 12 days.

◄ By the 1800s, warships, or "ships of the line," had as many as 100 cannons, arranged in rows along the decks to fire broadsides.

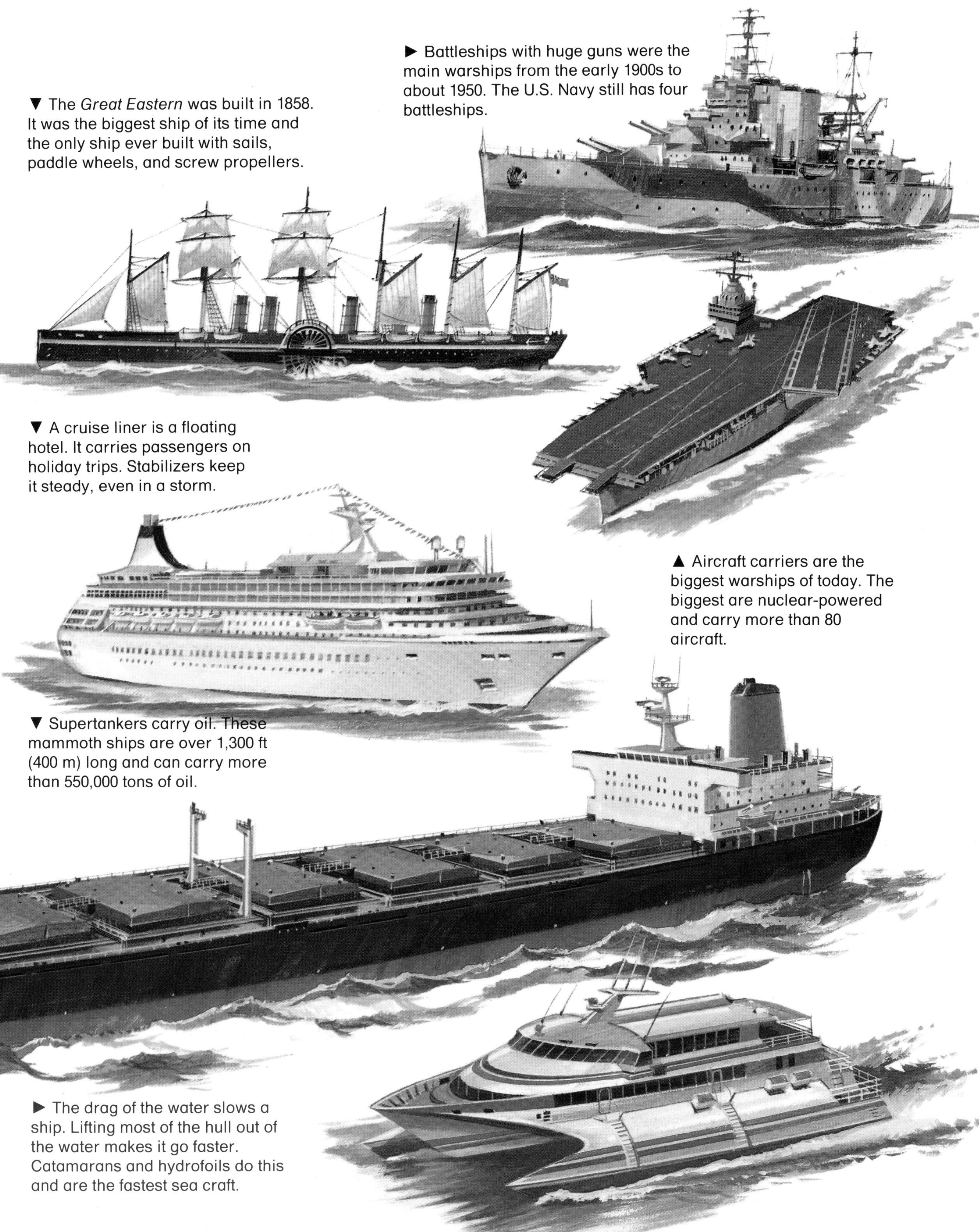

▼ The *Great Eastern* was built in 1858. It was the biggest ship of its time and the only ship ever built with sails, paddle wheels, and screw propellers.

► Battleships with huge guns were the main warships from the early 1900s to about 1950. The U.S. Navy still has four battleships.

▼ A cruise liner is a floating hotel. It carries passengers on holiday trips. Stabilizers keep it steady, even in a storm.

▲ Aircraft carriers are the biggest warships of today. The biggest are nuclear-powered and carry more than 80 aircraft.

▼ Supertankers carry oil. These mammoth ships are over 1,300 ft (400 m) long and can carry more than 550,000 tons of oil.

► The drag of the water slows a ship. Lifting most of the hull out of the water makes it go faster. Catamarans and hydrofoils do this and are the fastest sea craft.

S

shrimps and prawns
Shrimps and prawns are crustaceans. These animals have shells that are jointed, like suits of armor. They live in the sea and are related to crabs and lobsters. See **crabs and lobsters**.

silk
Silk is a beautiful smooth cloth. It is made from threads spun by the silk moth caterpillar. The silk is unwound from the caterpillar's cocoon and woven into cloth.

skeleton
The bones of your skeleton support and protect the soft parts of your body. The bones are held together by rubbery ligaments and hingelike joints. See **human body**.

▼ The skeleton holds the body together and supports its weight. The skeleton also protects the heart and other vital organs. An adult has about 206 bones. There are 29 bones in the skull alone.

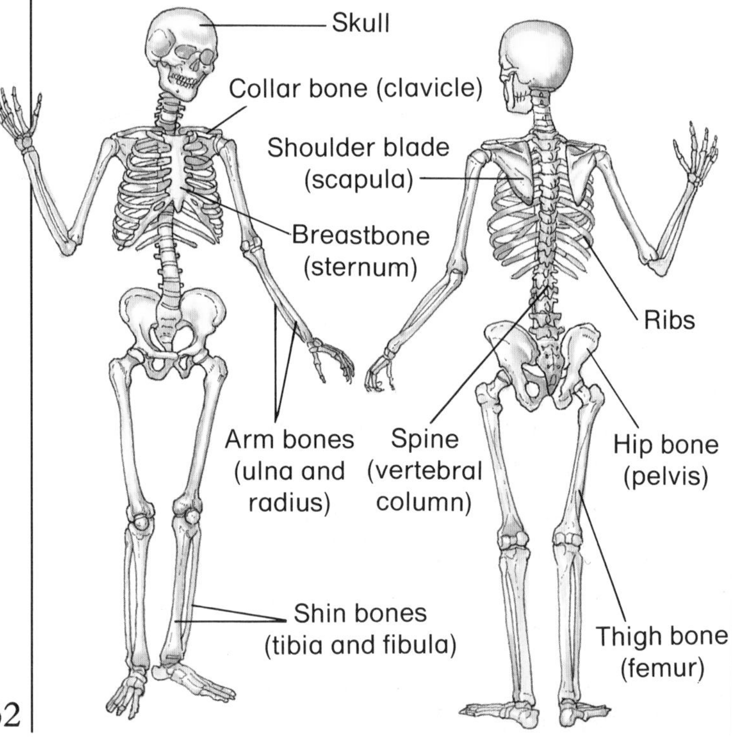

skin
Skin covers our bodies. It helps to keep out harmful germs and keeps us from getting too hot or cold. The skin's outer layer, the epidermis, grows all the time. The dermis beneath is thicker. It has nerves, blood vessels, hair roots, and sweat glands. See **human body**.

▶ The skunk squirts a foul-smelling liquid from a gland under its tail. The smell can cling to another animal's fur for days.

skunk
Skunks live in North America. They are related to weasels and badgers. Hungry animals keep away because the skunk squirts a smelly liquid if alarmed.

slave
Slaves are forced to work for someone else. They can be bought and sold. Once, prisoners of war became slaves. Africans were taken to America as slaves. Slavery was ended in the 1800s.

sleep and dreams
When we sleep, our bodies rest. Without sleep, people become tired and bad-tempered. Our brain works as we sleep, and our eyes move while our eyelids are shut. This happens when we dream. Children need more sleep than adults because their bodies are growing.

smell see **nose and smell**

sloth

The sloth lives in the forests of South America. This unusual animal hangs upside-down by its toes. It moves very slowly, usually at night, feeding on leaves. See **animals**.

snake

Snakes are reptiles. They have no legs but can climb, swim, or move quickly through underground burrows. To move, snakes zigzag or drag themselves along with the help of the scales on their skin. Snakes eat other animals. Some have poisonous fangs to bite their victims. Others grab their prey in their mouths. Some big snakes coil around their prey and crush it to death. See **reptiles**.

▼ These four snakes are found in warm countries of Europe. They hunt lizards, birds, and small mammals.

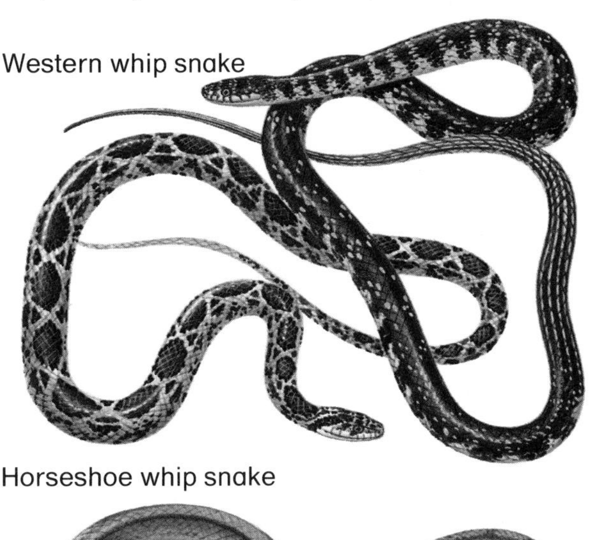

snow and hail

A snowflake is made of tiny ice crystals. Every snowflake is different, though all snowflakes have six sides. A snowstorm is a blizzard. Hailstones are balls of ice, made inside thunderclouds. See **crystal**.

soap

Soap is made from vegetable oil or animal fat. When you wash, the soap sticks to specks of dirt. The water then carries the soap and dirt away. Detergents are made from chemicals.

soil

Even a spoonful of soil is full of tiny plants and animals. Soil is made from rocks, worn down into tiny pieces by wind and water. Dead plants and animals enrich soil. Plants use the minerals in soil to make their food.

► Here is an experiment to see what soil is made of. Put some soil in a jar of water. Shake the jar. Stand the jar on a table and watch. The heavier particles sink to the bottom. The soil separates into layers.

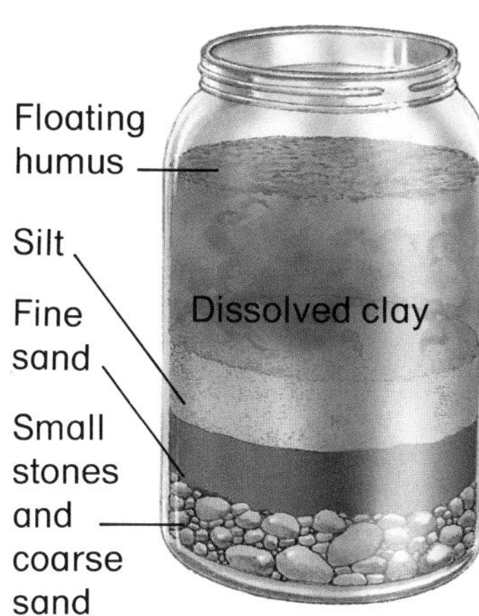

solar system

Our earth is one of nine planets moving in space around the star we call the sun. The sun and its family of planets form our solar system. Earth is the only planet that has air, water, and life. Spacecraft have discovered interesting things about the other planets but have found no signs of life.

SOLAR SYSTEM

The four planets nearest the sun (Mercury, Venus, Earth, and Mars) are rocky balls. Beyond them are the four giant planets (Jupiter, Saturn, Uranus, and Neptune). They are masses of liquid gas and ice. Between the orbits of Mars and Jupiter are about 30,000 tiny planets called asteroids. The most distant and smallest planet is Pluto.

◀ The Voyager 2 spacecraft was launched in 1977. It flew close to Jupiter (1979), Saturn (1981), Uranus (1986) and Neptune (1989). The robot craft sent back the first close-up TV pictures of these distant worlds.

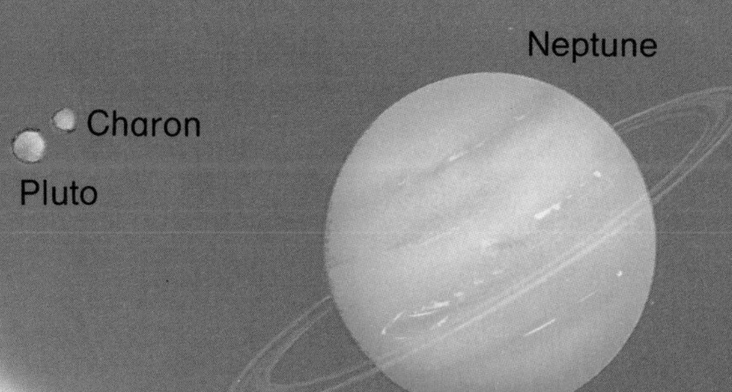

PLANETS IN ORBIT

The nine planets of the solar system move in orbits, or paths, around the sun. The four giant planets have rings of matter circling them. Here, relative sizes are correct, but planets are really much farther apart.

FACTS AND RECORDS

Planet	Distance from Sun	Number of Moons	Diameter	Interesting Facts
Mercury	36 million mi (58 million km)	None	3,032 mi (4880 km)	Its year lasts only 88 earth days.
Venus	67 million mi (108 million km)	None	7,519 mi (12,100 km)	The hottest planet, hidden by clouds.
Earth	93 million mi (150 million km)	1	7,926 mi (12,756 km)	The only planet known to have air, water, and life.
Mars	141 million mi (228 million km)	2	4,194 mi (6,794 km)	Nicknamed "the red planet" because of its rust-colored surface.
Jupiter	483 million mi (778 million km)	16	88,736 mi (142,800 km)	Twice the size of the other planets put together.
Saturn	886 million mi (1,427 million km)	18	74,978 mi (120,660 km)	Its famous rings have a diameter of over 186,000 mi (300,000 km).
Uranus	1,782 million mi (2,870 million km)	15	32,193 mi (51,810 km)	The first planet discovered with a telescope.
Neptune	2,793 million mi (4,497 million km)	8	30,775 mi (49,528 km)	Its year lasts 165 earth years.
Pluto	3,670 million mi (5,900 million km)	1	1,423(?) mi (2,290 km)	Almost 40 times as far from the sun as the earth is.

ASTEROIDS

There is a gap between the orbits of Mars and Jupiter. It is as if a planet is missing. Instead, there are about 30,000 mini-planets — rocky balls called asteroids. Even lumped together, they would be smaller than our moon.

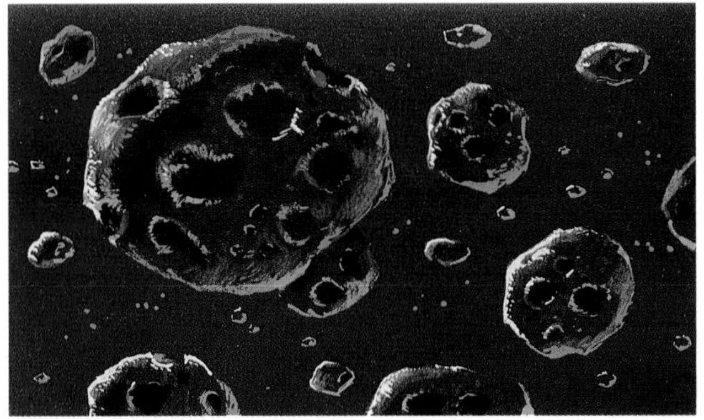

MILKY WAY

The Milky Way galaxy is our galaxy. It is a giant whirling mass of stars, shaped like a flat disk with a swollen middle. Our sun and its family of planets are toward the edge of the galaxy (marked by the red arrow).

Jupiter

Asteroid belt

Mars

Earth

Venus

Mercury

INSIDE THE SUN

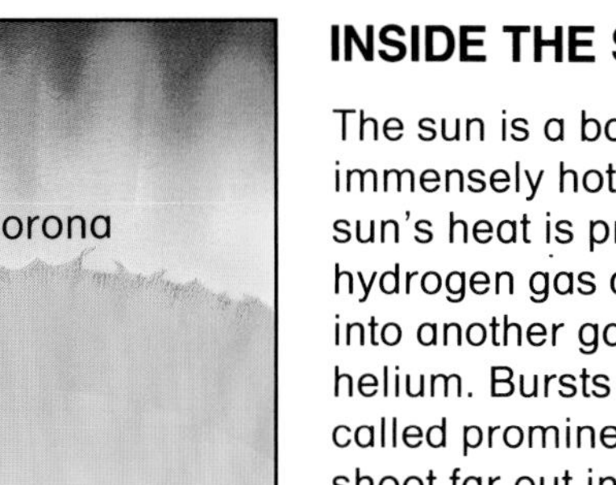

The sun is a ball of immensely hot gases. The sun's heat is produced as hydrogen gas changes into another gas called helium. Bursts of gas, called prominences, shoot far out into space. The surface of the sun is very hot, about 11,000°F (6,000°C). At the center, the sun is far hotter — about 27,000,000°F (15,000,000°C).

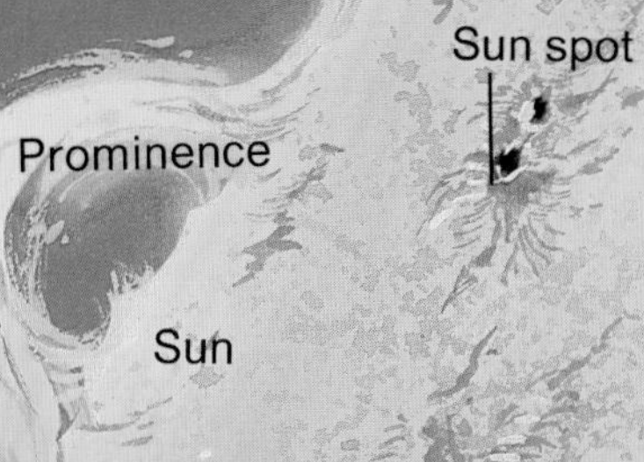

THE PATH OF A PLANET

Ellipse

The path a planet follows as it journeys around the sun is called its orbit. The shape of the orbit is a flattened circle, also called an ellipse.

WARNING

The sun's light can hurt your eyes. **Never** look directly into the sun, nor look at it through binoculars or a telescope.

S

sound

A sound is made when an object vibrates (moves backward and forward). Sounds travel in waves that spread out like ripples on a pond. We hear sounds when the waves reach our ears. Sounds can travel through air, water, and metals. When sounds get trapped inside a cave or a big room, the waves bounce back as echoes. Sound waves cannot travel through space, which is a vacuum (has no air). See **air**.

▲ Sound waves travel away from their source like ripples on a pond. They make vibrations in the air, which make our eardrums vibrate too, so that we can hear the sound.

▲ Take five bottles. Put different amounts of water in each. Tap each bottle with a spoon. The more air there is in a bottle the slower it vibrates and the lower the note produced.

South America

The continent of South America is joined to North America by the narrow isthmus of Panama. South America has jungles, forests, snow-capped mountains, and grassy plains. Its animals include llamas, jaguars, sloths, monkeys, rheas (ostrich-like birds), and anteaters. It is a continent rich in minerals, including oil, silver, tin, and copper. Despite this wealth, many South Americans are very poor.

▲ Trotsky (left) and Lenin were Communists who led the Russian Revolution. Trotsky was later murdered on Stalin's orders.

Soviet Union

The Soviet Union is also known as the U.S.S.R. It forms the world's biggest country, partly in Europe and partly in Asia. Until 1991, the Soviet Union had 15 republics with different peoples, languages, and customs. In 1991 the three Baltic States gained their independence. Russia is by far the biggest republic. Moscow is the capital city. Old Russia was ruled by tsars, or emperors, but in 1917 a revolution brought in Communist rule. This rule was ended in 1991. Despite natural wealth, the Soviet Union has old-fashioned farms and factories.

SOUTH AMERICA

South America is the fourth-largest continent. Some people are American Indians, but many are descendants of people from Europe, Africa, and Asia. Some natural wonders include the high Andes Mountains and the Amazon rain forest. Angel Falls is the world's highest waterfall (3,212 ft [979 m]).

▲ This statue of Jesus Christ (95 ft [29 m] tall) stands on a hilltop above the city of Rio de Janeiro in Brazil.

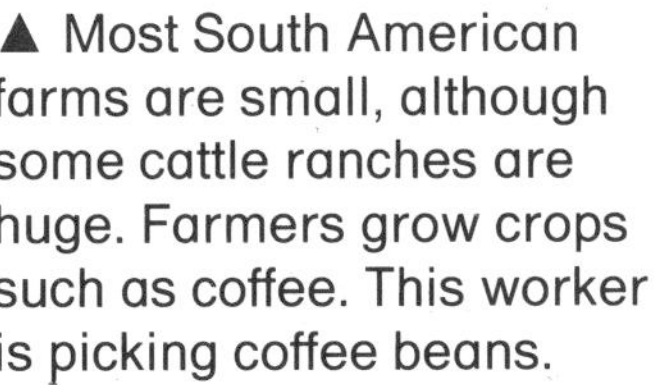

▲ Most South American farms are small, although some cattle ranches are huge. Farmers grow crops such as coffee. This worker is picking coffee beans.

▲ South America has high mountains, the Andes, running all the way along its western side. It has a long coastline, but few natural harbors.

FACTS AND RECORDS

Area: 6,795,000 sq mi (17,600,000 sq km)
Number of countries: 12
Population: 297,000,000
Largest country: Brazil (3,286,470 sq mi [8,511,965 sq km])
Largest city: São Paulo (Brazil) 18,052,000
Highest mountain: Mt. Aconcagua (Argentina)
Longest rivers: Amazon, Parana, Purus
Biggest lake: Lake Maracaibo (Venezuela)

SPACE FLIGHT

Most spacecraft have no people on board. They carry scientific instruments and cameras to study the stars and planets. Satellites stay in orbit around the earth. Probes travel deep into space to explore. Astronauts have been to the moon and have lived inside a space station for as long as a year. One day people may travel to Mars.

LIVING IN SPACE

There is very little gravity in space, so astronauts are weightless. They float about inside the spacecraft cabin. Food and drink float too unless kept in sealed containers! The astronauts wash in special vacuum showers that allow no drops of water to escape.

SPACE PROBES

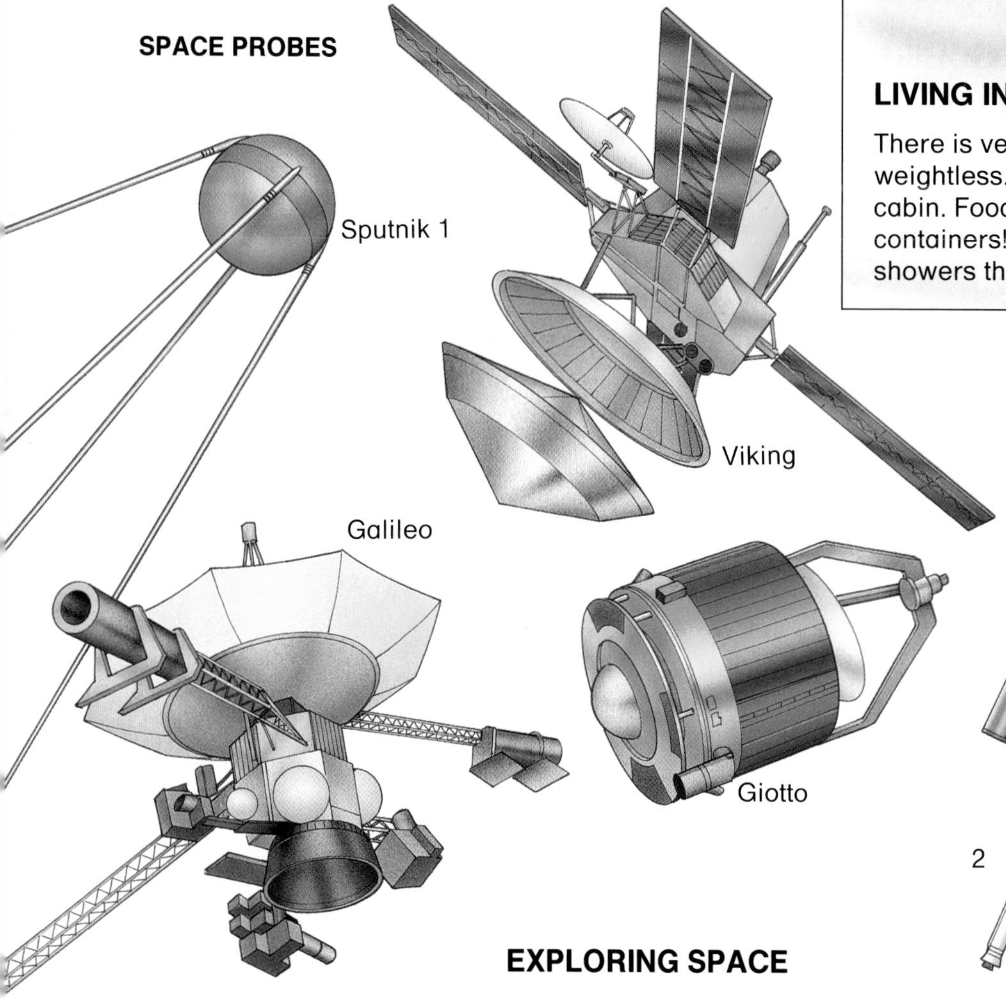

Sputnik 1

Viking

Galileo

Giotto

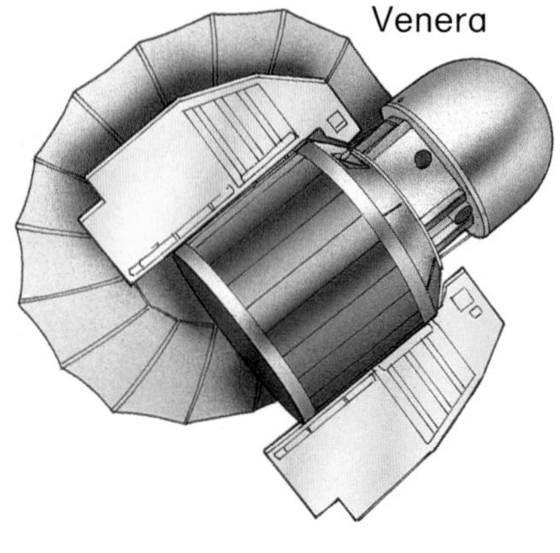

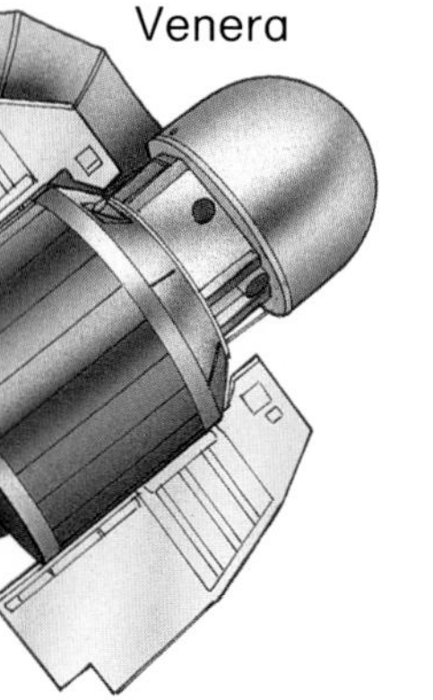

Venera

EXPLORING SPACE

Sputnik 1 (1957) was the first space satellite. The *Viking* craft landed on Mars in 1975. *Galileo* was launched to study Jupiter. *Giotto* flew close to Halley's comet in 1986. The Russian *Venera 7* probe explored the planet Venus in 1970.

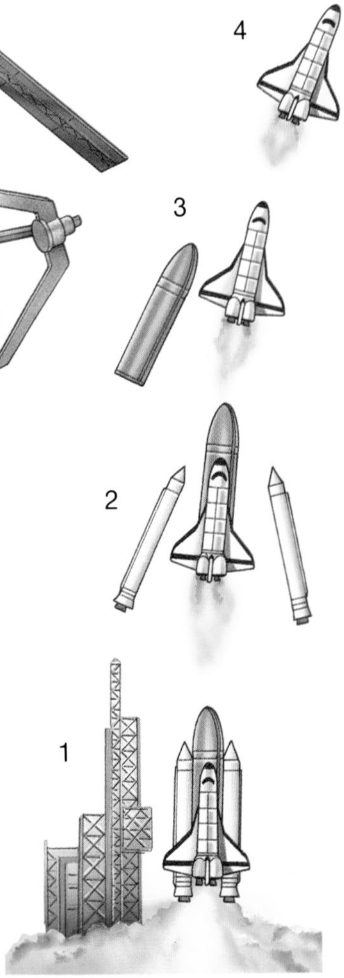

SHUTTLE LAUNCH

4

3

2

1

(1) The space shuttle has five rocket engines. It needs extra booster rockets to lift it off the ground.

(2) The engines burn chemical fuel from a huge tank. When the shuttle is about 28 mi (45 km) high, the used-up booster rockets fall away.

(3) When the craft is almost in space, the main engines are stopped and the empty fuel tank is dropped.

(4) The shuttle's orbital engines are used to send the spacecraft into orbit.

The space shuttle carries satellites, laboratories, and other important cargo into space, inside its huge payload bay.

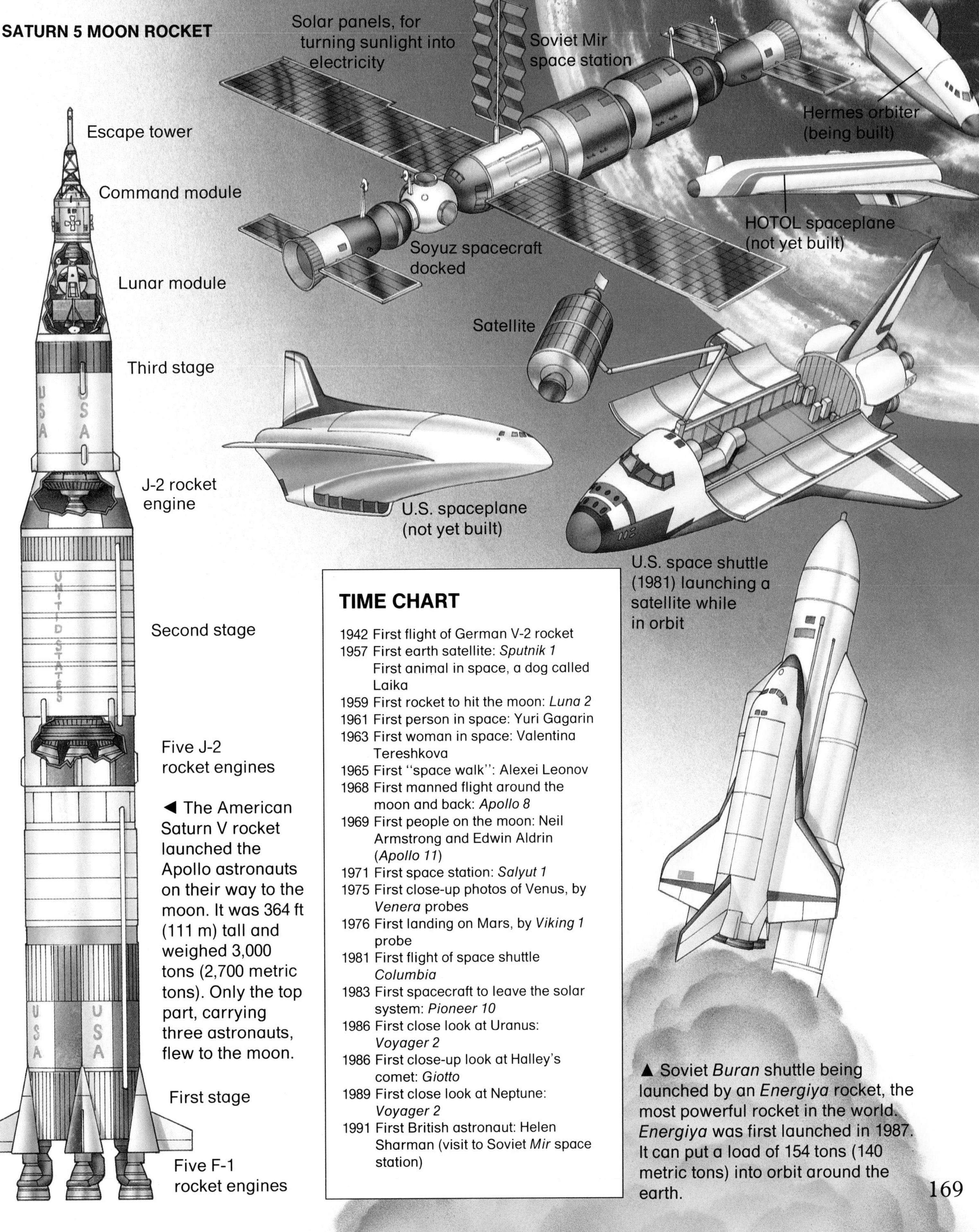

◀ The American Saturn V rocket launched the Apollo astronauts on their way to the moon. It was 364 ft (111 m) tall and weighed 3,000 tons (2,700 metric tons). Only the top part, carrying three astronauts, flew to the moon.

TIME CHART

1942 First flight of German V-2 rocket
1957 First earth satellite: *Sputnik 1*
First animal in space, a dog called Laika
1959 First rocket to hit the moon: *Luna 2*
1961 First person in space: Yuri Gagarin
1963 First woman in space: Valentina Tereshkova
1965 First "space walk": Alexei Leonov
1968 First manned flight around the moon and back: *Apollo 8*
1969 First people on the moon: Neil Armstrong and Edwin Aldrin (*Apollo 11*)
1971 First space station: *Salyut 1*
1975 First close-up photos of Venus, by *Venera* probes
1976 First landing on Mars, by *Viking 1* probe
1981 First flight of space shuttle *Columbia*
1983 First spacecraft to leave the solar system: *Pioneer 10*
1986 First close look at Uranus: *Voyager 2*
1986 First close-up look at Halley's comet: *Giotto*
1989 First close look at Neptune: *Voyager 2*
1991 First British astronaut: Helen Sharman (visit to Soviet *Mir* space station)

▲ Soviet *Buran* shuttle being launched by an *Energiya* rocket, the most powerful rocket in the world. *Energiya* was first launched in 1987. It can put a load of 154 tons (140 metric tons) into orbit around the earth.

S

speech

When you speak, your tongue, teeth, and lips work together to make sounds. Prehistoric people had a simple language. Languages developed over thousands of years. See **language**.

spider

Spiders look something like insects, but they aren't. Spiders have eight legs. Insects have six. A spider's body is different, too. It does not have feelers or wings. Spiders are hunters. Some chase their prey. Some hide in holes in the ground. Spiders can spin silken threads from inside their bodies. Many spiders use these threads to make sticky webs. When an insect gets trapped in the web, the spider kills it with a poisonous bite.

▼ Unlike most insects, some female spiders look after their young. When a fly is caught in the web, these baby comb-footed spiders hurry to make a meal of it.

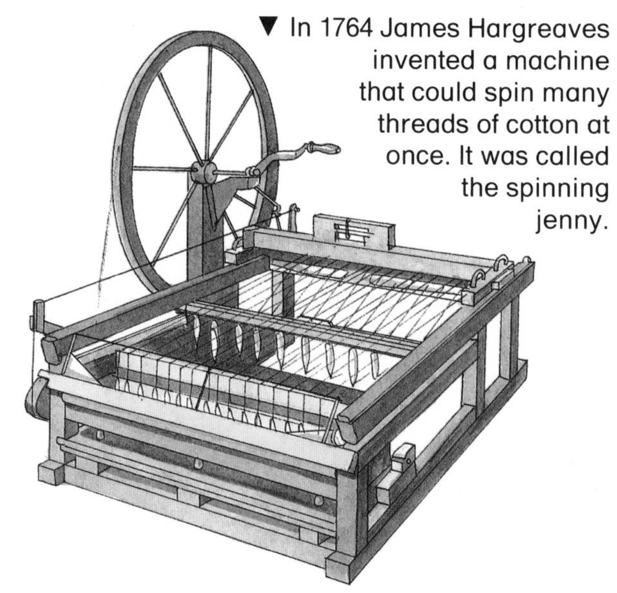

▼ In 1764 James Hargreaves invented a machine that could spin many threads of cotton at once. It was called the spinning jenny.

spinning and weaving

Spinning is twisting fibers together to make long threads. Cotton and wool are spun to make threads called yarns. The yarn is made into cloth on a weaving machine called a loom. One set of yarns is threaded in and out of the other, making a crisscross pattern. Spinning and weaving were done by hand until faster machines were invented in the 1700s, starting the Industrial Revolution.

sports

The oldest sports are hunting, racing, and sports related to war, such as wrestling and archery. The ancient Greeks started the Olympic games. The Romans enjoyed cruel sports such as gladiator fights.

Sports keep you fit and are fun, whether you play on your own, with a partner, or in a team. Professionals are paid to play their sports. There are games (football, tennis, hockey, baseball, soccer, basketball). There is "track and field" (running, jumping, throwing). There are water sports, auto sports, winter sports, and horse sports.

SPORTS

Sports began as a form of exercise, often used to train warriors for fighting. The ancient Greeks believed that sports were good training for the mind as well as for the body. During the 1800s, people in America and Europe began to think so, too. This is when the rules were first made for many of the sports we enjoy today.

▼ Skiing is an exciting winter sport, but you do not have to be a downhill racer to enjoy the fun. In slalom races, the skiers twist and turn around flagpoles. The skier with the fastest time wins.

▼ Baseball is a popular team sport in North America, Japan, and other countries. Here the batter is ready for the pitcher's throw.

▲ Water sports are fun for people of all ages. Sailing uses large or small boats. Swimming is good exercise and essential for water safety.

▼ Golf began in Scotland. A golf course has 18 holes. The object is to hit the ball into each hole, taking as few shots as possible.

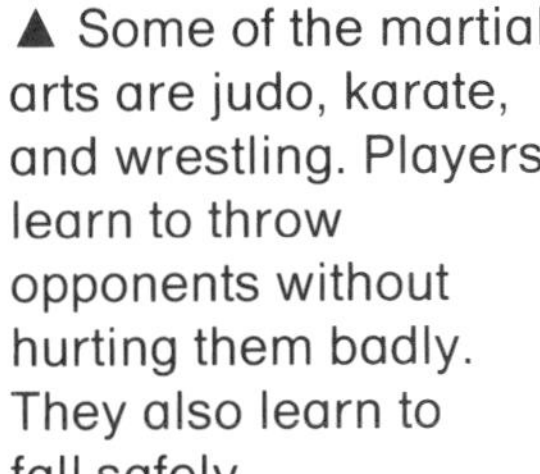

▲ Some of the martial arts are judo, karate, and wrestling. Players learn to throw opponents without hurting them badly. They also learn to fall safely.

▲ Athletes train hard for important races. These may be short or long.

► Horseback riding is exciting. Horses jump fences, gallop across country, or are ridden by jockeys in races.

S

squirrel

Squirrels are small furry rodents with long fluffy tails. Ground squirrels, like the chipmunk, live in burrows. Tree squirrels are expert climbers. Squirrels often bury supplies of food.

▼ The red squirrel lives in the pine forests of northern Europe. It has a bushier tail than the gray squirrel.

stamps

The first postage stamps were stuck on letters in Britain in the 1840s. Stamps made sending letters much simpler. Before their invention, the person receiving the letter had to pay for it.

star

There are millions and millions of stars. The sun is a middle-sized, middle-aged star. A star is born as a cloud of gas. It grows bigger, hotter, and brighter. After billions of years, it shrinks, cools, and fades. See **galaxy**, **sun**, **universe**.

Stone Age

The first tools were pebbles and flints. People chipped the edges of these stones to make cutters and scrapers. They made stone points for arrows and spears. About 5,000 years ago Egyptians had metal tools. Some peoples went on using stone tools into modern times.

submarine

Submarines are underwater boats. The first modern submarines were made in the early 1900s. Today a nuclear-powered submarine could travel around the world without ever surfacing.

▼ Scientists use small submarines, called submersibles, to explore the ocean depths. The submarine has electric motors and a mechanical arm to pick up objects. Its hull (body) is very strong.

sun

The sun is a star in the Milky Way galaxy. To us on earth, it is the most important star of all. Plants and animals need the sun's heat and light to live. Planets, asteroids, and comets move around the sun. See **solar system**.

swan

Swans are graceful water birds. They have webbed feet for swimming and long necks for feeding under water. Baby swans are called cygnets.

▲ A swan and cygnets

T

tapir
Tapirs are hoofed mammals that look like large pigs. Three kinds live in South America, and one in Asia. Tapirs live in forests near rivers. The tapir has a trunk like an elephant's, but shorter.

taste
Taste is one of our senses. It helps us remember which foods and drinks are pleasant and good for us. On the tongue are organs called taste buds. They can sense if food in our mouths tastes sweet, sour, salty, or bitter. Different parts of the tongue pick up different tastes. Older people have fewer taste buds, so they cannot taste things as well as children can. See **senses**.

FIND OUT FOR YOURSELF

Find your taste bud patches. Put a little sugar, lemon juice, salt, and vanilla extract into separate saucers. With a clean paintbrush, dab a little of each on different parts of your tongue. Where do you taste each flavor?

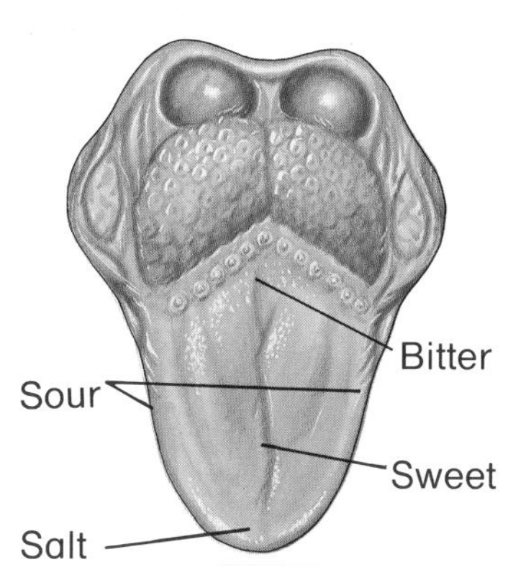

tea
Tea is drunk all over the world. It is made from the leaves of a small bushy plant. Tea plants are grown on big farms, called plantations, in Asia. The leaves are picked, dried, crushed, and roasted.

teeth
Teeth chew food to break it into pieces small enough to be swallowed and digested. An adult person has 32 teeth. The front teeth are pointed, for cutting and biting. The back teeth are flat, for grinding and crushing. A human baby is born with no teeth. By the time a child is about two and a half, it has 20 first teeth. The adult teeth grow in their place, starting when a person is about six.

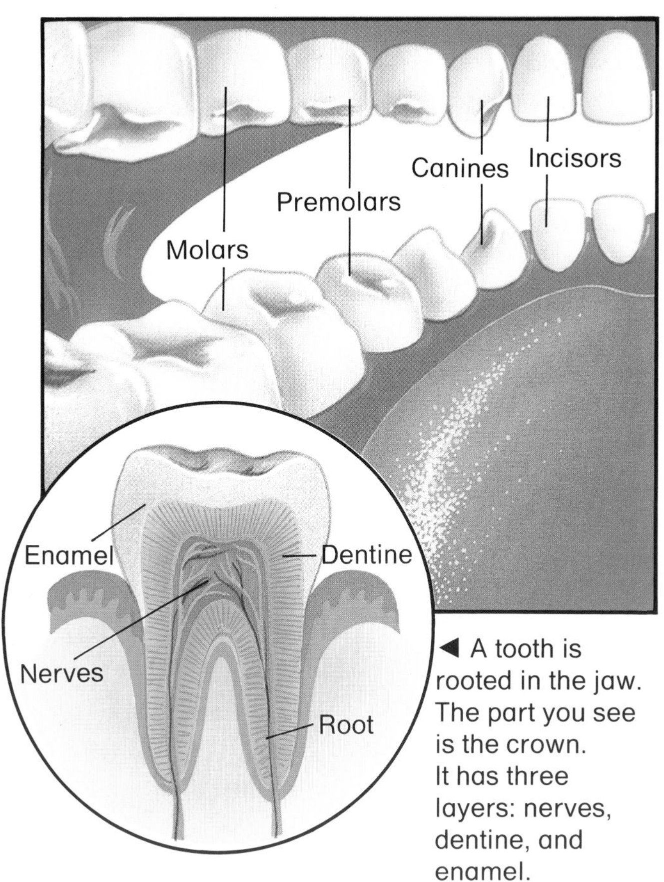

◀ A tooth is rooted in the jaw. The part you see is the crown. It has three layers: nerves, dentine, and enamel.

▲ Your teeth do different jobs. The molars grind and crush food. The canines tear. The incisors cut. We have all three kinds because we eat all kinds of food.

TELEVISION AND VIDEO

Television works by changing light waves into electric signals. These are broadcast as radio waves. TV antennas change the waves back to electric signals. Inside a TV set, signals are turned into color or black-and-white pictures.

Camera in TV studio

Sound microphone

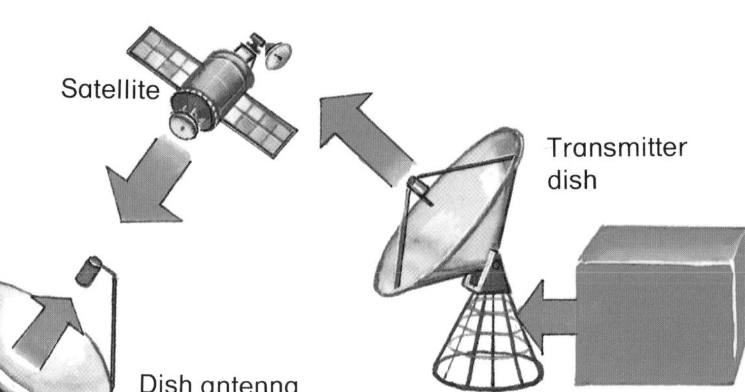

▲ Inside the TV camera, an electron gun changes the picture into electric signals. The signals are carried on radio waves to a TV antenna.

▶ Inside the TV set is a cathode ray tube. Its front is the screen. The signals make electron guns fire, lighting up chemical dots on the screen to make pictures.

Cathode-ray tube

Screen

▶ There are three electron guns in a color TV set. They fire beams of electrons at the back of the screen. The screen is covered with tiny chemical dots in groups of three: red, blue, and green. Each hit makes a flash of color, building up a picture.

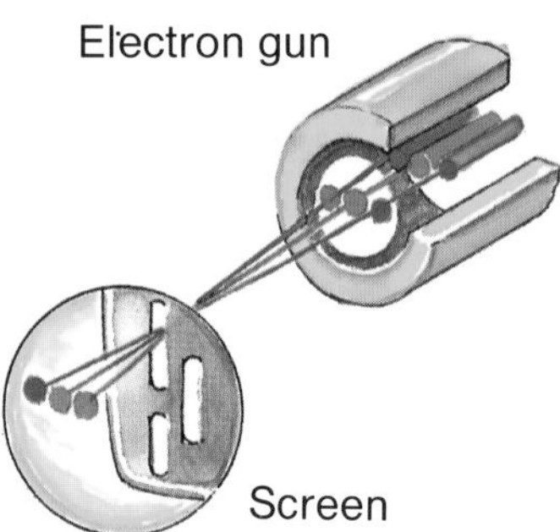

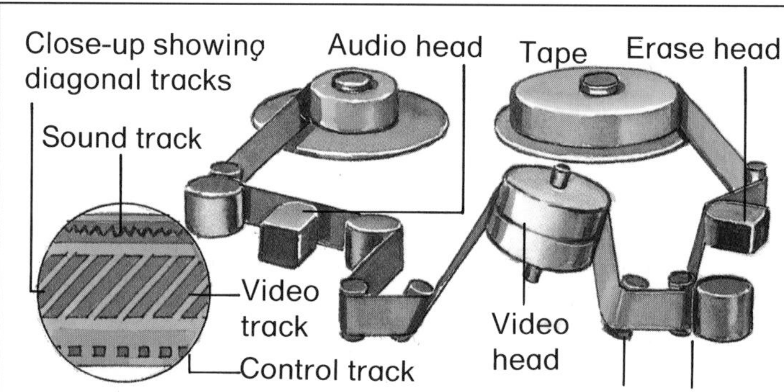

VIDEO RECORDERS

A video recorder stores the electric signals from a TV transmitter by recording them on magnetic tape. When the tape passes through the replay head of the video player, the signals are sent to the TV set and changed back into pictures.

TIME CHART

1926: John Logie Baird invented a mechanical television system. The electronic system used today was developed in the 1930s.
1936: first TV service, in Britain
1953: first color telecasts, in the United States
1962: first satellite TV pictures were sent across the Atlantic.

telephone
When you talk on the telephone, the sounds of your voice are turned into electrical signals inside the mouthpiece. The signals travel through wires or bounce off satellites in space. In the receiver, the electrical signals are changed back into sounds. A vibrating plate recreates the voice. Alexander Graham Bell invented the telephone in 1876. See **inventions and discoveries**.

telescope
A telescope has lenses inside that bend light to make distant objects appear larger. The first telescopes were made in the early 1600s. In 1688 Newton built a "reflecting" telescope. Most big telescopes used in astronomy are reflectors. Radio telescopes are dish-shaped antennas that pick up radio signals from very distant stars. See **astronomy, lens, light**.

▲ A refracting telescope (left) uses lenses to focus rays of light from the stars. A reflecting telescope (right) uses curved mirrors to direct light through a lens to the eye.

television and video
The word "television" means "far-seeing." TV shows us pictures from the far side of the world or from a spacecraft. Video recorders store and play back TV shows and films on tape.

▲ To make textiles, fibers are first spun into threads, which are then woven on powered looms.

textiles
A textile is a cloth made by weaving fibers together. Many fibers come from natural materials like cotton, wool, and silk. Other fibers are now made from chemicals. See **spinning and weaving**.

thermometer
A thermometer measures temperature. Inside it, there is a glass tube filled with liquid mercury or alcohol. The hotter the temperature is, the higher the liquid rises.

thunder and lightning
Thunderstorms happen when electricity builds up inside clouds, making sparks. Some sparks shoot to earth as lightning. The air heats up and explodes with a bang, called thunder. See **electricity**.

▼ In a thunderstorm you may see forked lightning. Lightning has a high electric charge and so is very dangerous.

tides and currents

The moon causes the tides. Its pull of gravity raises the water in the oceans. Two high tides happen every 24 hours. In between are two low tides. See **moon, oceans and seas**.

tiger see cats

time

We measure time with clocks and calendars. Over 3,000 years ago people in Babylonia figured out that the earth took 365 days to travel around the sun. One trip makes a year. The world is divided into time zones. At 12 noon in Greenwich, England, it is 7 o'clock in the morning (5 hours earlier) in New York and 3 o'clock in the afternoon (three hours later) in Moscow. See **clock**.

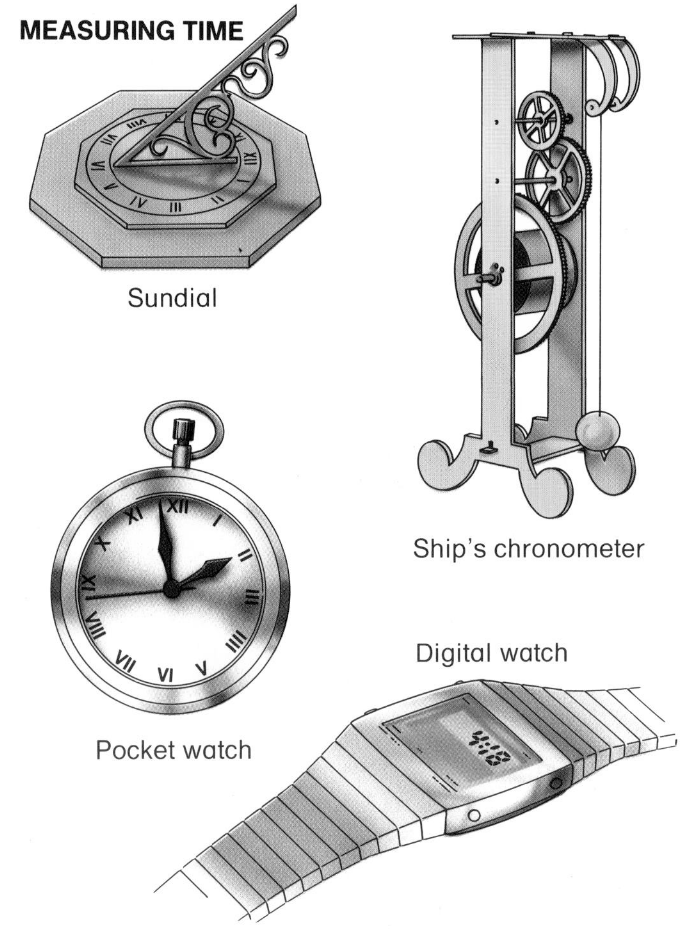

◀ A Hermann's tortoise from Europe. A frightened tortoise pulls its head and legs inside its shell.

▶ A stripe-necked terrapin. Terrapins are freshwater turtles and are flesh-eaters.

tortoises and turtles

Tortoises and turtles are the only reptiles with shells. Tortoises live on land. They walk very slowly and eat plants. The giant tortoise can live to be over 150 years old. Many turtles live in the sea, but lay their eggs on beaches. Their legs are shaped like flippers. They swim well, but crawl slowly on land. Terrapins are small freshwater turtles. Turtles and terrapins are meat-eaters. See **reptiles**.

toys

Some children's toys have not changed much in thousands of years. Children in ancient Egypt and Greece played with dolls, toy animals and carts, and balls. Clockwork toys were popular from the 1700s. So were dollhouses. Teddy bears are fairly modern. They first appeared in the early 1900s.

T

trade

Trade began when people first exchanged one good for another. Thousands of years ago traders, or merchants, traveled over land and sea. They set up markets and shops in towns. The goods that a country sells abroad are exports. The goods it buys from other countries are imports. Almost every country lives by trade. See **money**.

trees

Trees are tall woody plants. Most trees have one main stem, or trunk. Branches grow out from the trunk, and leaves sprout from the branches. Trees are the largest living things. A giant redwood tree can grow more than 360 ft (110 m) high. Some trees live for about 5,000 years. Deciduous trees drop their leaves in fall. They have flowers. Conifers, such as pines and firs, are evergreen. They make seeds in cones, not flowers. See **forest, plants**.

DID YOU KNOW?

Trees, like all plants, have tubes inside their trunks to carry food and water. In trees, these tubes form complete rings around the trunk. A new ring is added each year, so counting the rings shows how old a tree was when cut.

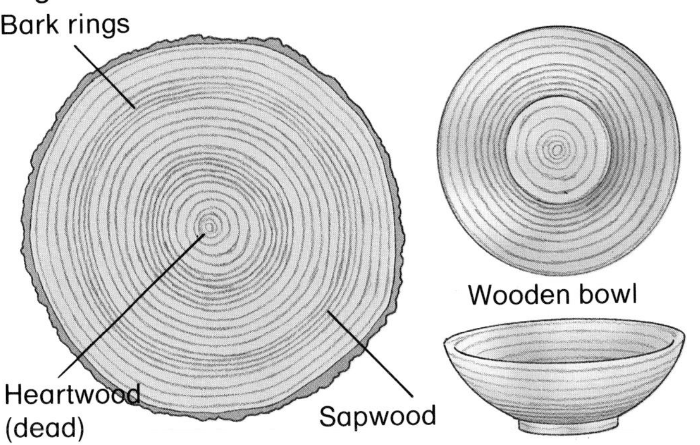

▲ Big trucks are used to carry all kinds of freight. On long journeys, the cab is the driver's home.

trucks and buses

Trucks are motor vehicles that carry goods. Some are no bigger than cars. Others weigh 55 tons. Buses carry people on short and long journeys. Horses pulled the first buses. Today, most trucks and buses have diesel engines. See **cars, engines**.

tunnel

Tunnels are dug underground. Some tunnels have roads through them. Others are used by trains. Tunnels also carry water to big cities. The world's longest tunnel is the Seikan railroad tunnel in Japan, which is nearly 34 mi (54 km) long. Nowadays, giant boring machines and explosives dig tunnels. The tunnels are lined with concrete. Trains will run through the new Channel Tunnel, which will link Britain and France under the sea.

► A modern tunnel-digging machine. It is called a mole and has rotating cutters in front to chew away the rock and clay. Conveyor belts carry away the loose soil. Powerful jacks push the machine along.

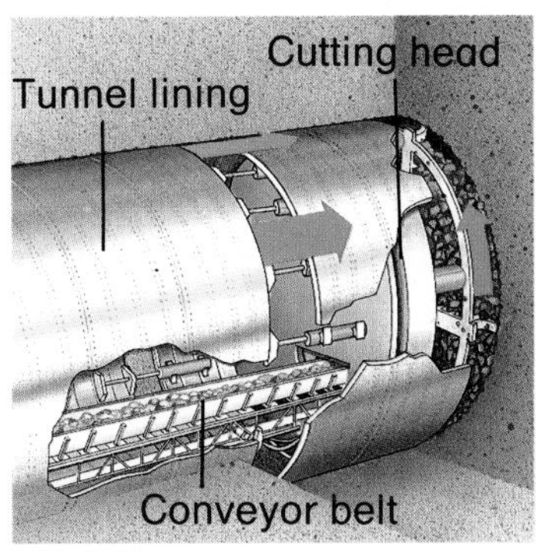

United Kingdom

The United Kingdom is a country made up of England, Scotland, Wales, and Northern Ireland. Great Britain includes England, Scotland, and Wales. Islands such as the Isle of Man and the Shetlands are also part of the United Kingdom. The south of the country is mostly flat, with rolling hills in parts. The north, especially the Highlands of Scotland, is more mountainous, though the highest mountain (Ben Nevis in Scotland) is only 4,406 ft (1,343 m) high. The longest river is the Severn. The United Kingdom is a crowded country, and most people live in towns and cities. London is the capital city. It has many old and famous buildings.

United Nations

Most of the countries of the world belong to the United Nations. This organization was set up in 1945 to keep the peace and to help people fight disease, famine, and poverty.

◀ The flag of the United Nations shows a map of the world. Around it is a wreath of olive leaves. The olive branch is an ancient symbol of peace.

United States

The United States of America is the world's richest and most powerful nation. It is the fourth-biggest (after the U.S.S.R., Canada, and China). The country is a republic, made up of 50 states. Forty-eight states are in the same part of North America. The other two are Alaska in the far north and the islands of Hawaii in the Pacific Ocean.

The Statue of Liberty greets ships arriving in New York Harbor. It was given by France in 1884. New York is the biggest city in the United States. It is famous for its skyscraper buildings.

The first Americans were the native "Indians" and Eskimos. Europeans started colonies in the 1500s, bringing black slaves from Africa. In 1776, 13 colonies rebelled against British rule and set up a republic. George Washington became its president. People from many countries have come to live in the United States. See **North America, Washington**.

U.S.S.R. see **Soviet Union**

universe

The universe is all of space and everything in it. It contains millions and millions of stars. The universe has no edges, because it seems to be getting bigger all the time. All the star groups, called galaxies, are rushing away from one another at enormous speeds. Many scientists think that all the matter making up the universe was once squeezed tightly together and then exploded. They call this the big bang. The big bang occurred between 10 billion and 20 billion years ago. Scientists measure light and other rays to study the most distant celestial objects, called quasars. Light from them takes thousands of millions of years to reach us. See **solar system**, **star**.

▼ These pictures show how the universe may have formed. (1) It began with the big bang. Matter flew apart and began to lump together (2) to form galaxies (3) which are still moving apart (4). The universe may never end, or it may shrink into itself in a "big crunch" (bottom).

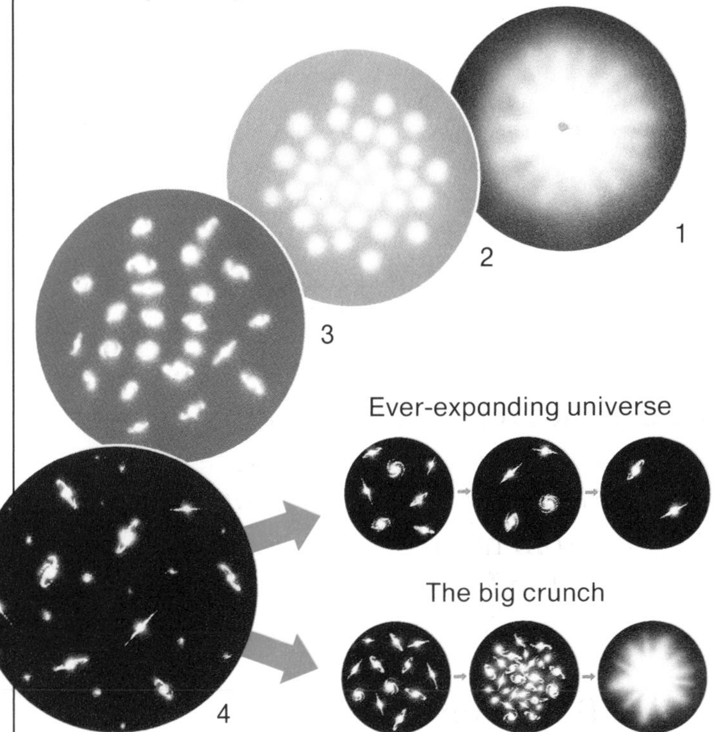

vegetables

Vegetables are edible plants. We eat leaves of lettuce, roots of carrots, and the tuber of potatoes. Peas and beans are seeds. See **food**.

Vikings

The Vikings were people who lived in northern Europe during the Middle Ages. They were bold sailors, traders, and fierce warriors. They settled in England and France, and journeyed as far as Russia and America. The Viking Age lasted from A.D. 800 to A.D. 1100.

The Vikings were feared warriors. One of their favorite weapons was the ax.

vitamins

Our bodies need vitamins to stay healthy. Vitamins are chemicals found in different foods. There are six kinds, called A, B, C, D, E, and K. We need vitamin C, for example, for healthy blood. See **food**.

volcano

A volcano is a hole in the earth's top layer, or crust. From deep below ground, melted rocks, gas, and ashes pour out of the volcano's mouth, or vent. This is an eruption. Some volcanoes trickle out streams of melted rock, or lava. Others explode violently. A volcano may be quiet, or dormant, for years, then suddenly erupt.

▼When a volcano erupts, hot magma is forced upward. Ash is thrown high into the air. Lava flows out of the volcano.

vulture

Vultures are big birds that scavenge, or feed on dead animals. They circle in the sky, watching for the next meal. Then they swoop down to feed. They have no feathers on their heads and necks.

walrus

The walrus is a large sea mammal related to the seal. It has two long tusks, or front teeth. It uses them for fighting and to scrape up shellfish.

wars

There have been many wars in history. Often wars start when a strong country tries to take over a weaker one. A civil war is a war between opposing forces within a country. An example is the American Civil War of 1861–1865. In the 20th century there have been two terrible world wars: World War I (1914–1918) and World War II (1939–1945). See **revolution**.

▼ The battle of Gettysburg in 1863 was a turning point in the American Civil War.

LIFE STORY

Washington

George Washington was the first president of the United States of America. He was born in Virginia in 1732. Virginia, like other American colonies, was then governed by Britain. Many Americans wanted to govern themselves. George Washington ran the family farm and worked as a land surveyor. In 1753 he helped defend Virginia against French soldiers. People admired his leadership and good sense.

In 1775 the American colonies voted to break away from British rule. It meant war. Washington was chosen to command the American army. He was a skillful general, and by 1781 the British were defeated. The 13 colonies became a new nation, the United States. In 1788 Washington was elected president of the new republic. He served as president until 1796, and he died in 1799.

wasp

Wasps are insects related to bees and ants. Unlike bees, wasps are hunters. They eat other insects and can sting.

water

Water is the most common substance on earth. All living things are mostly water. Your body is two-thirds water. Water falls to the ground as rain. Most of this rain flows into rivers and oceans. Rivers return water to the sea. The sun's heat turns sea water to vapor, which rises and cools to form clouds.

▼ The water we use comes from reservoirs. It is purified at treatment works, then pumped to homes. Waste water goes to sewage works for cleaning.

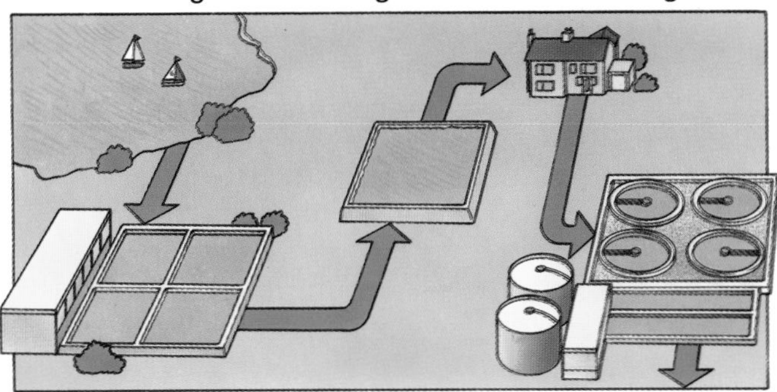

waves

Most sea waves are pushed along by the wind. Undersea volcanoes or earthquakes can cause huge waves called tsunamis. Other forms of energy, such as light, also travel in waves.

weapons

In ancient times, soldiers fought with spears, swords, and bows and arrows. They used giant catapults which hurled stones. Wars changed when guns were invented. Modern weapons include bombs, guided missiles, tanks, and guns. The most destructive weapon is the hydrogen bomb.

W

weather
Weather is caused by movements of air. For example, when a cold mass of air meets a warm mass of air, there is stormy weather with clouds, wind, and rain. The movement of the air is caused by the sun's heat. Weather varies from place to place. Climate is the weather pattern in one place over a period of time. The study of the weather is called meteorology. See **air**, **cloud**, **water**.

whale
Whales are sea mammals. They have lungs and must come to the surface to breathe. Whales give birth to live young. Some whales have teeth. They hunt fish and larger animals. Others have sieve-like mouths to strain tiny sea animals from the water. Hunting has endangered the whale. See **mammals**.

▼ Whales are the biggest of all mammals.

wheat see **cereal**

wheels and gears
A heavy load is much easier to move with the help of wheels. The wheels can be fixed to an axle on a cart, or they can be arranged, with ropes around them, as pulleys. The wheel was one of the most important human inventions. It was first used about 5,000 years ago.

Many machines have gears. These are wheels with teeth, or cogs, cut into their rims. The teeth of one wheel fit into the teeth of another wheel. Gears can increase or decrease the speed at which wheels turn. They can also increase or decrease the turning power of wheels. See **engines**, **machines**.

wind
Wind is moving air. As warm air rises, cool air takes its place. The strongest winds are hurricanes. See **weather**.

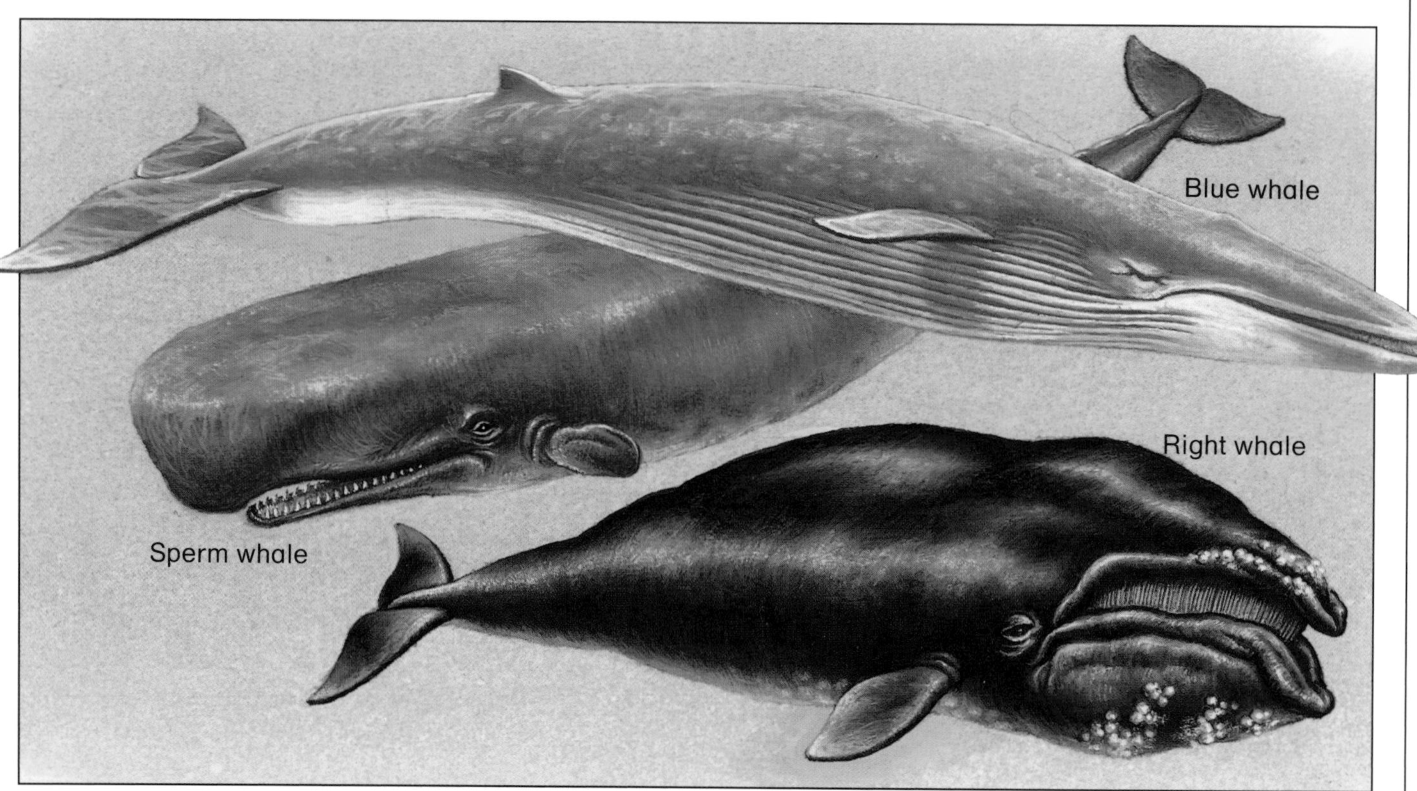

wolf
Wolves are the ancestors of dogs. They live in the wild in groups called packs. Wolves hunt deer and other animals; they very seldom hunt humans.

wood
Wood comes from different trees: hardwoods from deciduous trees, softwoods from conifers. See **forest**, **trees**.

wool
Wool is the hair of sheep, goats, and other animals, which is spun into cloth. See **spinning and weaving**, **textiles**.

▼ Sheep have been bred to give wool that is fine and long. The best wool comes from merino sheep.

word
New words are added to languages all the time. Examples are "astronaut" and "laser." Words are often borrowed from one language by another. For example, "algebra" came from Arabic. "Yacht" is a Dutch word. Each language has different words. "Yes" is "oui" in French and "ja" in German.

worm
Earthworms burrow in soil. Other worms live in ocean mud or sand. Some worms live inside other animals, as parasites.

LIFE STORY

Wright brothers
Wilbur and Orville Wright were brothers who made and flew the first airplane that could take off and land. Wilbur was born in 1867, Orville in 1871. They ran a bicycle-making business, but in their spare time they made model aircraft. People had flown in balloons and airships, and for short distances in gliders. No one had yet made a plane that had a motor and could take off and fly. The Wrights experimented with kite-like gliders. In 1903 they tried out a new plane with a gasoline engine they had built. It flew. The first flight lasted just 12 seconds, but the Wrights were soon making longer flights. Wilbur died of a fever in 1912. Orville died in 1948. See **aircraft**.

writing
The first writing was made with a stick in soft clay. The ancient Egyptians used picture symbols called "hieroglyphs." The pictures became letters, to form the alphabets we use today.

X ray

X rays are a form of energy that can pass through metal or the body. X-ray machines in hospitals make pictures of the body's insides. X rays are strong enough to burn. They can destroy harmful growths, such as cancers. X rays can show metal cracks and hidden weapons. See **medicine**.

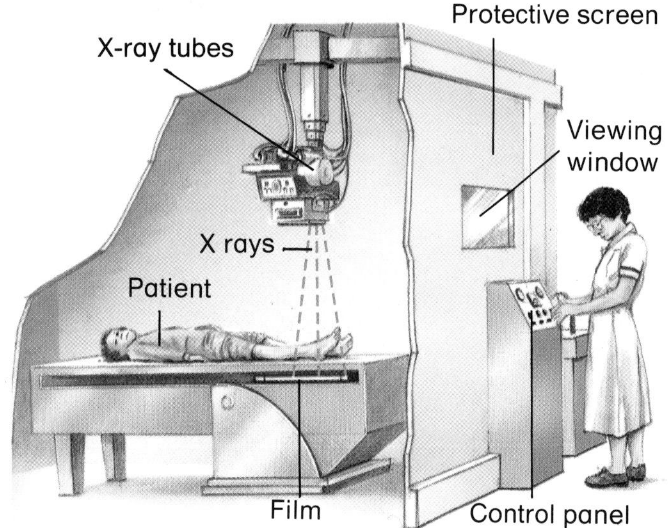

▲ X rays are aimed at the part of the body the doctors want to examine. The rays pass through the body and make a picture on a piece of film. This X-ray picture (right) shows the bones of the hand. Too much radiation is dangerous, so the operator works behind a screen.

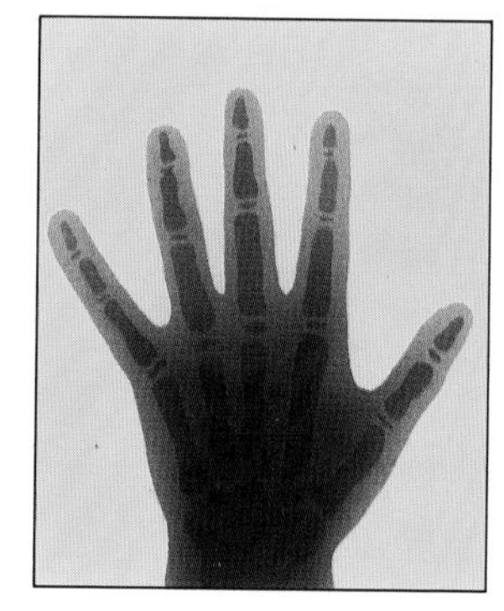

yak

The yak is an ox of the high mountains of northern Asia. Yaks have thick, shaggy coats of hair and can withstand the wind and snow. They have long, curving horns. Tame yaks are kept for their milk, meat, and hair. They also make good pack animals. Tame yaks are smaller and gentler than wild yaks.

year

The earth takes $365\frac{1}{4}$ days to orbit the sun. This is one year. A year on other planets is longer or shorter, depending on how long they take to journey around the sun. Because the calendar year is only 365 days long, we add an extra day every four years to make up the difference. The fourth year is called a leap year. See **solar system, time**.

zebra

Zebras are wild horses of Africa. Unlike horses, zebras are difficult to tame. No other horse has the zebra's bold striped coat. Zebras live in bands, or herds, for safety from predators. Zebras' stripes look like light and shadow. This helps zebras hide in tall grass. Their main enemies are lions. When lions attack, the zebras gallop away. See **animals**.

▼ Zebras live in herds. Like horses, male zebras are called stallions and females are mares. Each zebra has its own pattern of stripes.

zero

Zero in mathematics is shown as 0, sometimes written as "nought" or "nothing." Zero fills the space in a numeral; for example, 305 means three hundreds, no tens, and five ones. This use of zero began in Arabia and India. See **mathematics, numbers**.

zinc

Zinc is a metal with many uses. Steel coated with zinc will not rust. Brass is an alloy, or mixture, of copper and zinc. Electric batteries contain zinc.

zoo

Wild animals were kept in zoos 3,000 years ago in Egypt and China. For many years zoo animals were kept in cages. Today most people prefer to see animals roaming free in safari parks. Rare animals are studied and bred in zoos, and their young later returned to the wild.

Index